MELODY CHORDS for GUITAR

by Allan Holdsworth

Photo's courtesy of
Carvin Guitar
12340 World Trade Dr.
San Diego, CA 92128
Special thanks to Dave Flores

Special thanks to Jon Chappell
Guitar Magazine

ISBN 1-57424-051-X
SAN 683-8022

Contents

Allan Holdsworth
A true legend in our time

Allan Holdsworth was born August 6, 1946, in Leeds, Yorkshire, UK.

Guitar Virtuoso Allan started on saxophone and clarinet and took up the guitar at seventeen. He wanted the guitar to sound like a saxophone, more as if he were blowing it than plucking it. Coming to London at the end of the 1960s, he was one of the pioneers of jazz-rock-fusion music in the early 1970s. A highly individual stylist, with a gloriously fluid technique and an endless flow of linear ideas. He has said: "I tend to hear flurries of notes as a whole, from beginning to end, rather than hearing one note after the other".* As influential as John Coltrane, Django Reinhardt, Jimi Hendrix and Chuck Berry. Allan, a composer and band leader has influenced musicians and guitarists such as Frank Zappa, Scott Henderson, Eddie Van Halen, Joe Satriani, Carlos Santana, Neil Schon and many more.

*Jazz, The Rough Guide, © 1995 Published by The Rough Guides Ltd.

Allan at his home studio "the Brewery"
Courtesy of Carvin Guitar

With ALLAN HOLDSWORTH

"My approach to chords has always been as groups of notes that imply a certain scale," muses Allan Holdsworth. "I think of chords as belonging to a certain key, which implies a given diatonic scale. I can then play any note that is diatonically correct for that scale that sounds good to me. The chords I form may not be an inversion of any kind of C major chord, say, but just something that comes from that scale."

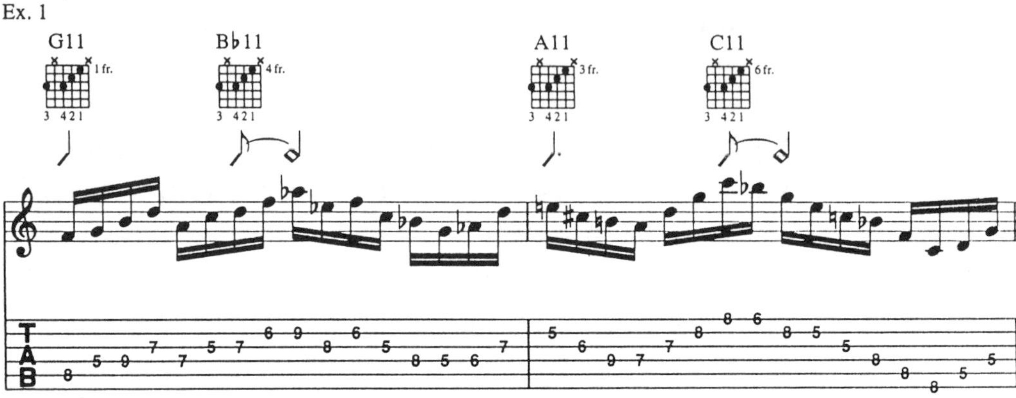

That may come as a bit of a shock to the jazz players who are used to approach ing progressions in terms of the harmonized scale, modes, and ii-V-I. "I don't know what any of that means," admits Holdsworth readily. "I don't really care about *what* it is, as much as the way that it *sounds*, so if I know that there's one scale leading to the next scale, and I like this group of notes that came from that scale moving to this group of notes coming from the following scale, then I'll use that. So I'm not even thinking of chords in a progression, actually."

Thus, Holdsworth sees chords as distinct units, not as group members of a key system. For example, in the typical fusion chord progression of G11 B♭11 A11 C11, Allan would consider each chord the tonic of its own key, and play one of his fav-orite scales, such as the Mixolydian with an added major 7 (1 2 3 4 5 6 ♭7 7). The result would look like Example 1, where each chord acts as a key and dictates the notes of the improvised scale.

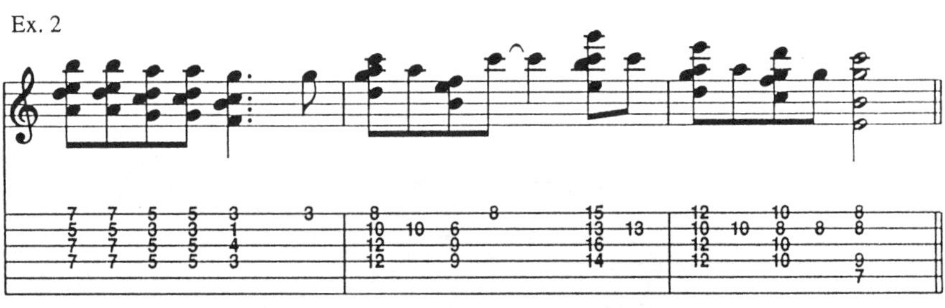

When he restricts himself to a certain diatonic key, as in this next example in C major, the chords can take on some pretty weird shapes—at least when viewed through conventional eyes. "This is a progression where all the chords relate to C major," says Holdsworth, but he doesn't shed any further light in defining their roles as major, minor or dominant chords (see Example 2), because he doesn't think of them that way.

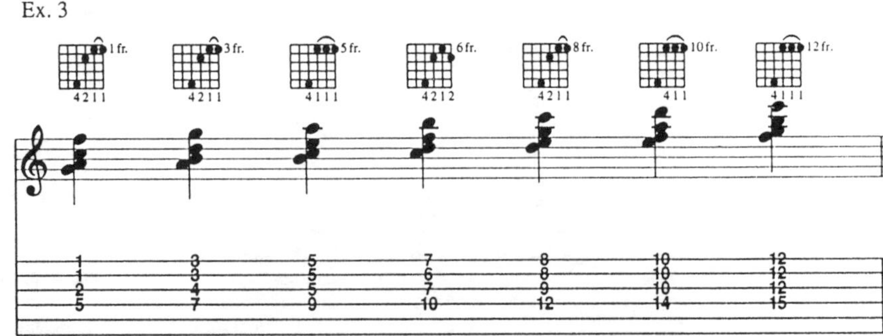

Even the harmonized scale in C major looks unfamiliar and knuckle-knotty when played by Holdsworth. It's C major in the sense that there are no sharps or flats, but the note groups don't form the reassuring major- and minor-7th forms we all learned when copping "jazz chords." Still, there is an internal logic to the sequence, and the sound is lovely and original (see Example 3).

Holdsworth didn't learn harmony conventionally, nor does he even hear things conventionally. "When I tried to go back many years to figure out the chords I liked to use and what I was going to call them, I realized I couldn't really call them something and show them to anyone else, be-cause those musicians wouldn't play the chord I was meaning. Maybe that's why when I harmonize something, what happens is different, because I'm not looking at the chords in the same way. I don't even see it like that. It's impossible for me to see it like that. I just hear it. Obviously, everybody has a different harmonic sensibility, and sometimes you might want to do something that someone else might not want to do, or might not even like. So I just base it on that—I base it on instinct. One has to analyze the harmony, obviously, and I have to do it in my own way, and I have my own symbols that I write out so I can get through something. If I've learned it, and the band and I have played it regularly, then I always try to improvise, so I always try to do something different each time. It's not like I have one way to do it, because that's what improvising is."

Edited by Jon Chappell

PREFACE

The aim of this book is to provide the guitarist with a simplified method of learning chords, in diagram form, for playing accompaniments in orchestral and instrumental performances of modern popular music and also for playing popular melodies in "chord-solo" style.

Since all pop-songs consist of the notes of the keys represented by the chord symbols given, in most song sheets, for the harmonic accompaniment, I have grouped the chords for each scale note in the order in which they ascend and descend the scale according to the key signature indicated by each one of the various chord symbols.

The order just mentioned includes, naturally, chord forms which are well known to the majority of guitarists and, therefore, provides for individual selection to be made, by each reader, of chords for general use.

The chords may be learned in any order to suit personal preferences as most of the chords are readily mastered, in all keys, by regular practice.

Knowledge of music theory and an ability to read music notation is not a prerequisite in this system and for this reason I have attempted to explain such technical matters as are necessary, in references to scales and chords, in terms which may be easily understood by the reader.

Chord Diagram

The chord diagrams given in the following pages are presented in the order in which the "leading note" of a chord - (I.E., the top note) - occurs in the scale when the latter is played from the open position to the highest convenient position, (fret), on the same string.

Scale notes and "altered" scale notes, in chord form, are usually played on the first string, second string and, for three and four-string chords, on the third string.

It will be noted that some of the chords are practical on guitars which are provided with a "cut-away" portion but which are practically impossible to play on models having no more than twelve frets up to where the neck joins the body. "Not to worry" however, there are many chords available for the "non-cut-away" models, including those in which unwanted strings are prevented from sounding by lightly touching them with a part of the finger, or of the hand, which is not employed in the fingering of the chord.

Examples are illustrated in the keys, G Major, G Minor and in the "Dominant" and "Diminished Dominant" scales of those keys - (the latter are explained in the section which deals with them).

Excepting for chord forms in which open strings are featured, all chord forms are easily played on various positions on the fingerboard, thus producing the same chords in any key by simply keeping the fingers of the left hand fixed in the "pattern" of the selected chord and then moving the hand and arm up, or down, the fingerboard, as the case may be, to the position required for producing the chord in any desired key.

Reference tables are given for the purpose of readily locating the fret position for any scale note and any "altered" scale note of Major, Minor and Dominant scales in all keys. The "altered" scale notes, incidentally, are those which are lowered, or raised, a half-tone, (or fret).

Signs and Terms

N.P. Nut Position
O Open String

A number, in brackets, on the left of a chord diagram indicates the fret on which the first finger of the left hand is placed, thus 'stopping' the string at this position.

Numbers nearby the black dots, (notes), on a diagram indicate the left hand fingering. Alternative fingerings are given immediately under a diagram.

A number, or sign, beneath a diagram represents the bass note of the chord; alternative bass notes are shown in brackets.

Numbering of the Scale Notes

Scale notes are numbered, as counted from the fundamental note, in numerical order in the ascending scale, in accordance with the key signature and including the fundamental note in the count. The note on the eighth scale step is the "octave" of the fundamental note on step number one and, therefore, this octave of the fundamental may be regarded as the first step of the continuation of the scale ascending to the next higher repeat of the fundamental.

The distance, in scale steps, between any two scale notes is known as an "interval" and this is represented by a figure which indicates the distance which separates the two notes. This figure always refers to the uppermost of the two notes and there are two main kinds of intervals, viz. "Simple" intervals, (meaning less than an octave in size) and "Compound" intervals, (meaning those greater than an octave in size).

The simple intervals are 2nds., 3rds., 4ths., 5ths., 6ths., and 7ths. Compound intervals are 8ths., 9ths., 10ths., 11ths., 12ths., and 13ths. The intervals which are greater than the 13th need not concern us.

The compound intervals just referred to are, of course, the same, in harmony, as the simple intervals, except they are an octave higher. Of these compound intervals, 8ths., 10ths., and 12ths., are never used in chord symbols because they are simply the notes of the common chord, (or "triad" as it is commonly called), and this is always represented by nothing more than the name of the fundamental, or root note, e.g., the symbol G represents the common triad built upon G and consisting of the keynote, third and fifth notes of the G Major scale.

"Altered" scale notes are those which are raised a half-tone, (or fret) and are known as "augmented" intervals, and those which are lowered a half-tone, (fret), and are known as "minor" intervals when applied to major intervals, and as "diminished" intervals when applied to the 5th and to the 7th interval of the dominant chord when the latter is converted to a "diminished seventh" . The term "altered" scale note applies to both simple intervals and compound intervals, e.g., the "augmented 4th" is the same, in harmony, as the "augmented 11th" except it is an octave below the latter. Either of these two terms may be used in chord symbols.

It is important to remember that, in minor keys, the 'minor 3rd', 'minor 6th' and 'minor 7th' are actual scale notes in the descending "melodic minor" scale, while the "Major" 6th and "Major" 7th are actual notes in the ascending "melodic minor" scale. "Altered" notes, in minor scales, are limited to the "augmented 4th" or "diminished 5th", (same sound), and, infrequently, the 'minor 9th'/'minor 2nd'.

Reference Table of Scale Notes

Fingerboard positions of the scale notes and "altered" scale notes in the key of G major are represented by figures denoting the Scale-Step position of each note, as counted from the root upwards in accordance with the key signature: thus,

Diagram 1.

Octave 1							(1)	2	(3)	4	(5)	6	7	(8)
(G)	A	(B)	C	(D)	E	F♯	(G)	A	(B)	C	(D)	E	F♯	(G)
(1)	2	(3)	4	(5)	6	7	(8)	9	(10)	11	(12)	13	14	(15)
							Octave 2							

THE FINGERBOARD IS DIVIDED INTO 5 SECTIONS

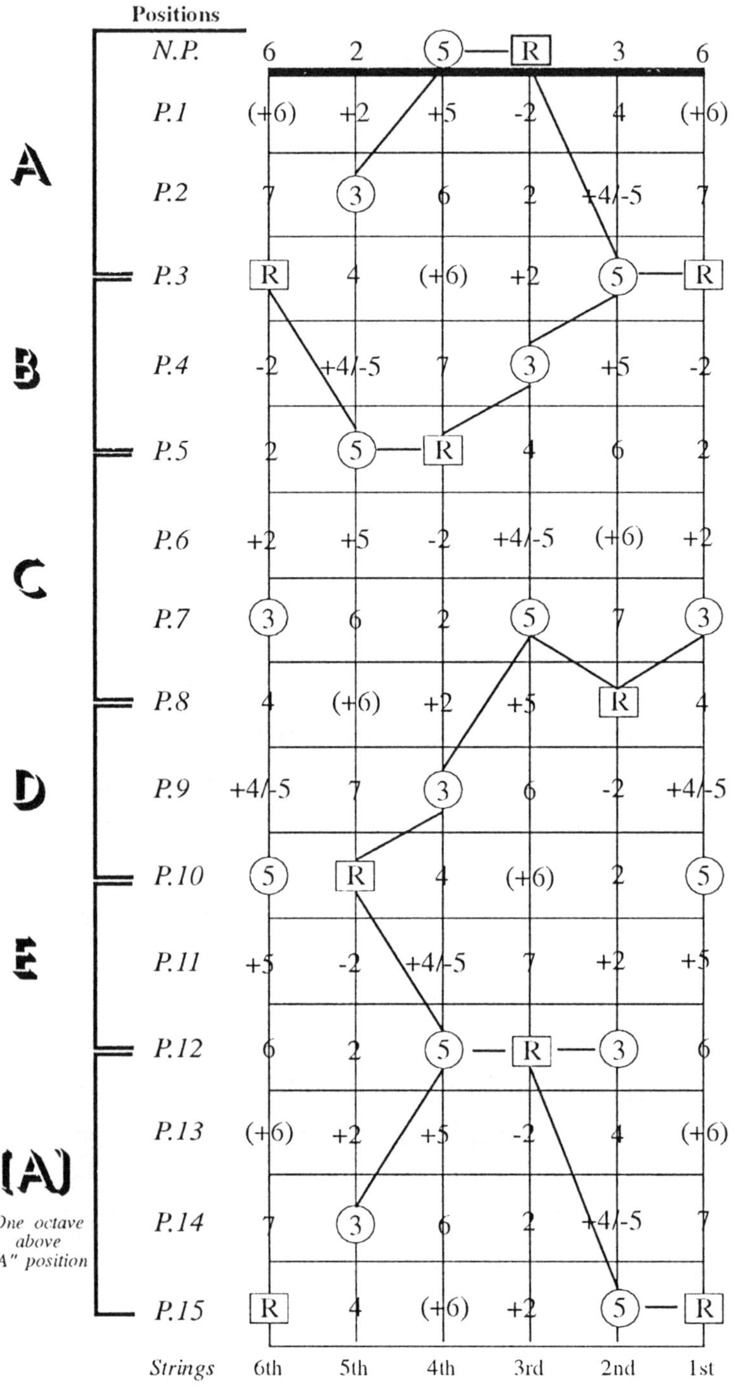

The notes of the common major chord,(triad) are shown in the circles in ***Diagram 1*** and the table to the left. The chord is represented in symbol form simply by the name of the root "G". The boxed "R" represents the root.

*The left table is a visual guide to forming the the "standard" major chord shapes around the root positions (in any major key). (Note that that **A** and **B** have the root on the **1st** and **6th** strings at the same fret).*

ALTERATIONS

-2 (A♭) : +2 (A♯) : +4 (C♯) :

+5 (D♯) : -5 (D♭) : +6 (E♯)

-9 (A♭) : +9 (A♯) : +10 (C♯)

The 2nd, when added to the triad, is always represented by the number "9", it's compound equivalent. The 4th is represented as such and also as an 11th. the augmented 6th is never used in symbols because it is identical to the minor 7th interval known as the "dominant" 7th.

Standard Forms / G Major

The lines on the table below indicate the notes of the common triad in the key of G Major. In the right table, figs. A-J show the "standard" chord forms of the common triad in Guitar chord diagram form.

Symbol Terms

+4 : +11 = Aug 4th / Aug 11 +5 = Aug 5th +2 : +9 = Aug 2 / Aug 9 2 : 9 = Maj 2nd / Maj 9 -2 : -9 = min 2nd / min 9	-5 = dim 5th 4 : 11 = 4th / 11th (Aug 6th not used in chord symbols)

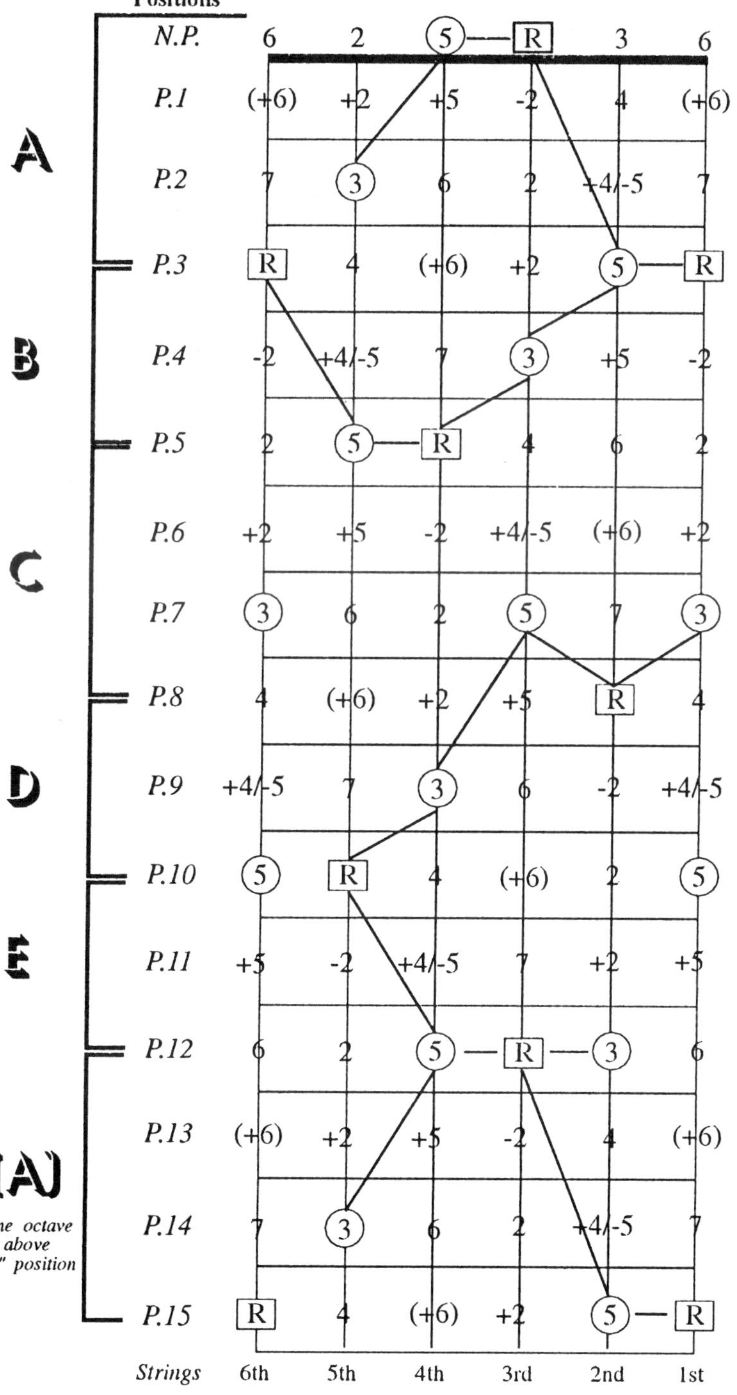

To form the chord shapes in any key, first find the *Root* positions and then form the chord shapes around these positions.

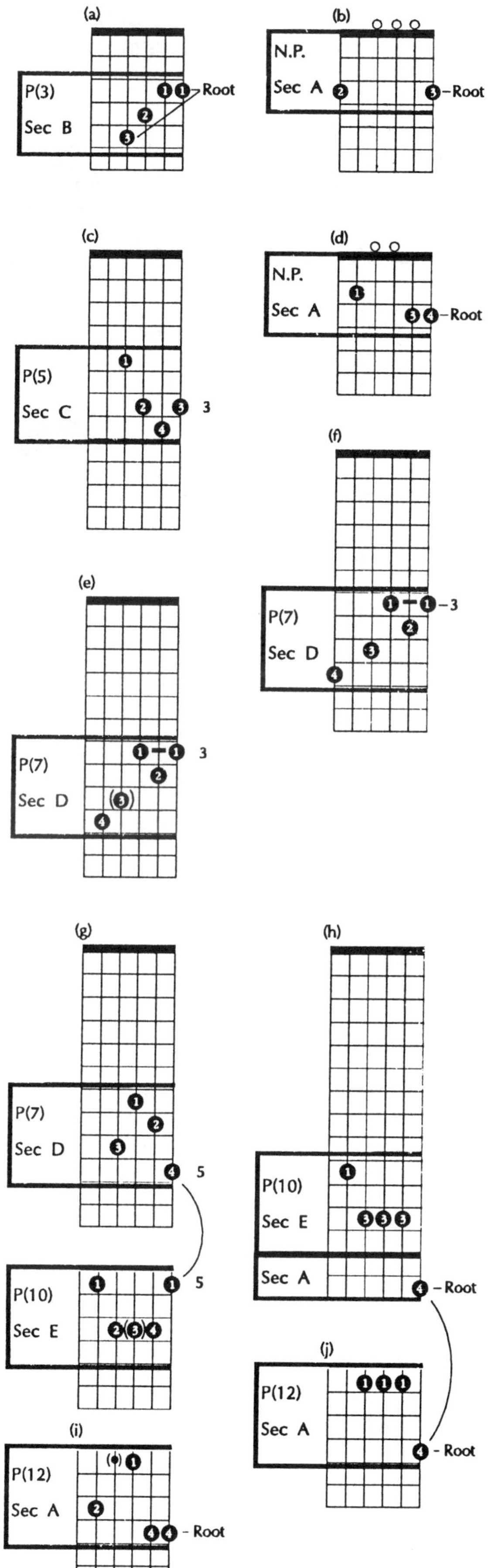

In the case of chord symbols in popular song accompianments, the indication of major chords with other scale notes added or chords with "altered" scale notes are easily obtained by making simple adjustments to the "standard forms" as shown in ***Fig. 3.***

Fig. 1 shows the table of fingerboard positions of the scale notes of G Major. Note the "markers" placed on the positions occupied, in chord diagrams, by the black dots, (notes) The "markers" are the circular shapes. (Note that the Roots are enclosed by a square.) These are most useful in marking out the notes of chord forms on the table leaving both hands free when sketching out chord diagrams derived from adjustments made to "common chord" forms, as mentioned above and as illustrated in ***Fig. 3.***

Fig. 1

Positions
N.P.
P.1
P.2
P.3
P.4
P.5
P.6
P.7
P.8
P.9
P.10
P.11
P.12
P.13
P.14
P.15
Strings
6th
5th
4th
3rd
2nd
1st

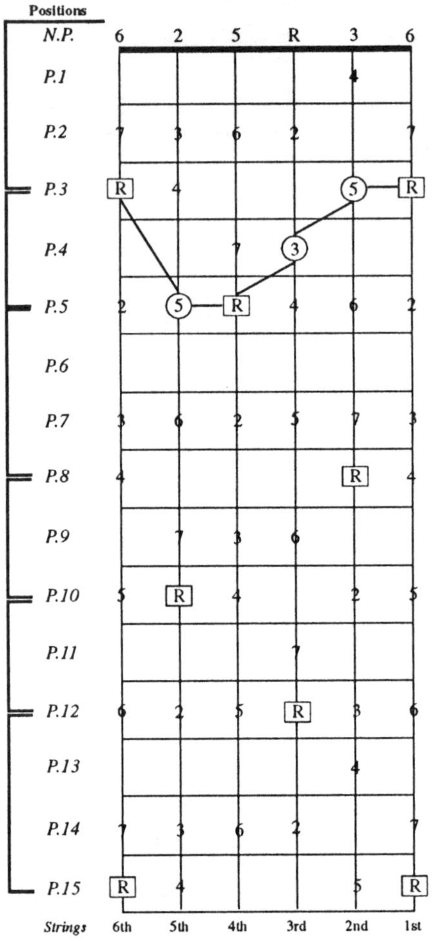

Fig. 2

Standard forms of the common chord in G major

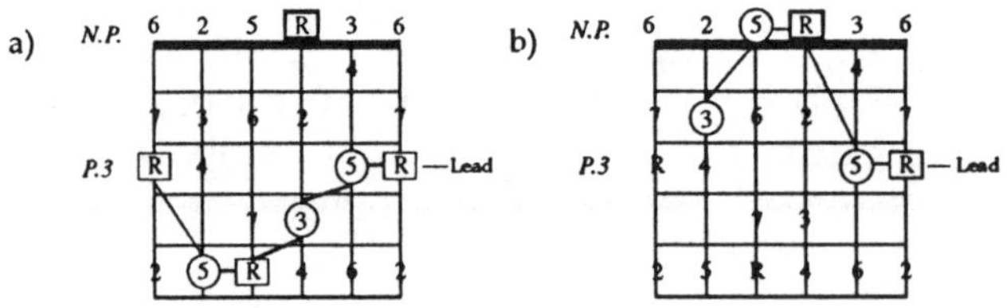

a)
N.P.
P.3
Lead
b)
N.P.
P.3
Lead

Fig. 3

Standard forms (above) adjusted to include "added" or "altered scale notes in the harmony parts. (Root lead)

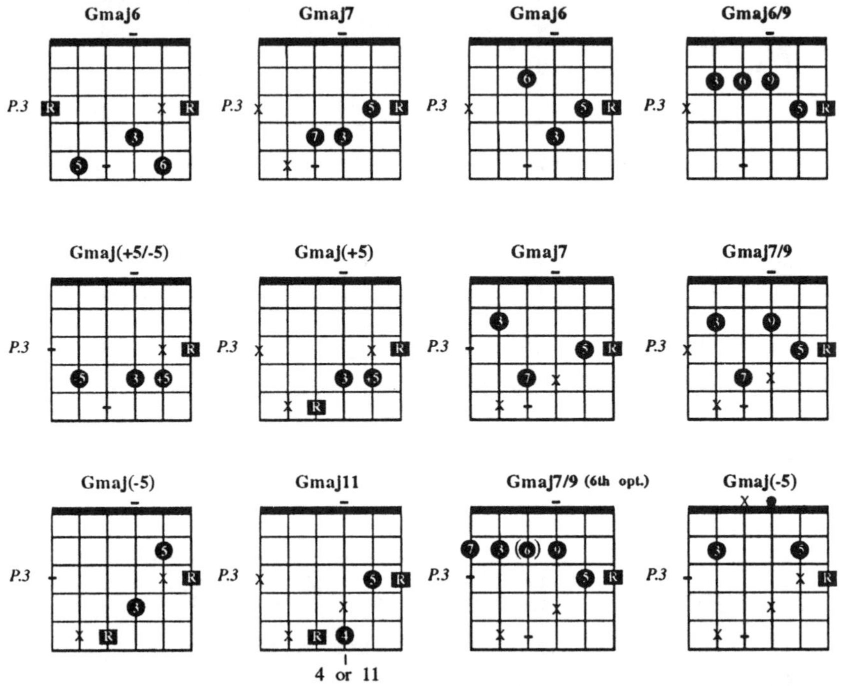

GmaJ6
GmaJ7
GmaJ6
GmaJ6/9
GmaJ(+5/-5)
GmaJ(+5)
GmaJ7
GmaJ7/9
GmaJ(-5)
GmaJ11
GmaJ7/9 (6th opt.)
GmaJ(-5)
4 or 11

Gmaj6
Gmaj6 and Gmaj7
Gmaj6
Gmaj6/9
Gmaj+11
+4 or +11
Gmaj6
Gmaj6

With the markers placed in position, as shown in ***Fig. 1***, make a visual note of the positions, ajacent frets, nearby postitions on each string and any other scale notes which are to be included in the harmony parts as shown in ***Fig. 2.*** (*For the time being, leave the "lead" note on the first string unchanged.*) Later on this note too may be adjusted.

Note that the "6th" may replace the "5th" on the same string, and that the displaced "5th" may be restored on an alternative position (*On the 5th string.*) The "6th" may also replace the "doubled" Root, likewise the "maj7". For other adjustments, a few moments spent on comparing each of the chords in ***Fig. 3.*** with the common chord in ***Fig. 2.*** will prove most helpful as a guide to making adjustments to a given chord form.

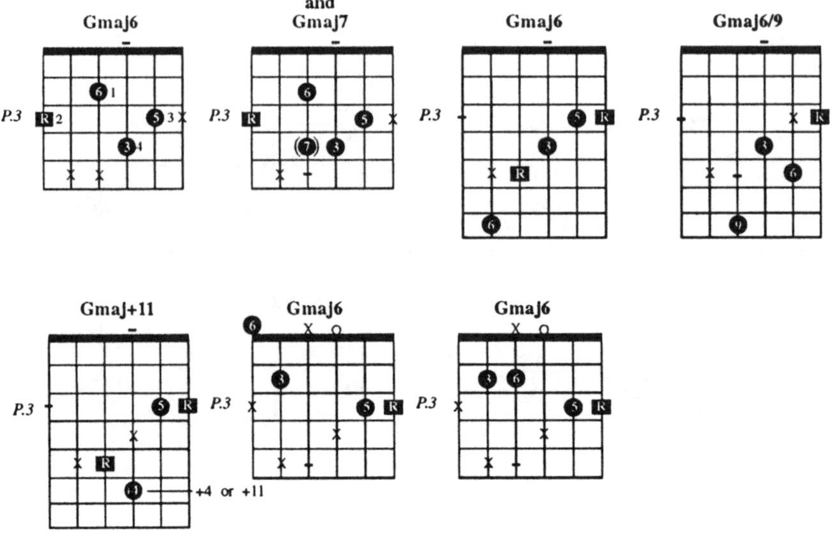

Part One

Scales in Chord Form

Scales in G Major

R.N. represents the Root; the remaining scale notes and "altered scale notes" are represented by figures which indicate the positions of the notes in the scale ascending from the root 1 and from the root 8, the octave root 1. Alternative chord diagrams for each scale note are given to allow for individual selection by the reader.

See page 6 for directions on producing the same chord forms in any other major key and page 20 for reference tables showing the positions of the fingerboard and of the scale notes in all major keys.

FIG. 1. SCALE NOTES AND "ALTERED NOTES" ON THE FIRST STRING

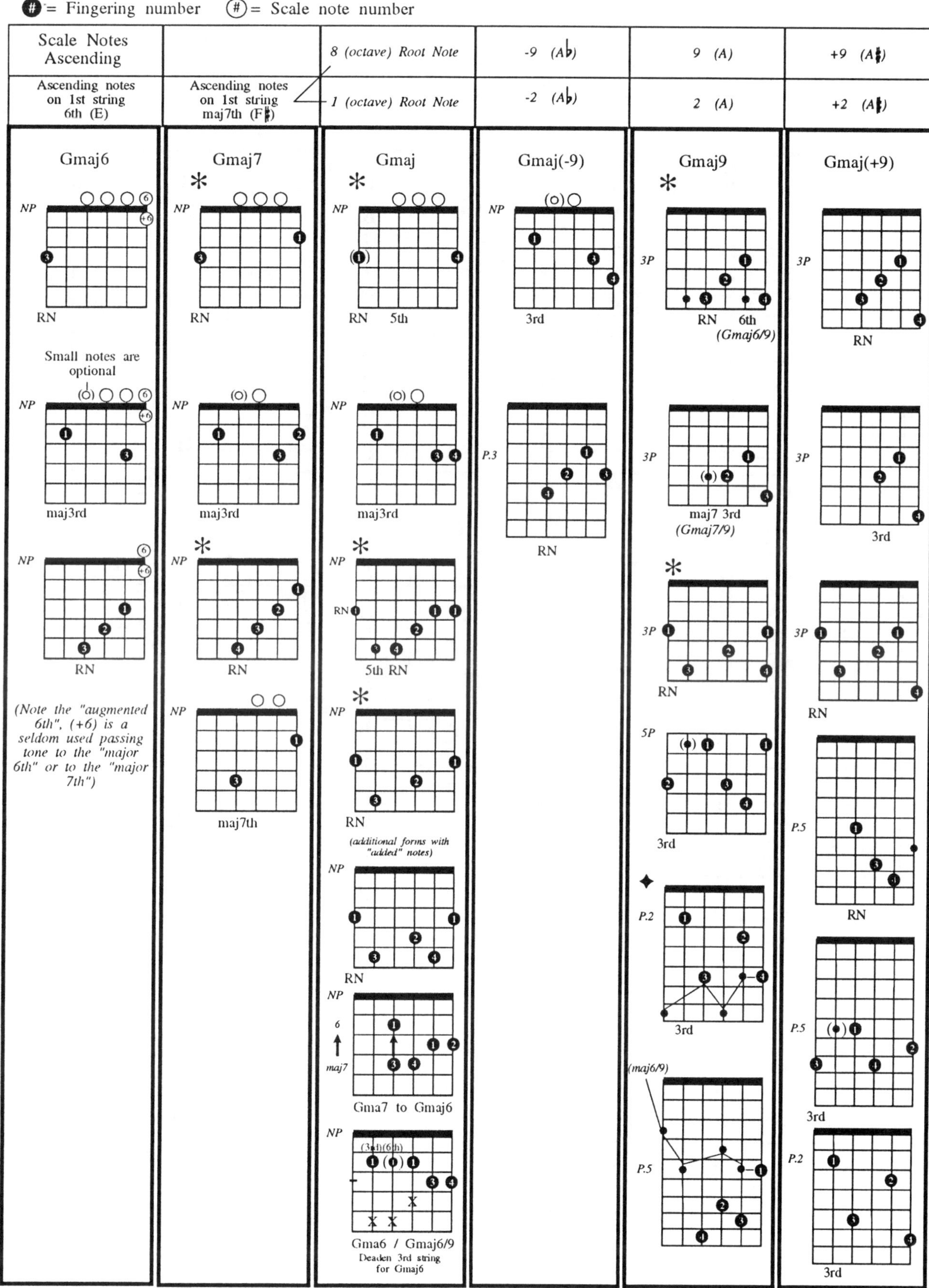

✻ *Chord forms frequently used in general accompaniment work.*

✦ *Chord forms thus marked are easier to play on higher positions.*

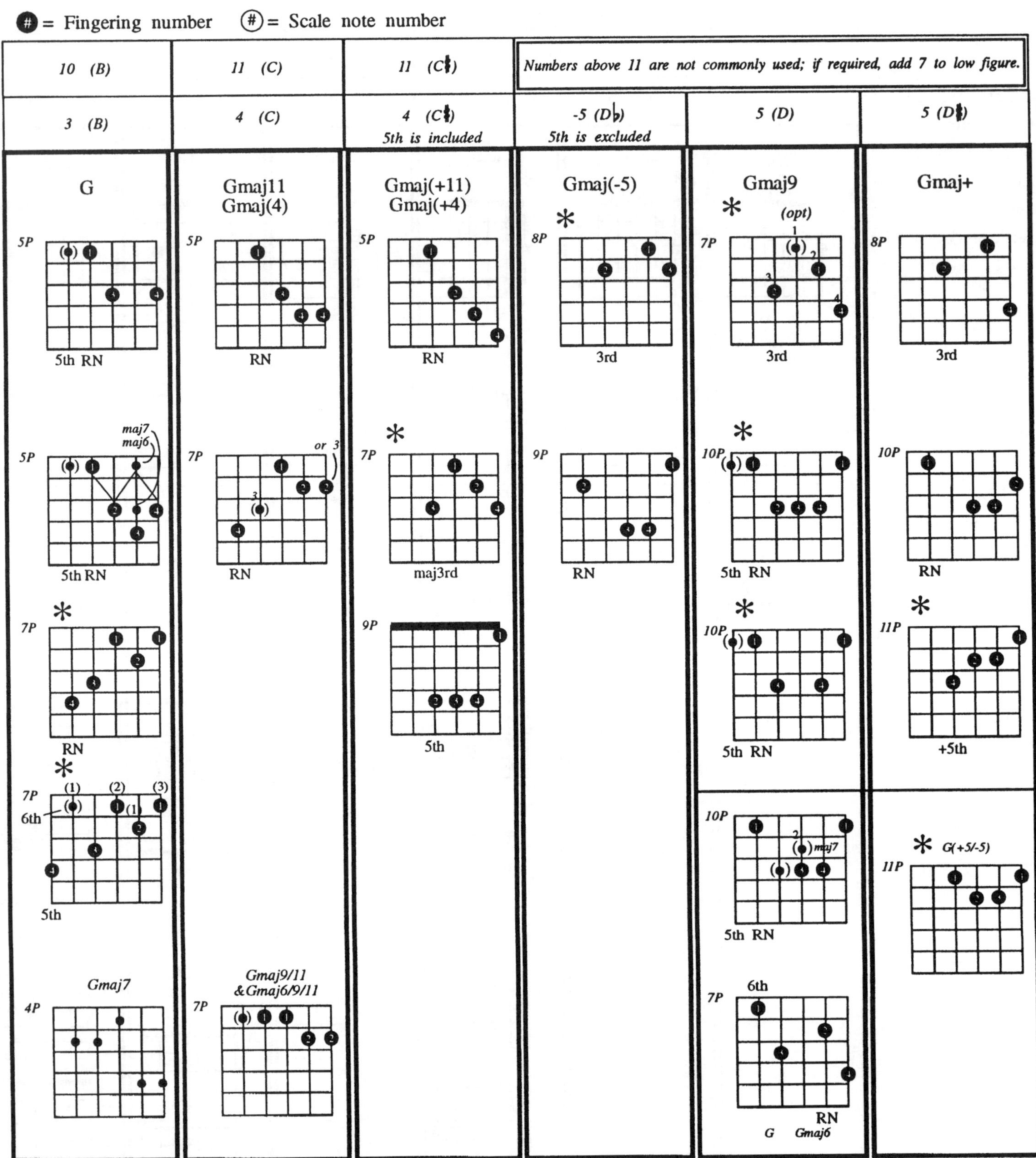

✻ *Chord forms frequently used in general accompaniment work.*

✦ *Chord forms thus marked are easier to play on higher positions.*

Scale Notes and "Altered" Notes cont.

Chord Sequences in Harmony Accompaniments

Instead of playing the "standard" chord for all 8 beats, you can often substitute chords which contain "added" or "altered" scale-notes as in the example below.

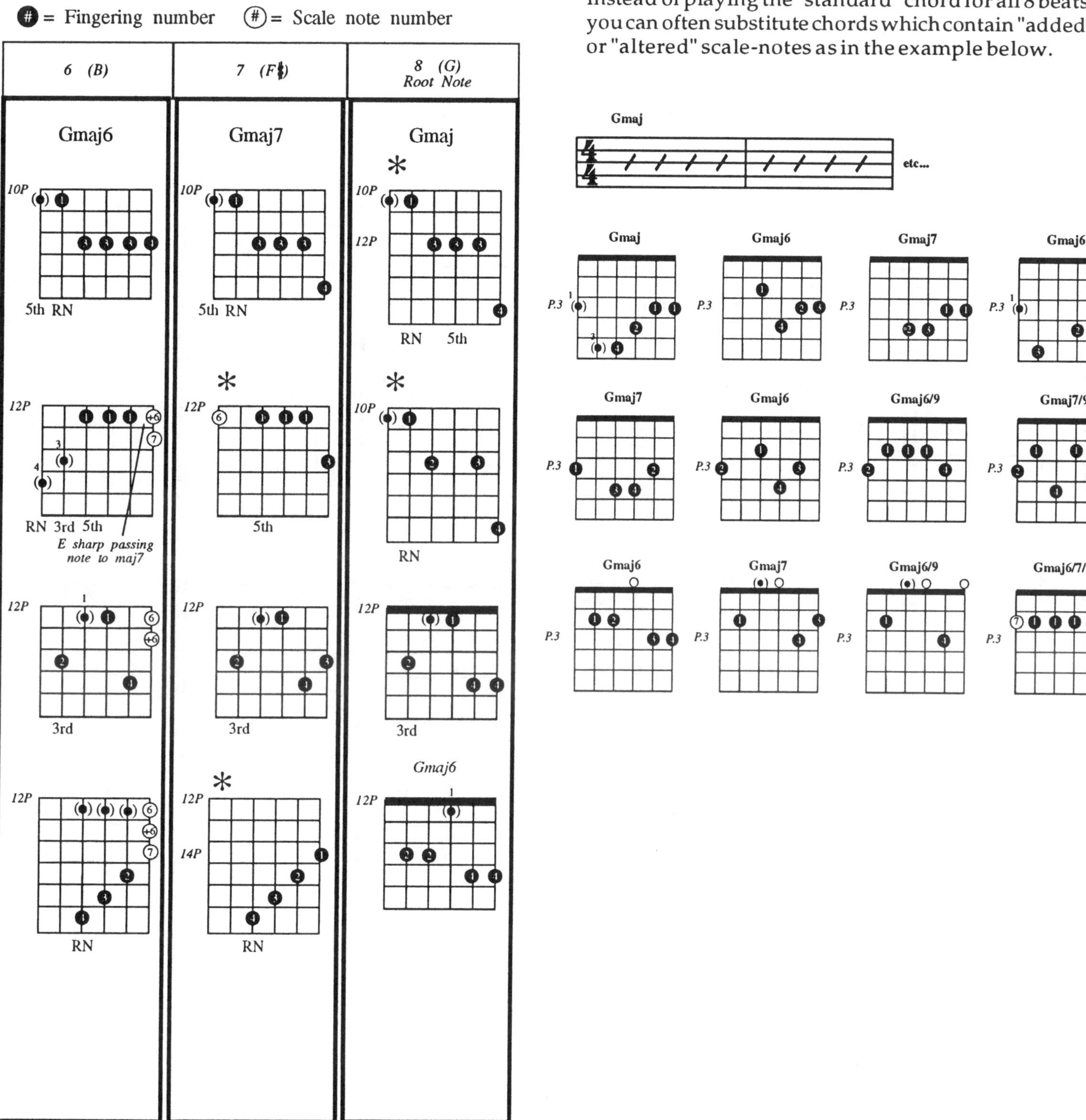

✱ *Chord forms frequently used in general accompaniment work.*

✦ *Chord forms thus marked are easier to play on higher positions.*

SCALE NOTES AND "ALTERED NOTES" ON THE 2ND STRING

Fig. 2 is the same as Fig. 1 except the scale notes and "altered" notes are on the 2nd string. These chord forms provide for notes in the scale ascending from the 6th (E), of G major, on the open first string to the 3rd (B), on the open 2nd string and also "inside" chord alternatives to the chords for scale notes up to fret position ten, on the first string for the 5th, (D).

SCALE NOTES ASCENDING FROM B, (*THE THIRD*), IN G MAJOR

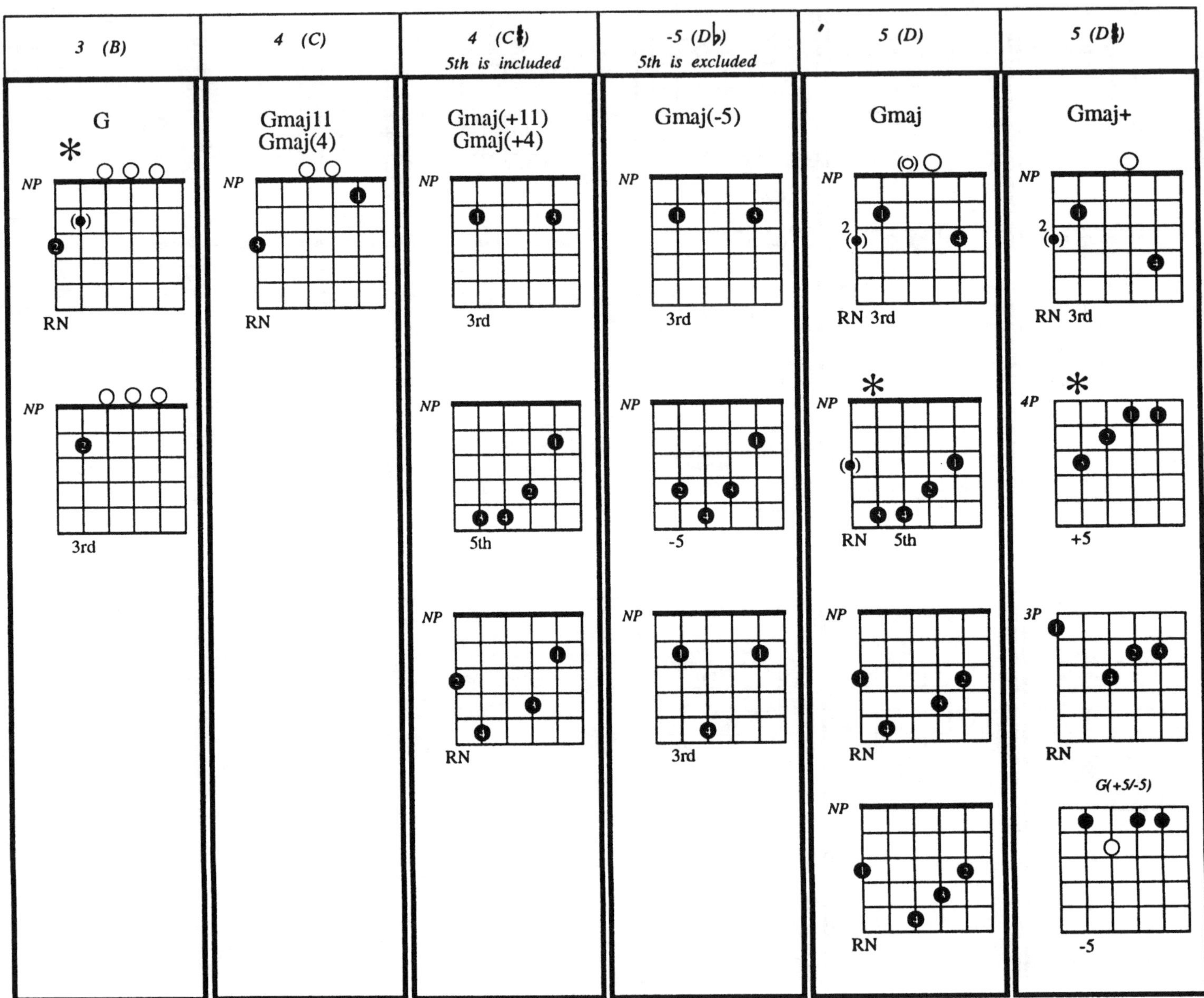

✱ *Chord forms frequently used in general accompaniment work.*

Scale Notes and "Altered Notes" on the 2nd String cont...

Scale notes ascending from B, (*the third*), in G major

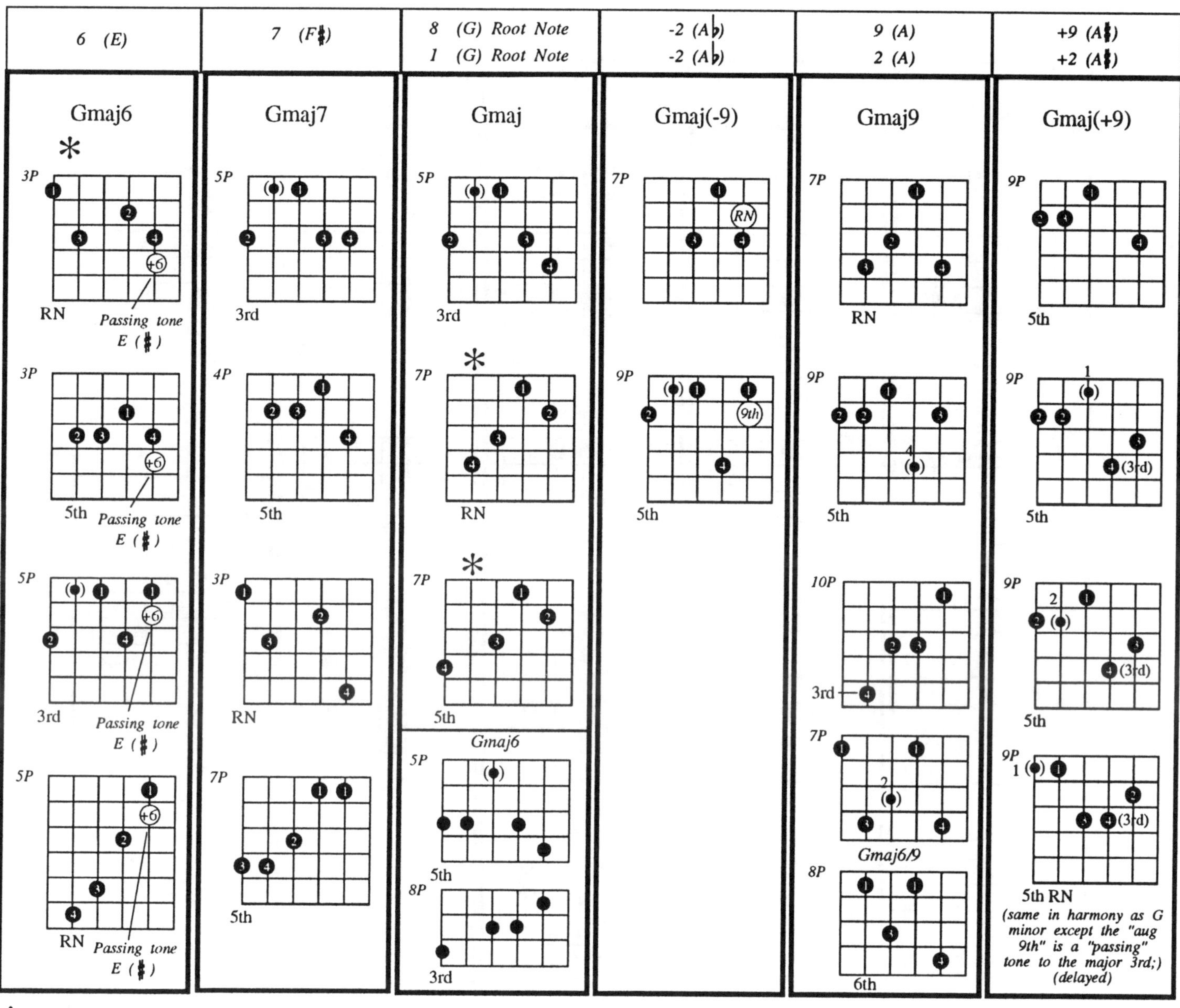

* Chord forms frequently used in general accompaniment work.

Scale Notes and "Altered Notes" on the 2nd String cont...

Scale notes ascending from B, (the third), in G major

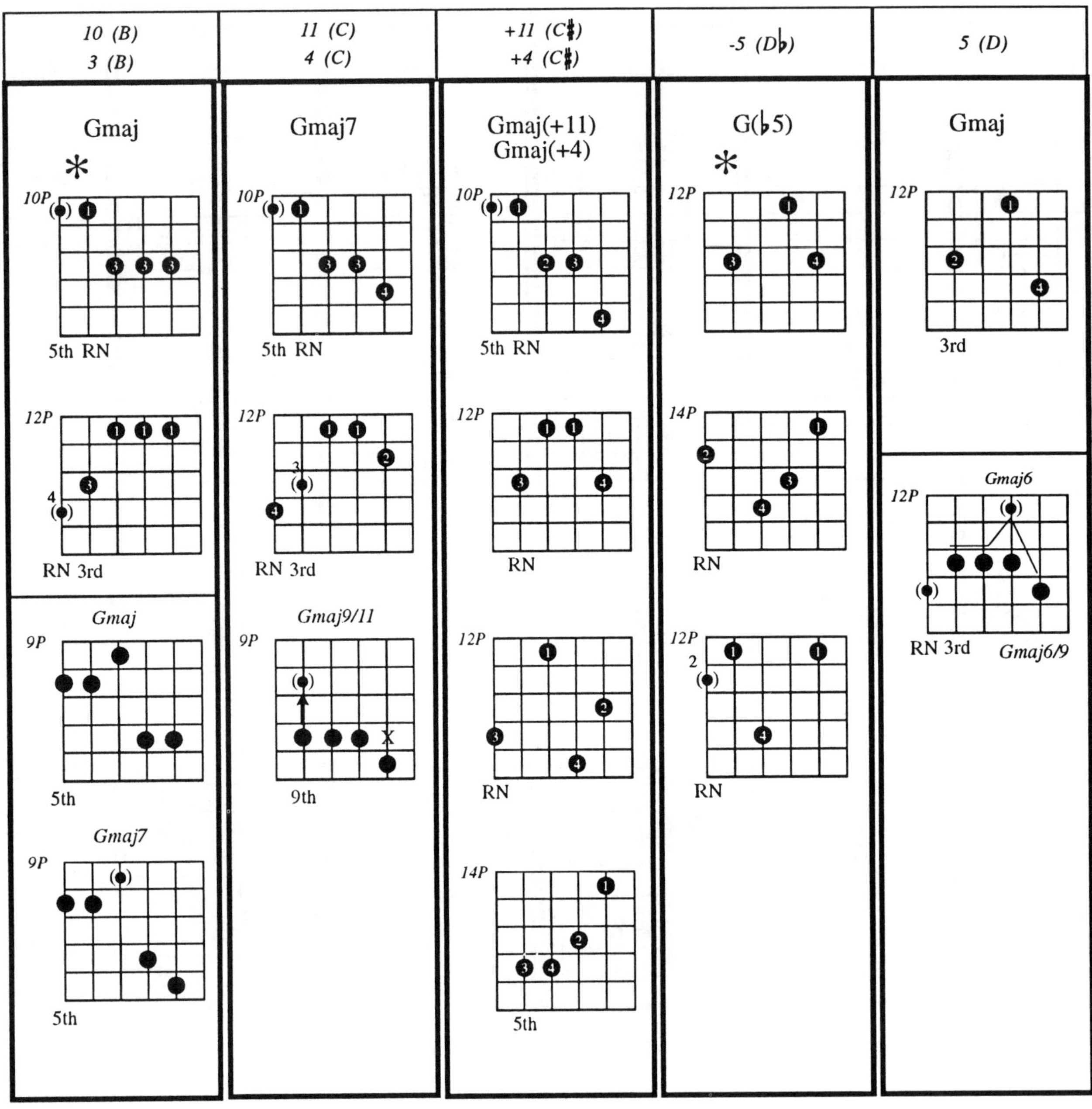

✱ *Chord forms frequently used in general accompaniment work.*

SCALE NOTES AND "ALTERED" NOTES ON THE 3RD STRING

Fig. 3 is the same approach as *Figs 1* and *2* but the scale notes and "altered" scale notes on the third string. These chord-forms provide for notes of the G major scale descending from the note B, (3rd), on open second string to G, (rootnote), on open third string, and also the "alternative" forms for notes ascending the scale to the "octave" of the latter Rootnote

SCALE NOTES ASCENDING FROM THE ROOTNOTE, (G), ON THE OPEN THIRD STRING

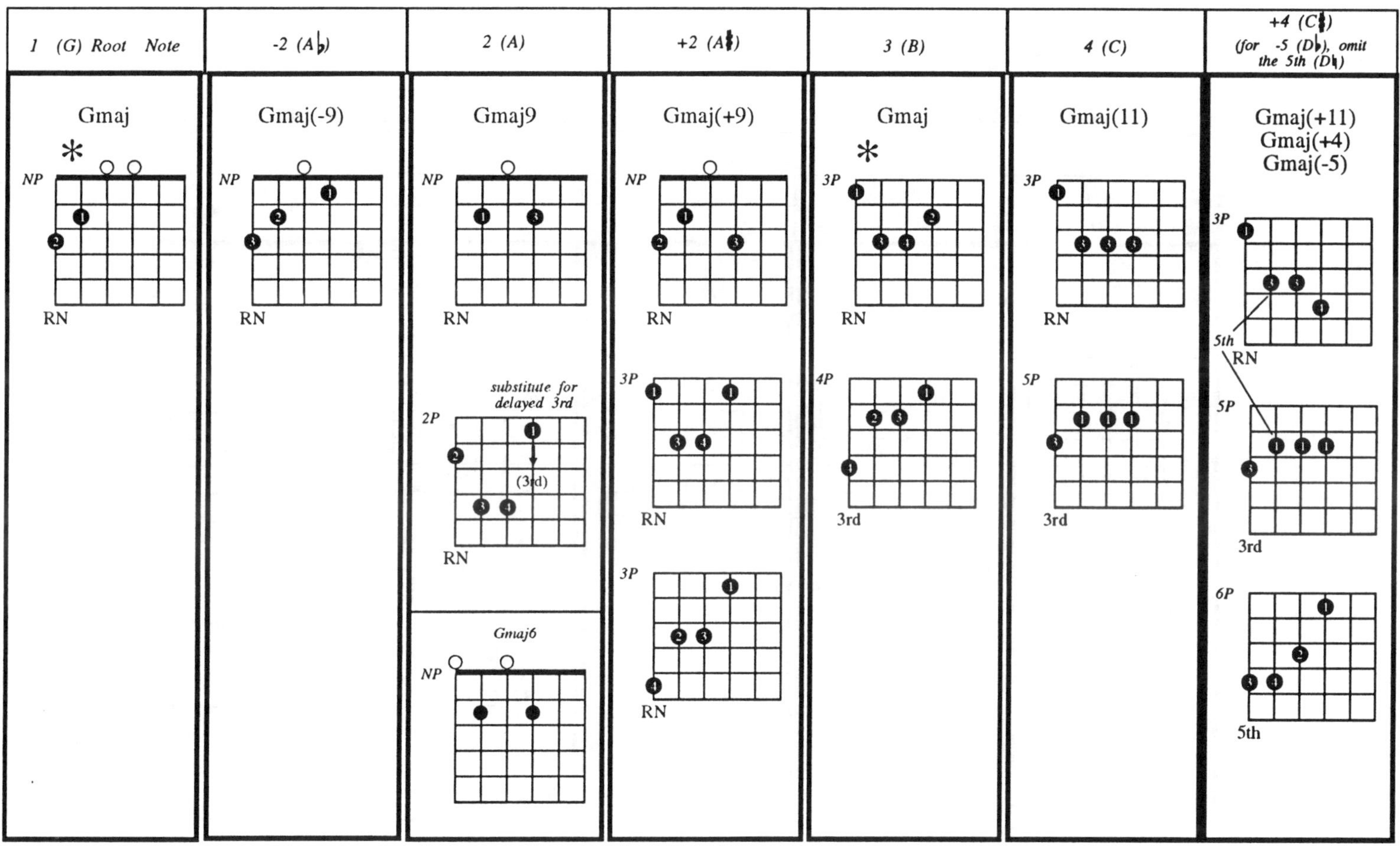

✻ *Chord forms frequently used in general accompaniment work.*

Scale notes and "altered" notes on the 3rd string cont...

The chords given in Fig. 1, 2 and 3 provide a complete range of scale notes and "altered" scale-notes of the key of Gmajor to produce the same range in any chosen major key. Refer to the "Reference Tables: Major Keys", on page 20. The table given shows the positions for the fingerboard, each scale note, and all six strings.

To adjust any of the "standard" chord-forms in any selection key, follow the directions given on page 10. The examples show how "added" or "altered" scale-notes can be included in the harmony parts of a chord according to the chord symbol. (Given in the harmonic progression for any particular popular song you are dealing with at any given time.) Such adjustments apply equally to chord selection for use in accompaniments or in "chord solo" playing.

Scale notes ascending from the Rootnote, (G), on the open third string

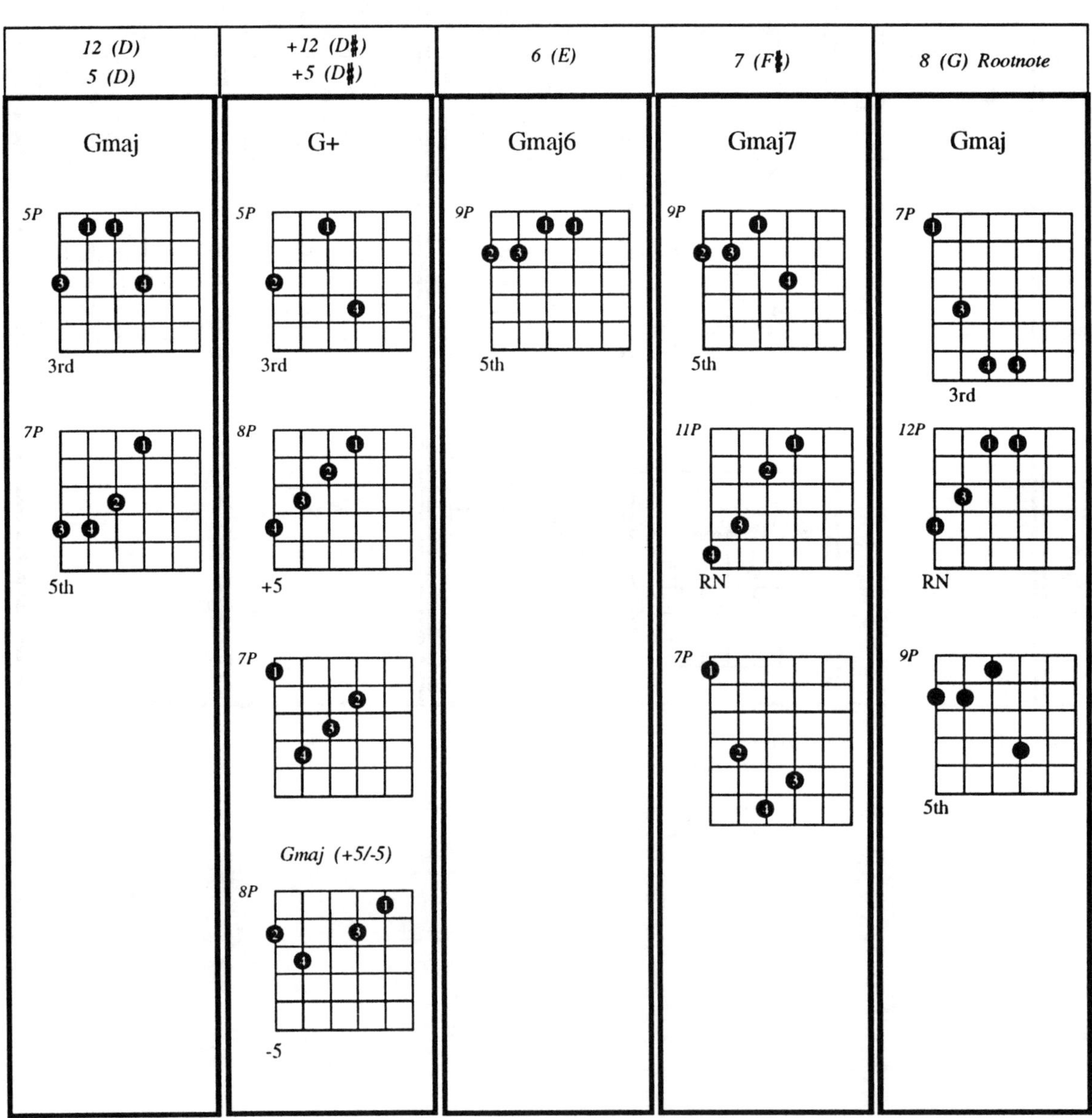

"CHORD SOLO"
PLAYING SELF ARRANGED

As already mentioned, the notes of any popular song are scale notes and 'altered' scale notes, including 'passing notes', belonging to the keys indicated by the chord symbols given for the harmonic accompaniment. Therefore, to play a melody in chord style it is only necessary, as a preparatory step, to work out the positions on which the notes will be played on the finger board. Some will be on the first string, some on the second, and if required, some on the third.

The next step is to take each chord symbol in turn, preferably dealing with those given in the first four bars of the melody, followed later on by the succeeding four bars and so on, in stages, through the whole chorus.

Refer to the 'Reference Tables; Major Keys'. For each major chord symbol in the 'four bar extract', turn to the table given for the symbol so that you can locate the 'scale note' name for the melody note- (You will already know the position of the note on the guitar, assuming that you have worked out the positions in the preparatory step just mentioned.) Then turning to figures 1, 2 and 3, make a rough sketch on paper of chord diagrams given for the same melody note in G major, but this time with the lead note of the chord diagram to be placed on the scale note in your chord solo. (See page 91 and 92, on which the latter page is given a chord solo of an extract from 'Greensleeves').

After dealing with the major chord symbols and their scale notes which occur in the melody line, take each minor chord symbol and melody notes in turn and deal with them in the same way. Follow this with dominant chord symbols and their melody notes and last diminished.

The method just explained is somewhat more convenient than the one which involves switching back and forth from major chords to minors, back to majors, then dominants and so on. In the final linking together of the 'melody chords', your ear and instinct for good harmony will be the deciding factor in devising an interesting solo.

The table on the right is an example in C major showing the distance using whole steps and half steps between any two scale notes and the interval distance between the root note and each note of the ascending scale.

'Altered' notes are in brackets.

C major scale on the 2nd string

Position	2nd string	Note
N.P.	7	-B
P1	R	-C (circled)
P2	(-2)	-D♭
P3	2	-D
P4	(+2)	-D♯
P5	3	-E
P6	4	-F
P7	(+4/-5)	-F♯/-G♭
P8	5	-G
P9	(+5)	-G♯
P10	6	-A
P11	(-7)	-B♭
P12	7	-B
P13	R8	-C (circled)
P14	(-9)	-D♭
P15	9	-D

Reference Tables: Major Keys

Scale notes in all major keys and their positions on the fingerboard. Directions are the same as those given on page 7, and for scale notes and 'altered' scale notes in G major, page 8. Note particularly the pattern of root note positions. Play these in 'octave form' to become familiar with these positions, then form the various chords around the octave positions. To find the figure for a 'compound' interval, simply add 7 to the figure for the equivalent 'simple' interval, i.e.,2 plus 7 =9, 4 plus 7= 11.

Figure 1- Tables for the 'open' key and the cycle of flat keys from F major to D flat major. For G flat see F sharp major.

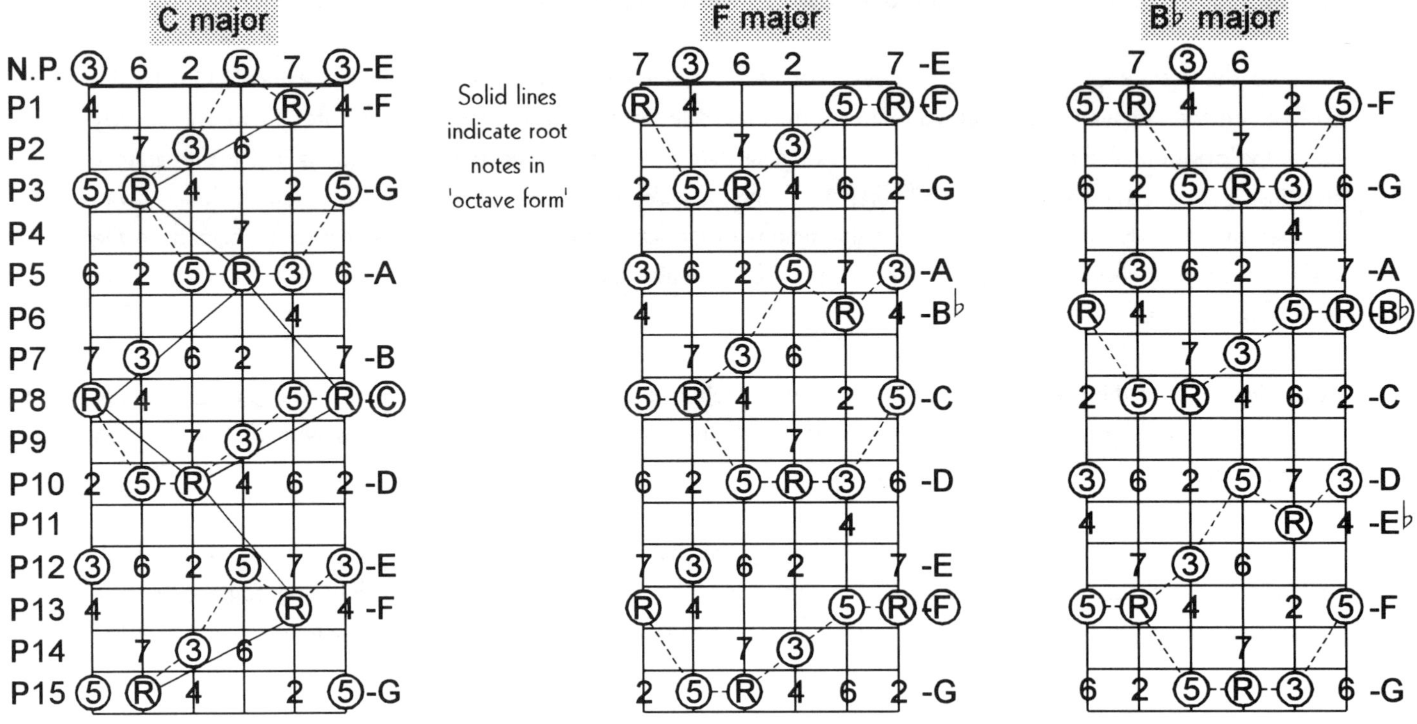

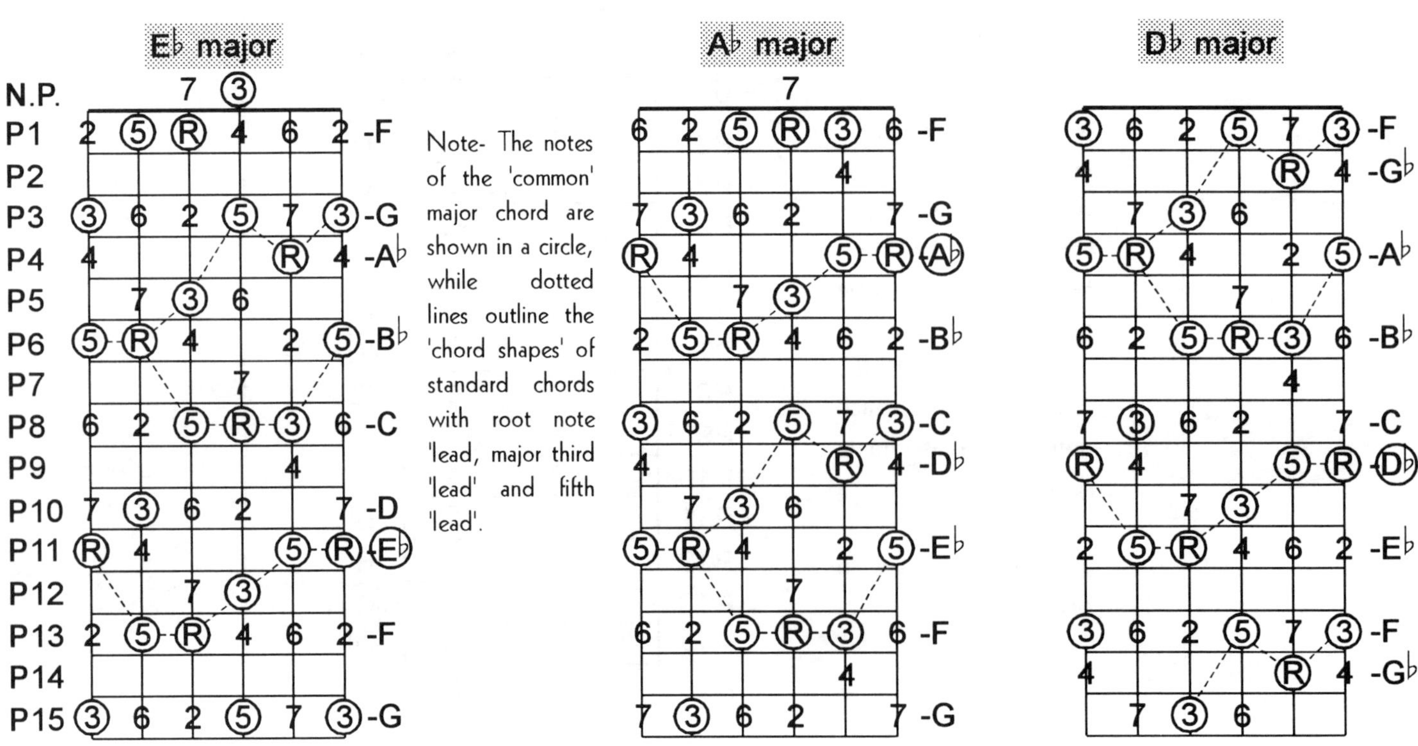

Figure 2- Tables for the cycle of sharp keys.

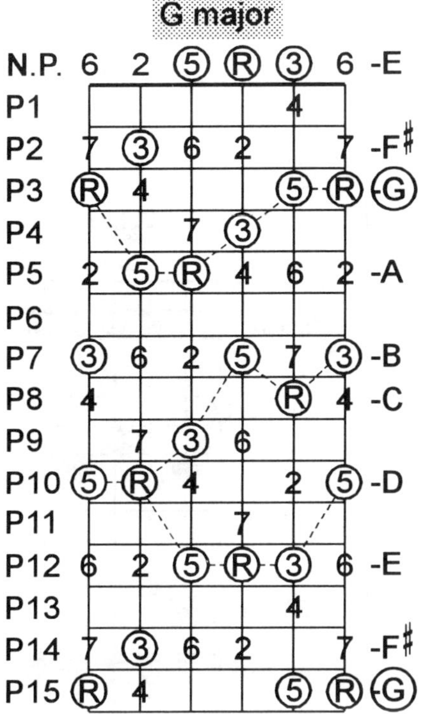

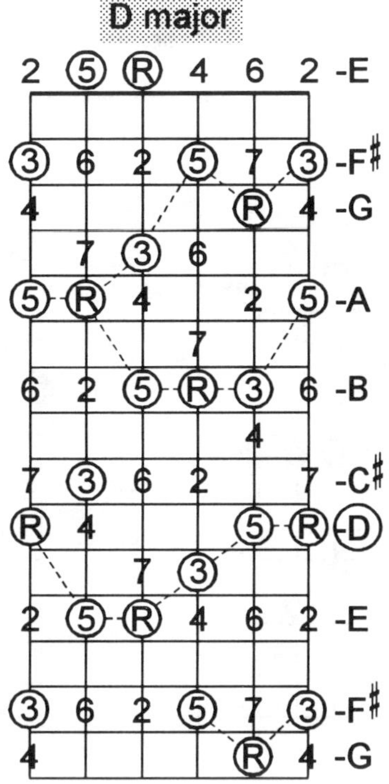

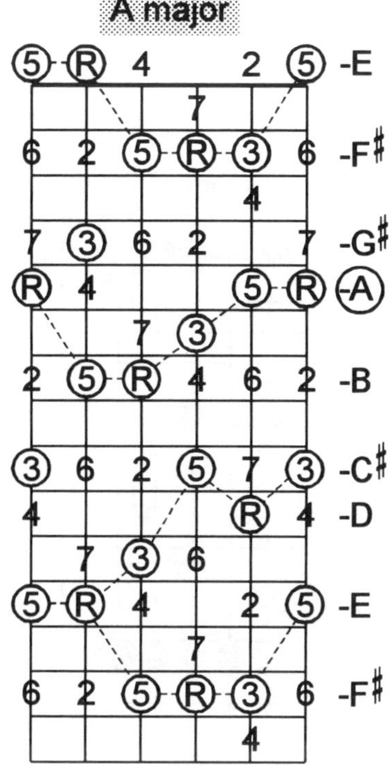

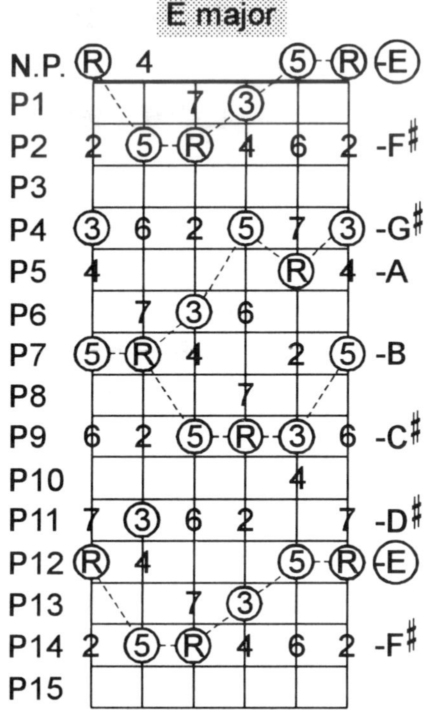

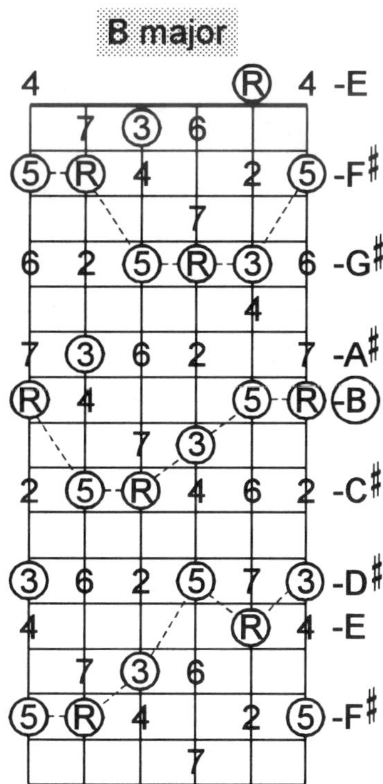

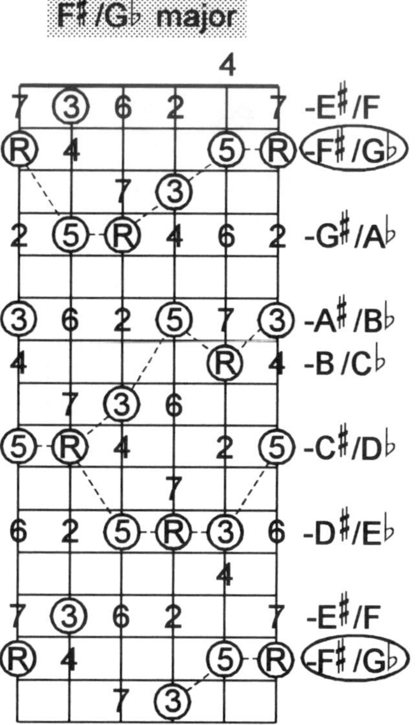

Example in transposing the chord form from '6th' lead in G major to C major, E♭ major and A major. Try some of your own transpositions in other keys as well. Note the finger allotted to the lead note.

Fingers used for chord shapes are in black dots- ❶

Circled fingers are the '6th' as lead note- ③

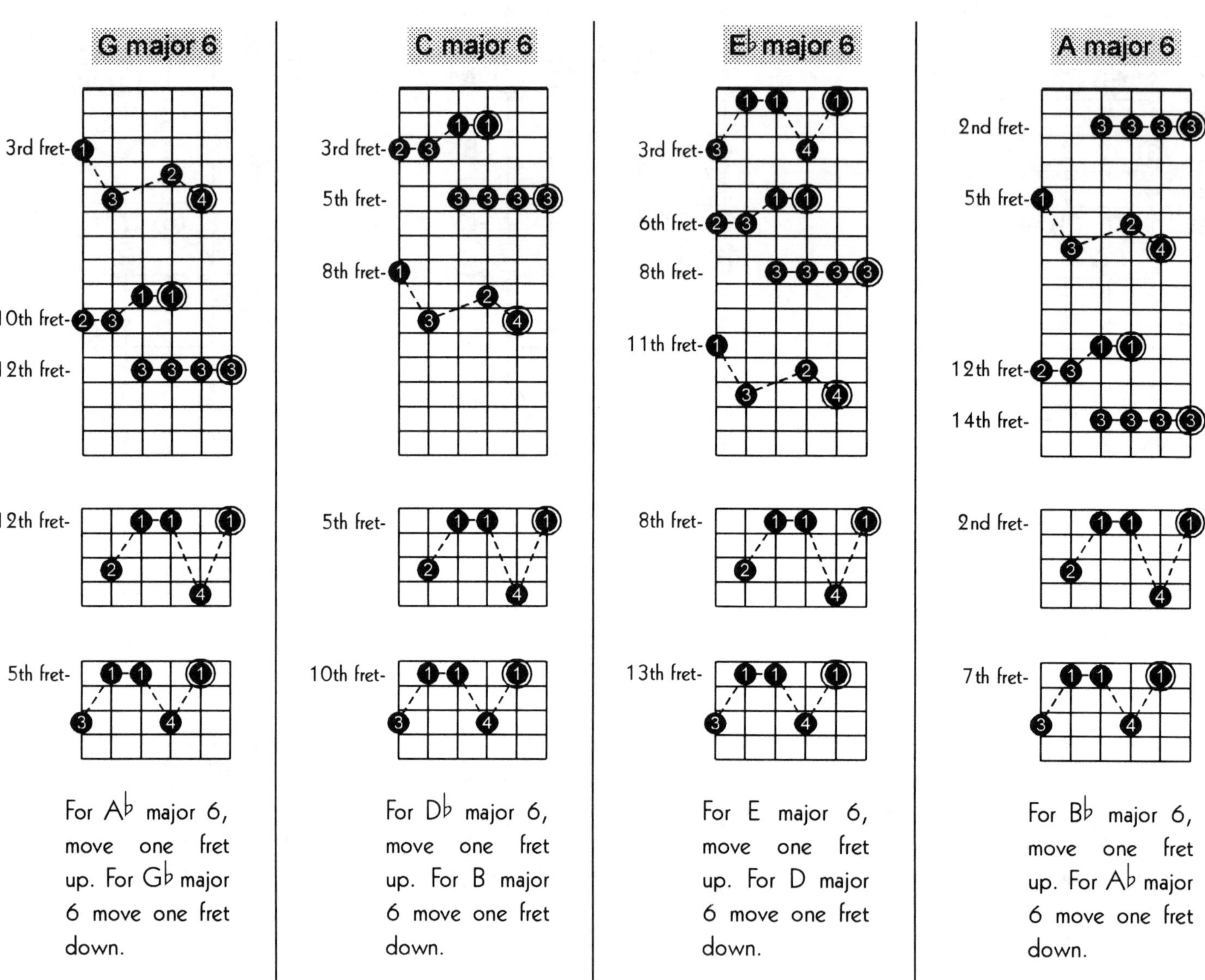

For A♭ major 6, move one fret up. For G♭ major 6 move one fret down.

For D♭ major 6, move one fret up. For B major 6 move one fret down.

For E major 6, move one fret up. For D major 6 move one fret down.

For B♭ major 6, move one fret up. For A♭ major 6 move one fret down.

Experiments With Chords Forms

In concluding part 1, the following extension method described on page 10, for adjusting the 'common' or standard chord form, (for major key harmony), in order to include other scale notes and/or altered notes in the harmony parts, may be of some interest to readers who wish to make use of what are often referred to as progressive chords.

1 - Refer to figure 1, page 11, and look for chord diagrams in which the sixth string is not used. For this experiment, simply transfer the note given for the first string to the same first position on the sixth string. In the case of chords having a scale note other than the root note, third or fifth in the lead, the result of the transferring of the lead note to the sixth string will be to include an added or altered note in the harmony parts, in the bass part.

The following examples show some of the chord forms produced by the experiment:

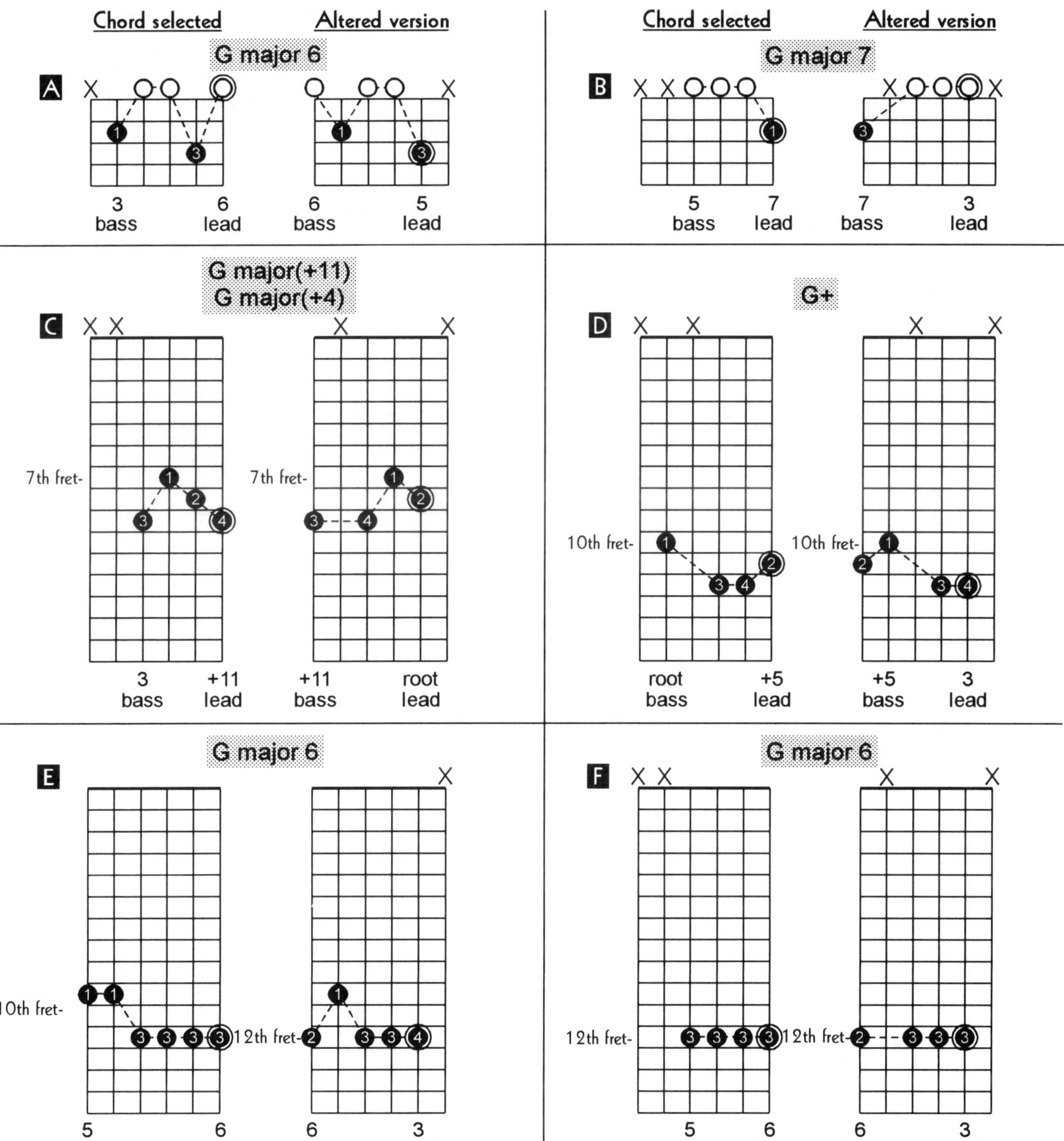

The above experiment can be applied to minor, dominant and diminished chords with the 'lead' on the first string and the sixth string vacant. Some discretion should be used in the case of chord forms having the 9th and minor 9th in the bass, particularly in major and minor chords. Though the minor 9th is effective in dominant chords, as are other "added" and "altered" notes except the 6th(or 13th), which is frequently used in the bass part for major and minor chords but is not so good in dominant chord harmony. Much depends upon the chord which immediately follows the chord with "passing" bass note. The 9th can descend a whole tone to the root or sometimes to the "delayed" 3rd; the "aug.4th"/"dim.5th" to the "natural"5th or again to the delayed 3rd while the 7th can descend to the 6th or ascend a half-step to the root note. When such sequences are played "by ear" the latter will be the best guide.

2 - This one is the opposite to #1. Refer to fig. 2 page 14 and select forms which have a note on the sixth string. Transfer this note from the sixth string to the same position on the first string or simply duplicate it on the first string.
The note on the sixth string will be one of the notes of the triad , i.e., the root note, 3rd or 5th, and this note will become the new "lead". Though in this case the harmony notes will contain an "added" or "altered" note. In some instances the note which you transferred to the first string may be subsequently moved one or two frets up or down where practical, while other notes stay put. A few moments spent on a little pondering of the following examples will be sufficient for the reader to understand the procedure.

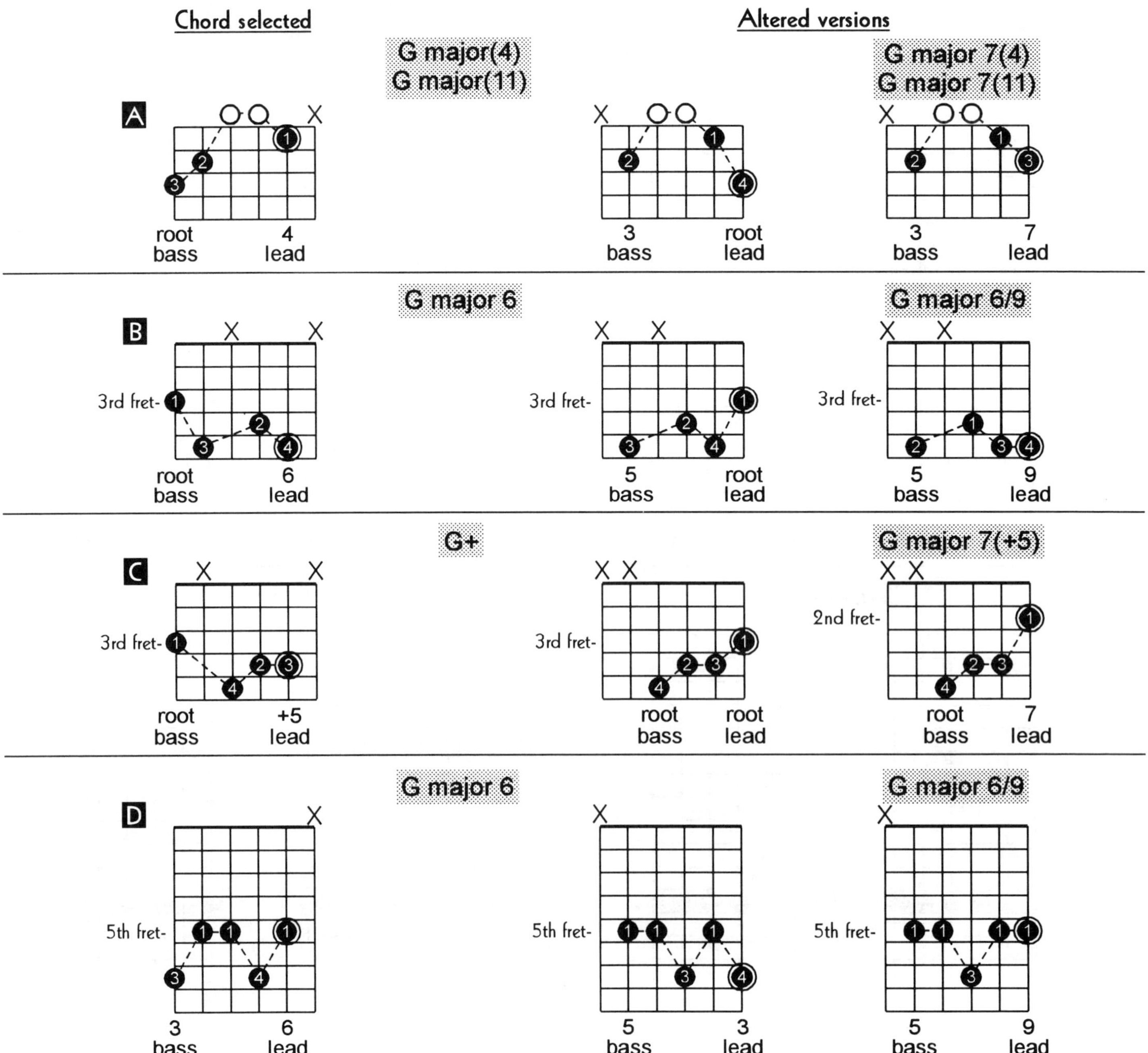

There is plenty of scope for individual experiments on the methods outlined above since you can treat minor chords and dominant chords in the same manner.

3 - Again refer to fig. 2. For this experiment simply add a note to the vacant first string. The added note will belong to the same scale as the notes of the chord. Examples are:

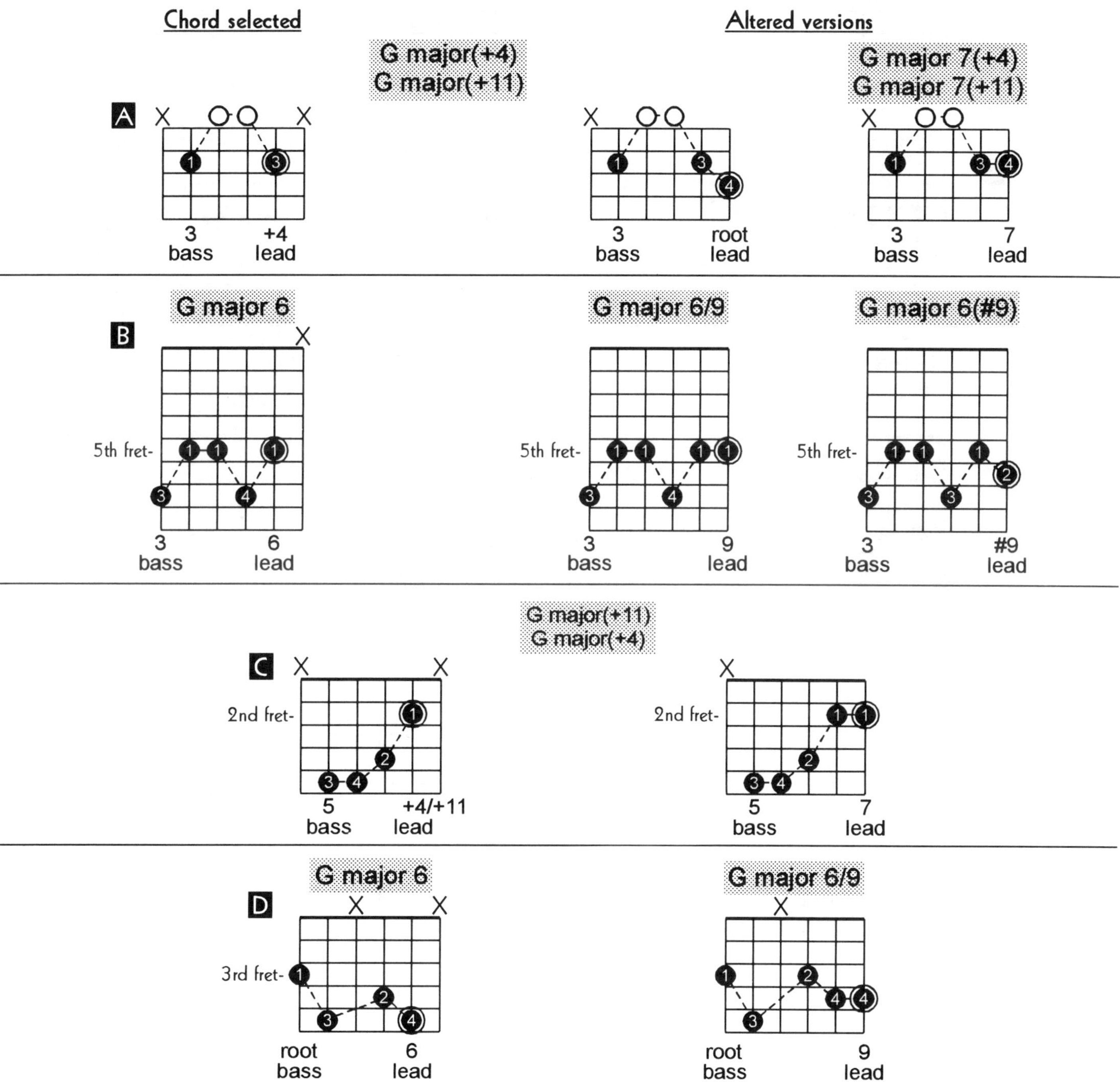

4 - The present experiment is less productive than the previous three. Refer to fig. 3, page 17, and select from the chords with the lead on the third string, those forms which allow for adding a scale-note or an altered scale note on the vacant second string. The examples given here are practically self explanatory and perhaps less confusing.

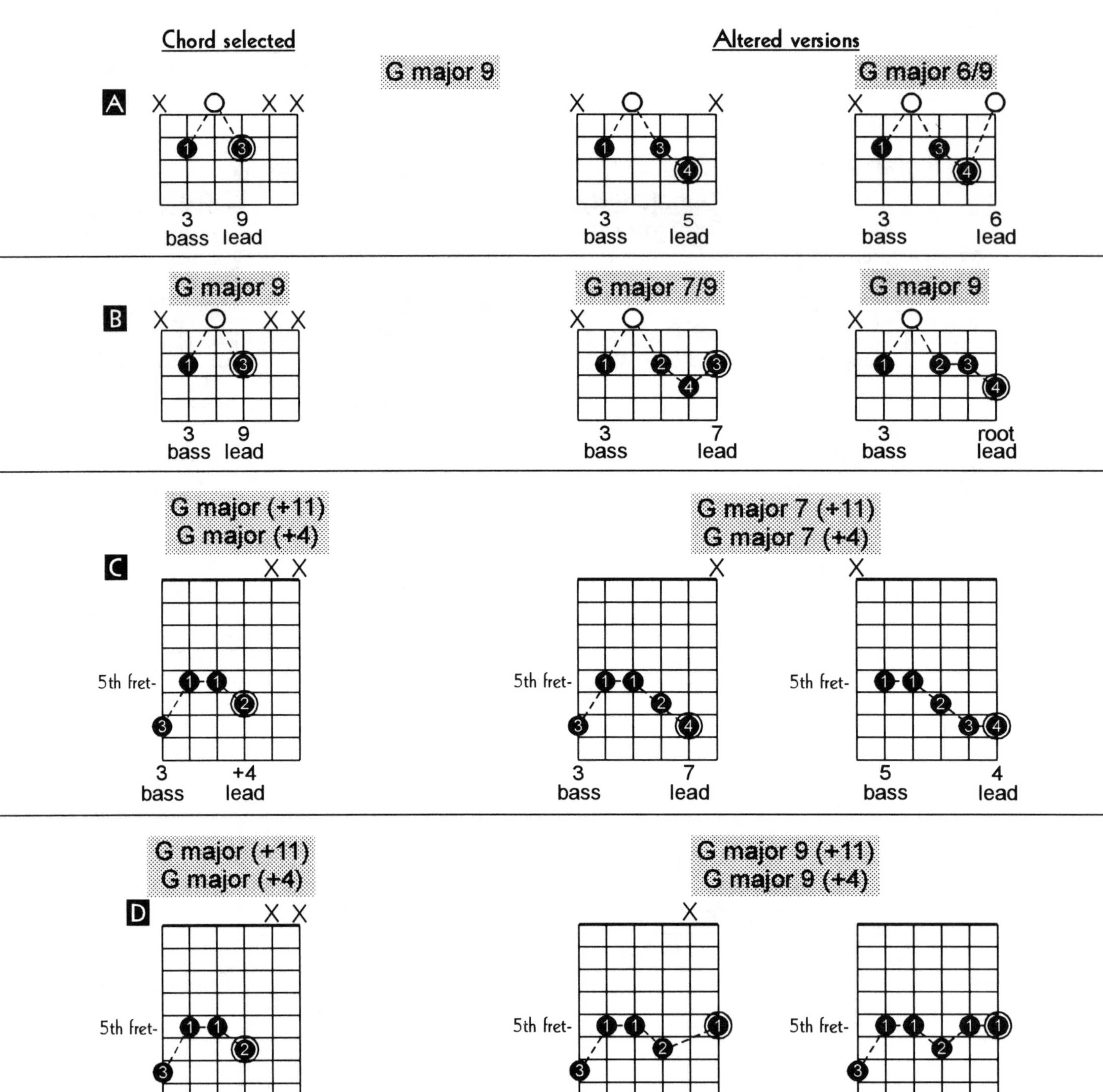

5 - The method described in this experiment is completely different from those in experiments 1- 4, and more involved. It is the readers priviledge to take it or leave it.

The purpose of the experiment is to devise an appropriate chord form to use for a particular lead note for a given chord symbol in which an added or altered scale-note is called for in the harmony part. First attempts are best confined to dealing with chords which contain no more than one added or altered note. Therefore, should the given chord symobol indicate the inclusion of two added notes, you could omit one of the two notes.

Suppose the lead note is the 5th and the chord symbol is a G major 6 as below in Figure 1. On a sheet of paper, write down the four notes of the chord, in vertical order with the lead note, D(the5th) at the top and the remaining notes of the chord in the order as they occur in the G major scale descending from D.

Figure 1

G major 6

D .... 5th lead
B 3rd
G .... rootnote
E .... 6th bass

These notes are in close harmony form and in most cases this form is challenging on the guitar because of the wide expansion of the hand required for their execution. In this instance the close formation is often used by guitarists.

Referring to the table on page 32 titled "Notes produced on the strings at each fret" and following the directions given on page 10, place a marker on D(3rd fret on second string) or on position ten on the first string. Then place markers on the notes B, G, and E on adjacent inner strings. The notes should be in order exactly as you have written them down. The illustrations in figure 1 shows the markers in position on the table of fingerboard positions.

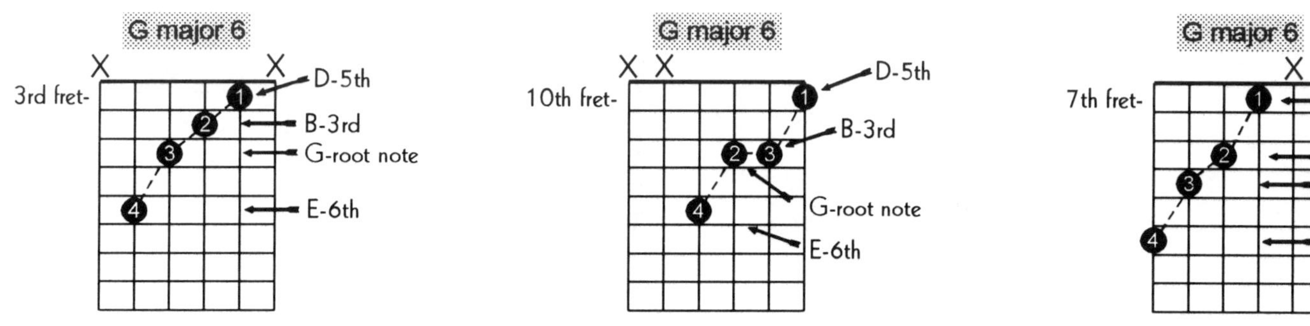

The fret position stopped by the first finger can be indicated either at the side of the diagram. The latter figure indicates the fret position next in the direction towards the nut position and is convenient for use with chord diagrams close together.

Besides the close harmony forms for the four-note chord given in figure 1, we can also have the same four notes arranged in open or extended harmony and these are ideally practical for playing on the guitar.

Close harmony

a)

D	lead	D	lead
B	3rd	B	3rd
G	root note	E	6th
E	6th	G	root note

A simple method for rearranging the three notes in the harmony parts, while maintaining the same lead note, is shown in this eample of the regrouping of the notes of figure 1. The notes in harmony parts of the close harmony form were, in descending scale order: B, G and E. Keeping the note B in the same position we can alter the notes G and E to read E and G.

Open or extended harmony

b)

D	lead	D	lead
G	root note	G	root note
E	6th	B	3rd
B	3rd	E	6th

In this example, take G as the top note of the harmony parts in descending scale order G, E, B and G, B, E.

c)

D	lead	D	lead
E	6th	E	6th
B	3rd	G	root note
G	root note	B	3rd

Take E as the top harmony note. We have E, B, G and E, G, B thus completeing the permutation order of the three notes, as shown in this example.

The notes in the open and extended forms are in descending order of the scale below the lead note, except each note is, in turn, moved an octave lower.

Take each of the extended harmony forms, from the previous page, in the order given and place markers on the position of the notes on the table of fingerboard positions. As to allow for easy sketching the chord diagrams on a sheet of graph paper, or on plain paper, the chord diagram froms thus obtained are as shown in the illustration following:

A

D .... lead
B 3rd
E 6th
G .... root note   bass

G major 6

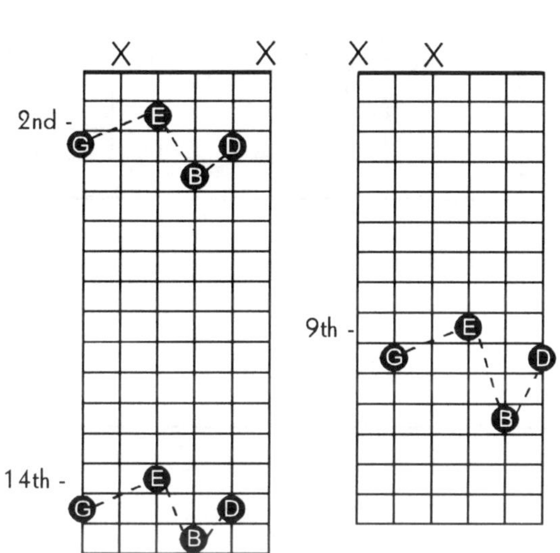

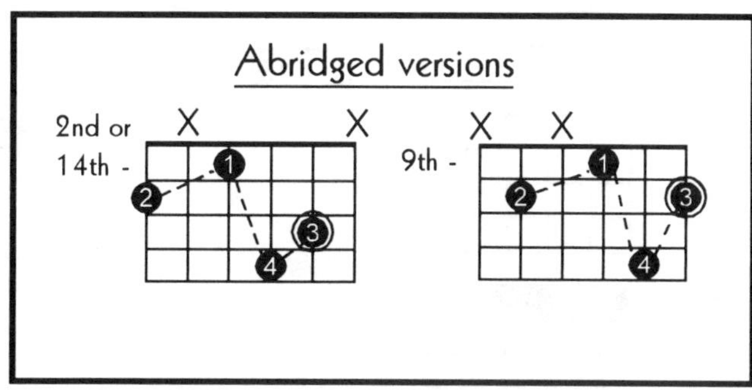

B

D .... lead
G .... root note
E 6th
B .... 3rd   bass

G major 6

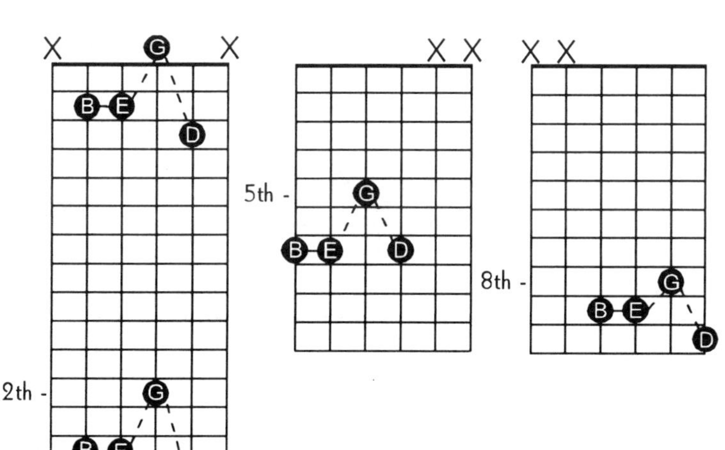

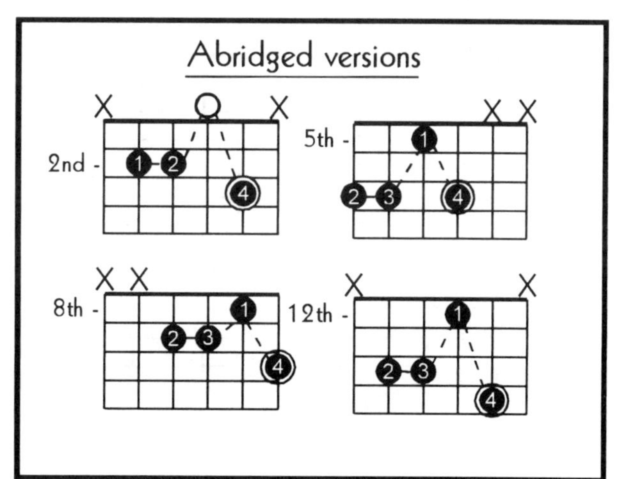

C

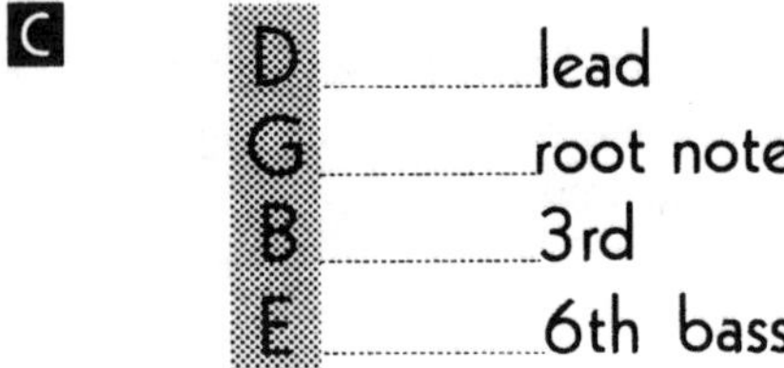

G major 6

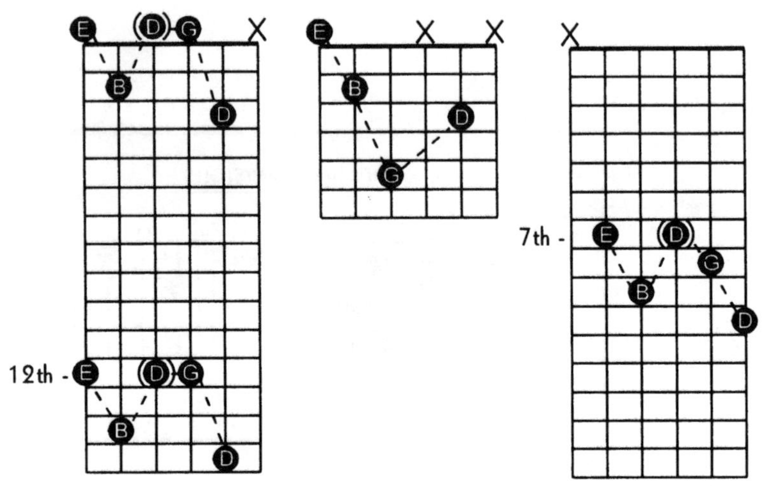

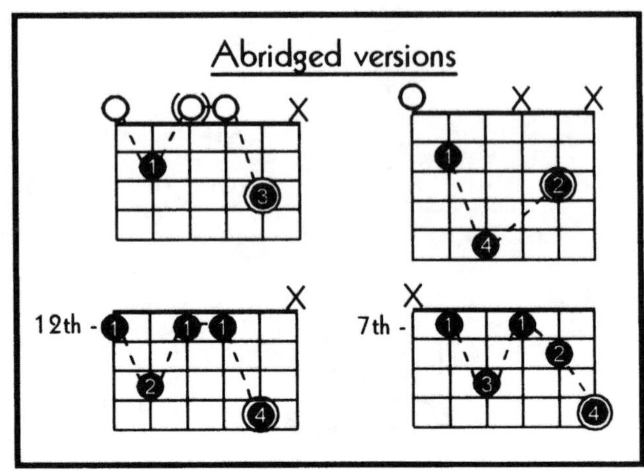

D

D lead
E 6th
B 3rd
G root note bass

G major 6

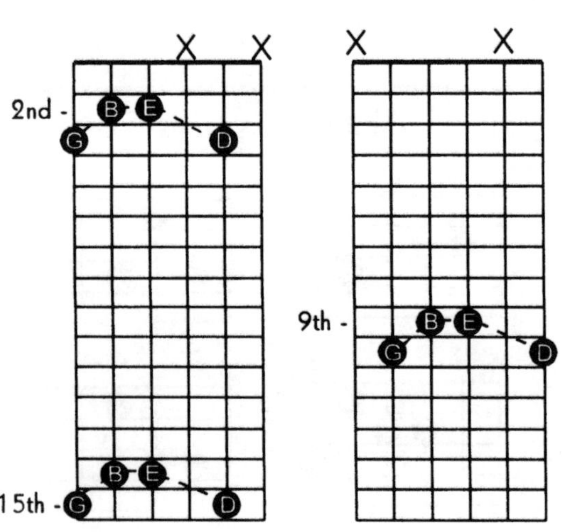

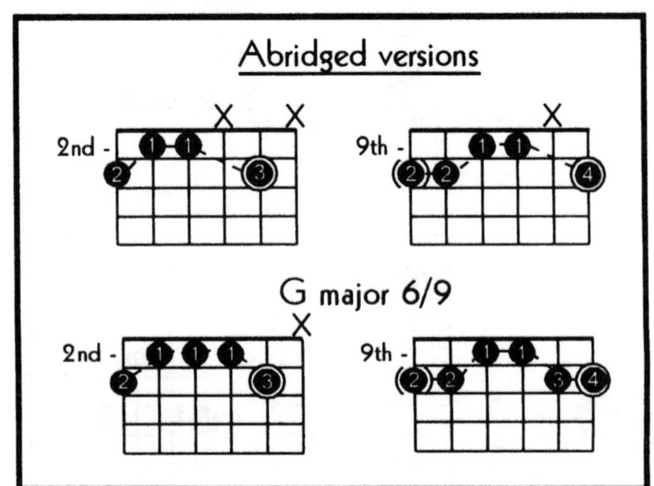

The second grouping in figure **D** is impractical on the guitar due to the wide intervals which are contained in the extension. Except in isolated instances in which the gaps can be filled in with doubled notes as in the example given below.

G major 6

E

G	root note lead
B	3rd
D	5th
E	6th bass

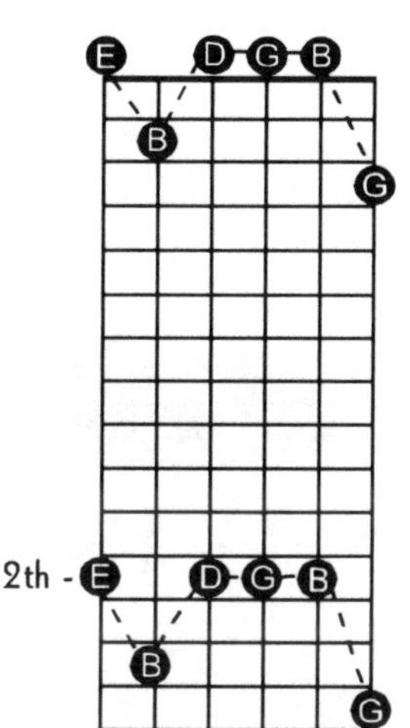

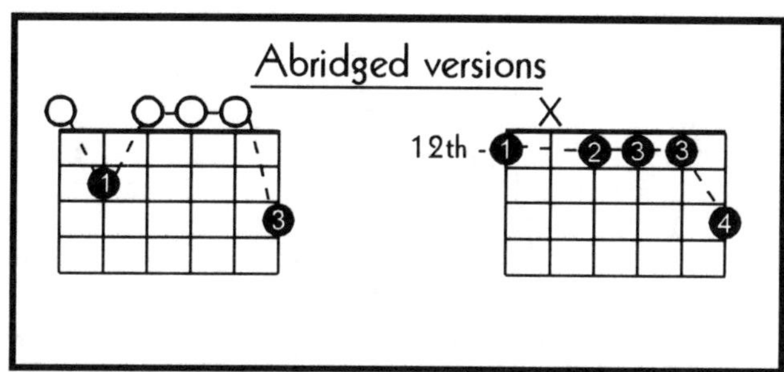

Experiment #5 can also be used when any of the other three notes of the G major 6th chord are in the lead position. So when this chord is called for in accompaniment work it is possible to obtain a large selection of chord diagrams for this symbol, and when moved up and down the fingerboard to various positions the chord of the major sixth in any major key. Additionally, all other four-note chords with minor and dominant harmony can be treated in the same manner.

In the case of chord symbols which call for two added notes such as major 6/9, major 7/9, minor 6/9, minor 7/9 and dominant 7th chord with added 9th or minor 9th. These chords can be converted to four-note chords by omitting the 5th. Except when the 5th and 3rd are in the lead, omit the root. In the case of dominant chords, the same rule applies, except when the 5th and 9th are in the lead, it is preferred to omit the root. As for G 11 with added 9th, a six-note chord, omit both 3rd and 5th except when the 5th is the lead, omit the root and 3rd.

The five experiments with chords will provide readers who have the time to devote to such projects with an extensive repertiore of chord forms covering practically every kind of chord symbol used in popular music. It will be sufficient to work out the chord forms for one particular symbol letter-name: C major, C minor and C dominant. Since the chord diagrams for these chords are easily produced for any other symbol-letter name in the usual manner.

As a supplement to the reference tables of scale notes and altered scale-notes in all major and minor keys, the table of notes produced on the strings at each fret on page 32 gives the alphabetical names of the notes while on page 71 the reference table shows the notes in music notation.

Notes Produced On The Strings At Each Fret Including "Enharmonics"

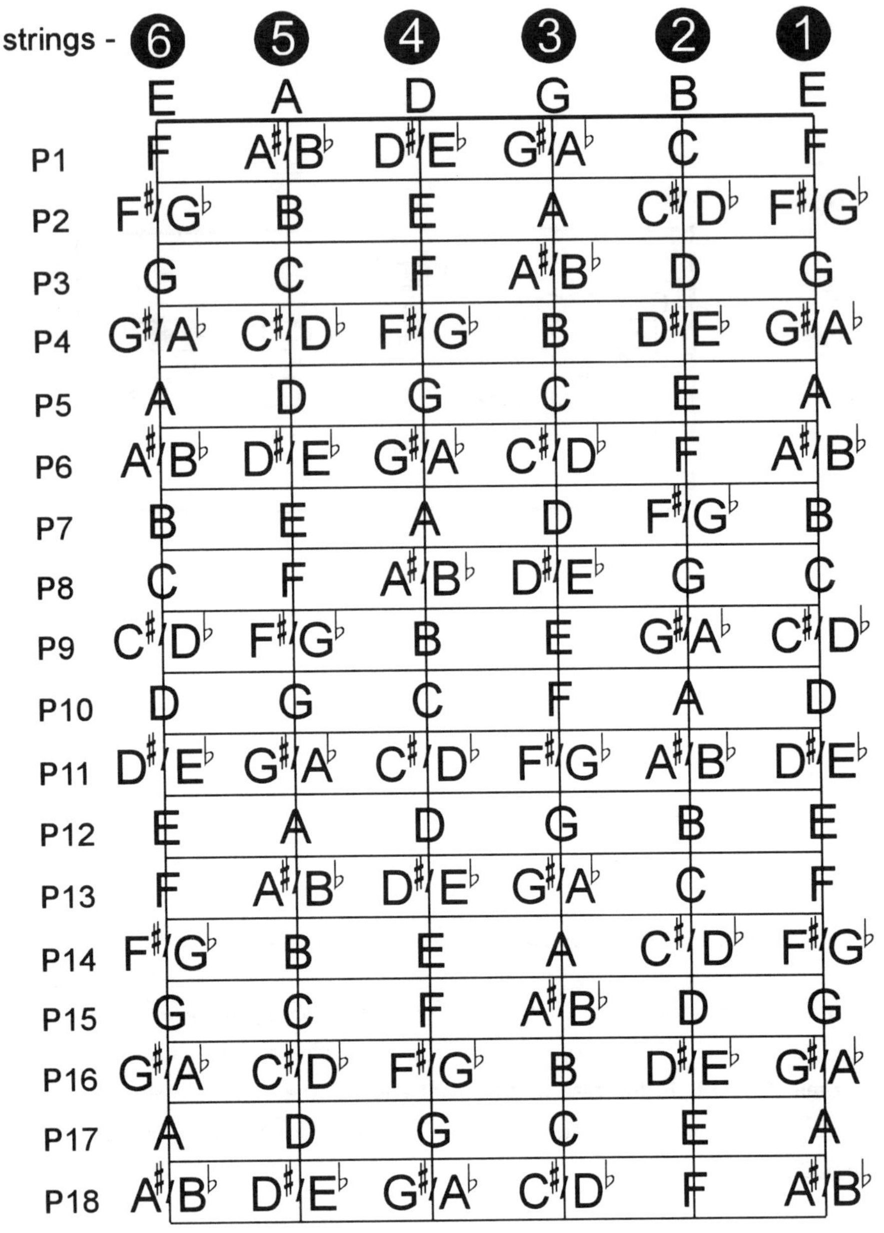

strings -	6	5	4	3	2	1
	E	A	D	G	B	E
P1	F	A♯/B♭	D♯/E♭	G♯/A♭	C	F
P2	F♯/G♭	B	E	A	C♯/D♭	F♯/G♭
P3	G	C	F	A♯/B♭	D	G
P4	G♯/A♭	C♯/D♭	F♯/G♭	B	D♯/E♭	G♯/A♭
P5	A	D	G	C	E	A
P6	A♯/B♭	D♯/E♭	G♯/A♭	C♯/D♭	F	A♯/B♭
P7	B	E	A	D	F♯/G♭	B
P8	C	F	A♯/B♭	D♯/E♭	G	C
P9	C♯/D♭	F♯/G♭	B	E	G♯/A♭	C♯/D♭
P10	D	G	C	F	A	D
P11	D♯/E♭	G♯/A♭	C♯/D♭	F♯/G♭	A♯/B♭	D♯/E♭
P12	E	A	D	G	B	E
P13	F	A♯/B♭	D♯/E♭	G♯/A♭	C	F
P14	F♯/G♭	B	E	A	C♯/D♭	F♯/G♭
P15	G	C	F	A♯/B♭	D	G
P16	G♯/A♭	C♯/D♭	F♯/G♭	B	D♯/E♭	G♯/A♭
P17	A	D	G	C	E	A
P18	A♯/B♭	D♯/E♭	G♯/A♭	C♯/D♭	F	A♯/B♭

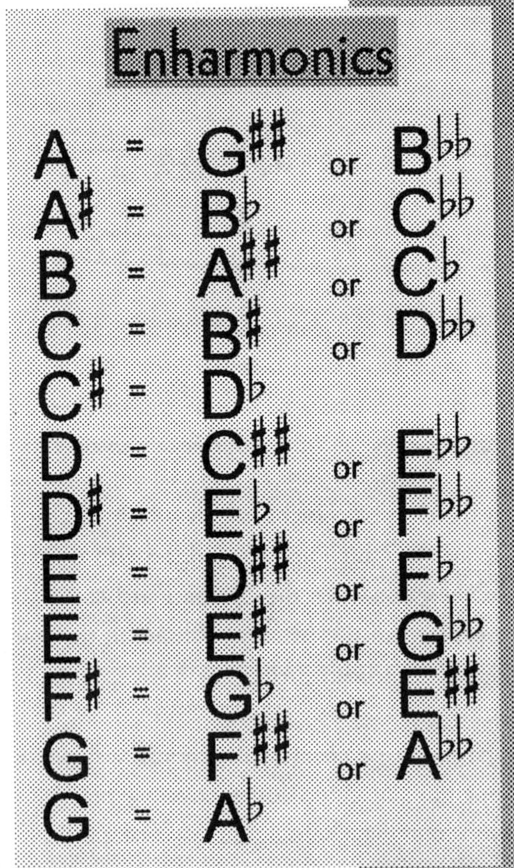

Enharmonics

A	=	G♯♯	or	B♭♭
A♯	=	B♭	or	C♭♭
B	=	A♯♯	or	C♭
C	=	B♯	or	D♭♭
C♯	=	D♭		
D	=	C♯♯	or	E♭♭
D♯	=	E♭	or	F♭♭
E	=	D♯♯	or	F♭
E	=	E♯	or	G♭♭
F♯	=	G♭	or	E♯♯
G	=	F♯♯	or	A♭♭
G	=	A♭		

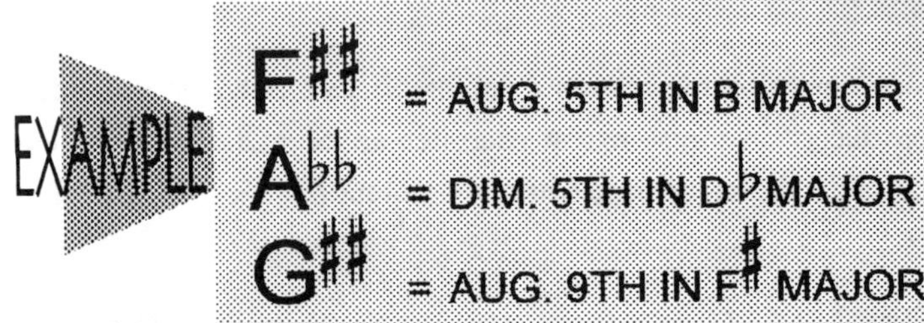

Part Two

Minor Scales In Chord Form

All examples of scale notes and altered scale-notes in part 2 are given in key G minor, from which the chord forms may be easily transposed to all other minor keys.

The scale notes and altered scale-notes in chord form include the two standard forms of the minor scale, example: the "**melodic minor**" scale and the "**harmonic minor**" scale. The melodic minor scale ascends a natural minor scale with a raised 6 & 7(maj6 and maj7) and then descends with a flat 6 & 7(min6 and min7).

The raised scale notes are shown in the brackets given below and also on the reference table of scale notes in key G minor.

Melodic Minor Scale

The sixth and seventh notes of the ascending scale are identical to the notes of the major scale which shares the same root note. However, these two notes are each lowered a half-tone to produce the minor sixth and minor seventh notes on the scale in descending order.

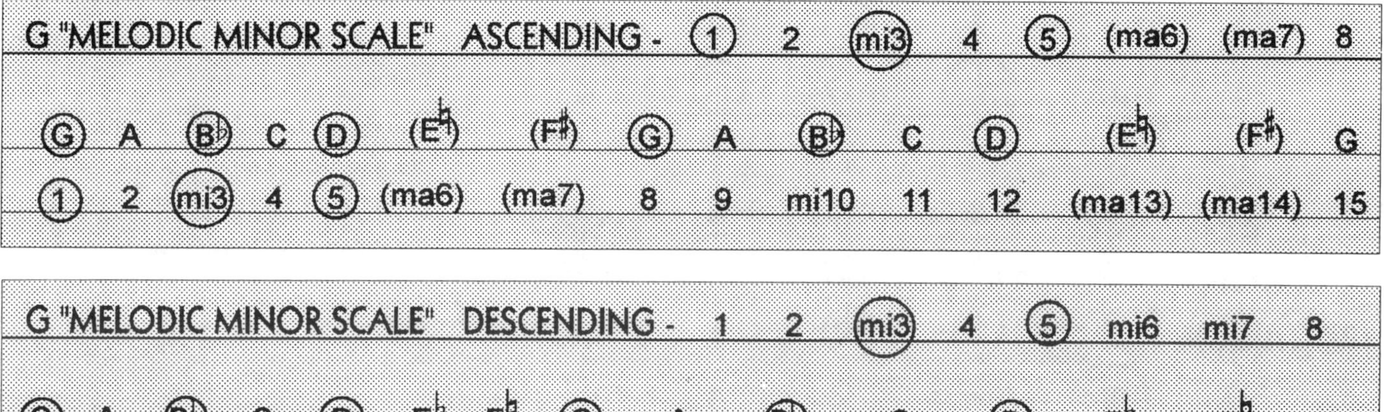

G "MELODIC MINOR SCALE" ASCENDING - 1 2 mi3 4 5 (ma6) (ma7) 8

G	A	B♭	C	D	(E♮)	(F♯)	G	A	B♭	C	D	(E♮)	(F♯)	G
1	2	mi3	4	5	(ma6)	(ma7)	8	9	mi10	11	12	(ma13)	(ma14)	15

G "MELODIC MINOR SCALE" DESCENDING - 1 2 mi3 4 5 mi6 mi7 8

G	A	B♭	C	D	E♭	F♮	G	A	B♭	C	D	E♭	F♮	G
1	2	mi3	4	5	mi6	mi7	8	9	mi10	11	12	mi13	mi14	15

(Read the descending scale from right to left.)

Harmonic Minor Scale

In this scale only the seventh note is raised a half tone; the sixth note of the scale is a minor sixth. This scale has the same notes in both ascending and descending order.

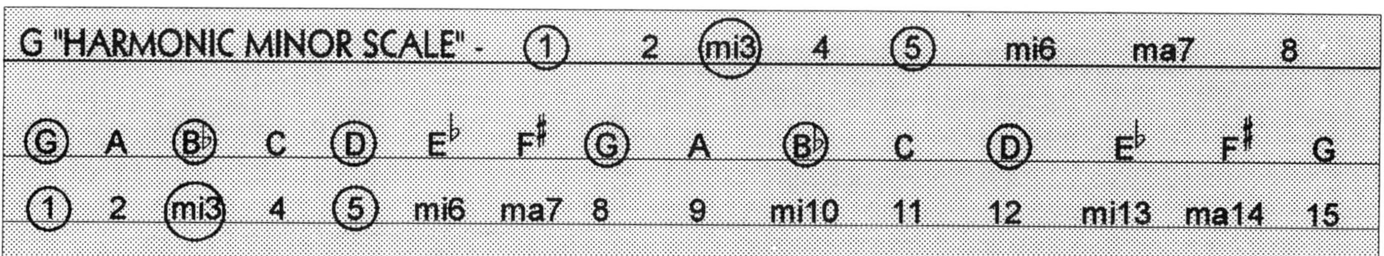

G "HARMONIC MINOR SCALE" - 1 2 mi3 4 5 mi6 ma7 8

G	A	B♭	C	D	E♭	F♯	G	A	B♭	C	D	E♭	F♯	G
1	2	mi3	4	5	mi6	ma7	8	9	mi10	11	12	mi13	ma14	15

(This scale ascends and descends the same notes.)

Reference Table of Scale Notes and Altered Scale Notes In G Minor

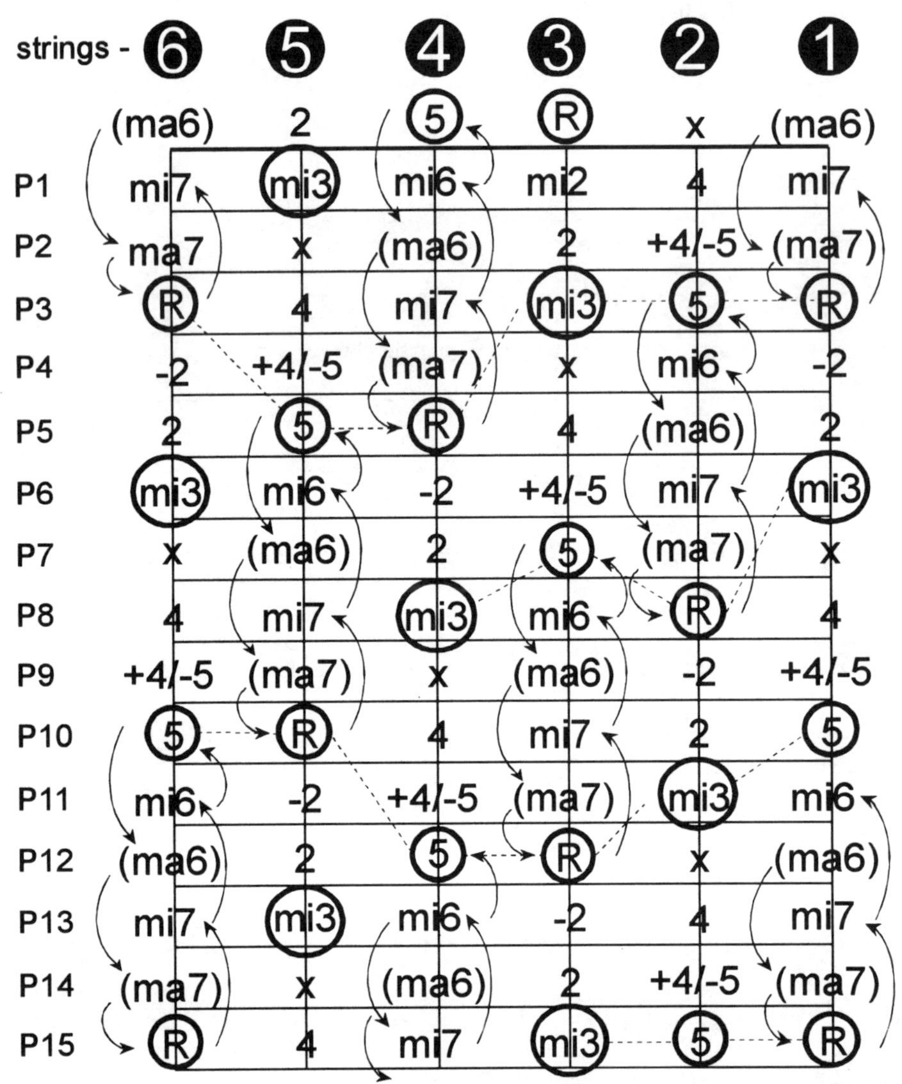

Directions are similar to those given on page 8 in the reference table of scale and notes and altered scale-notes of key G major.

The raised sixth and seventh notes of the scale are represented on the table as (ma6) and (ma7), while R represents the root note.

Notes of the common triad - rootnote, minor third and the fifth are shown in a circle. In chord symbol form the triad is indicated by the name of the root note suffixed with the term m, mi or min. EXAMPLE: Gm stands for the common minor chord in key of G minor.

Standard chord forms for the G minor triad are given on the right of the table. Each note of the triad takes its turn as the lead note of the minor chord.

Symbol Terms

X = major third(a note that is foreign to the minor key but may occassionaly be used as a passing note)

Arrows between notes on the same string indicate the steps in the ascending scale with raised 6th and 7th and in descending the minor 7th and minor 6th.

+4.	aug.4th
+11.	aug.11th
-5	dim.5th
-9.	min.9th
9	maj.9th
-6 or ♭6. . .	min.6th
6	maj.6th
-7	min.7th
ma7 or ♮7. .	maj.7th

Common Minor Triad

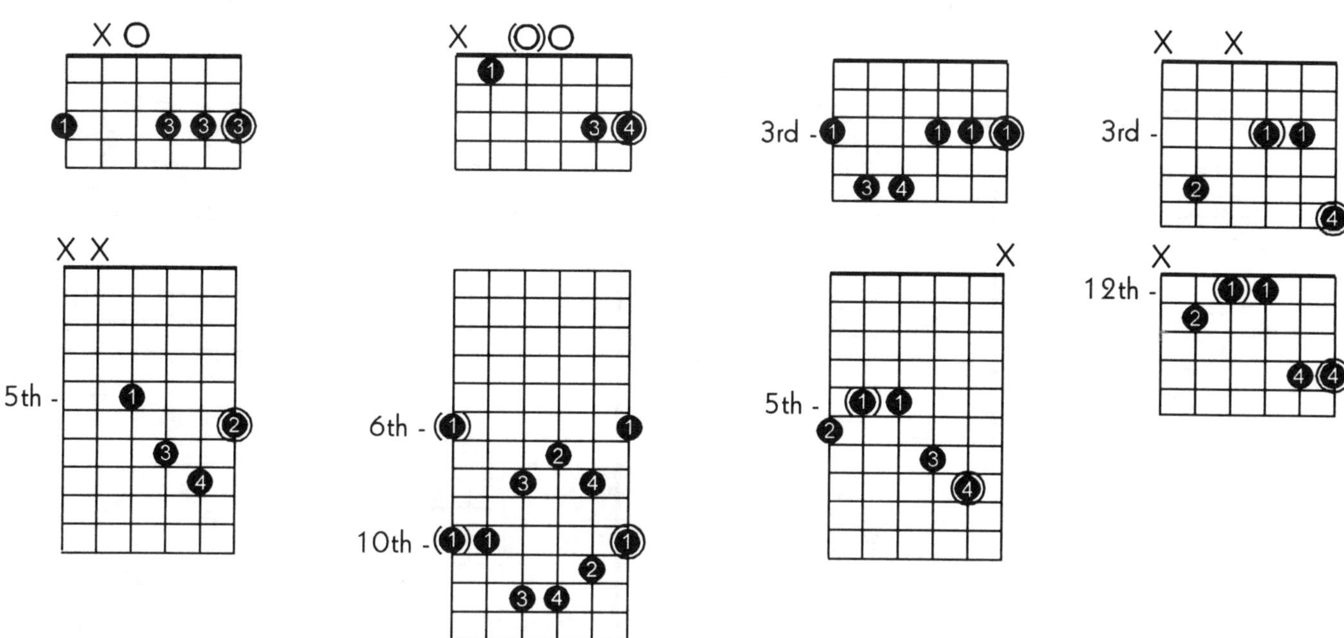

Scales In Chord Form
Minor Chords

Examples in key of G minor. Notes in the harmony parts are those of the common minor triad, (root note, minor 3rd and the 5th); to include added or altered notes in the harmony parts follow the directions given on page 10 and in the "Experiments with chord forms", page 23.

FIG. 1

Scale notes and altered notes on the first string, commencing with the raised or major sixth in the key of G minor.

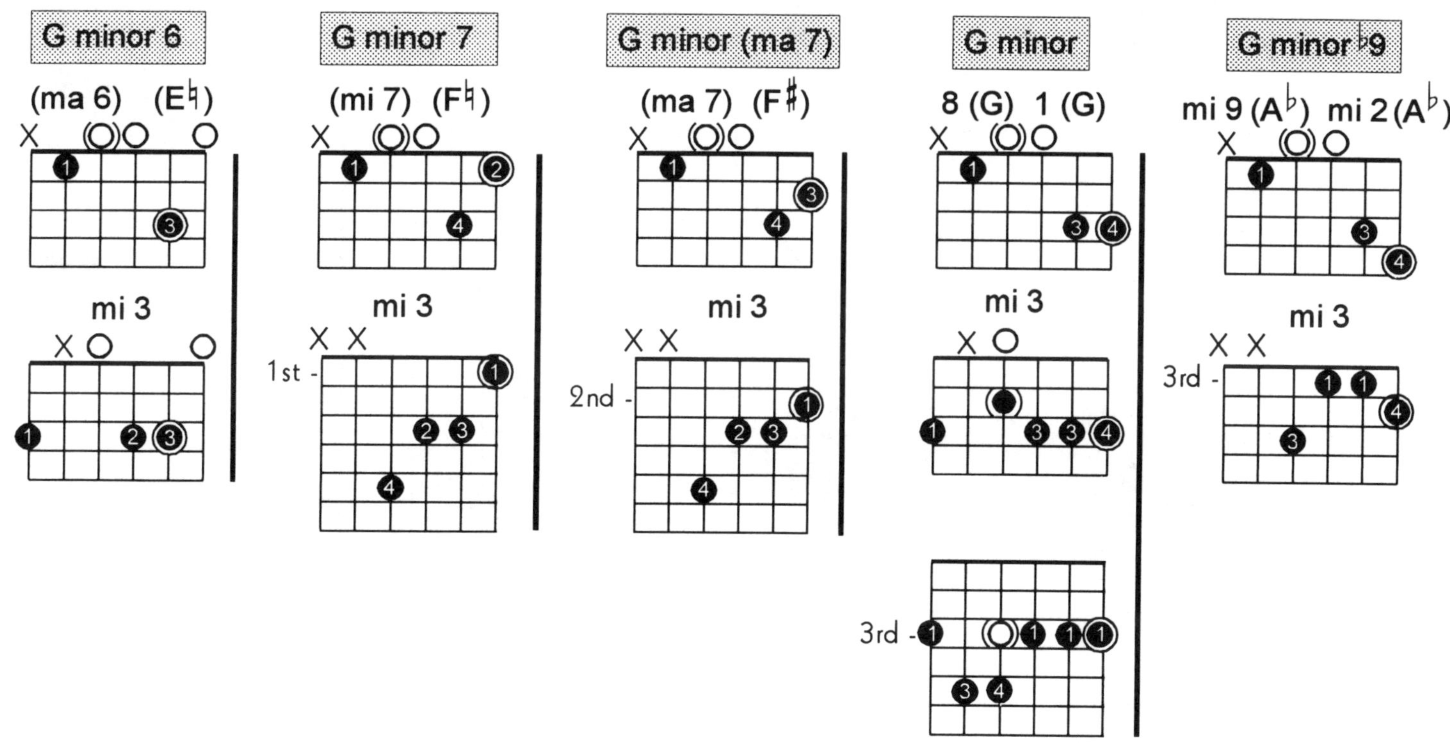

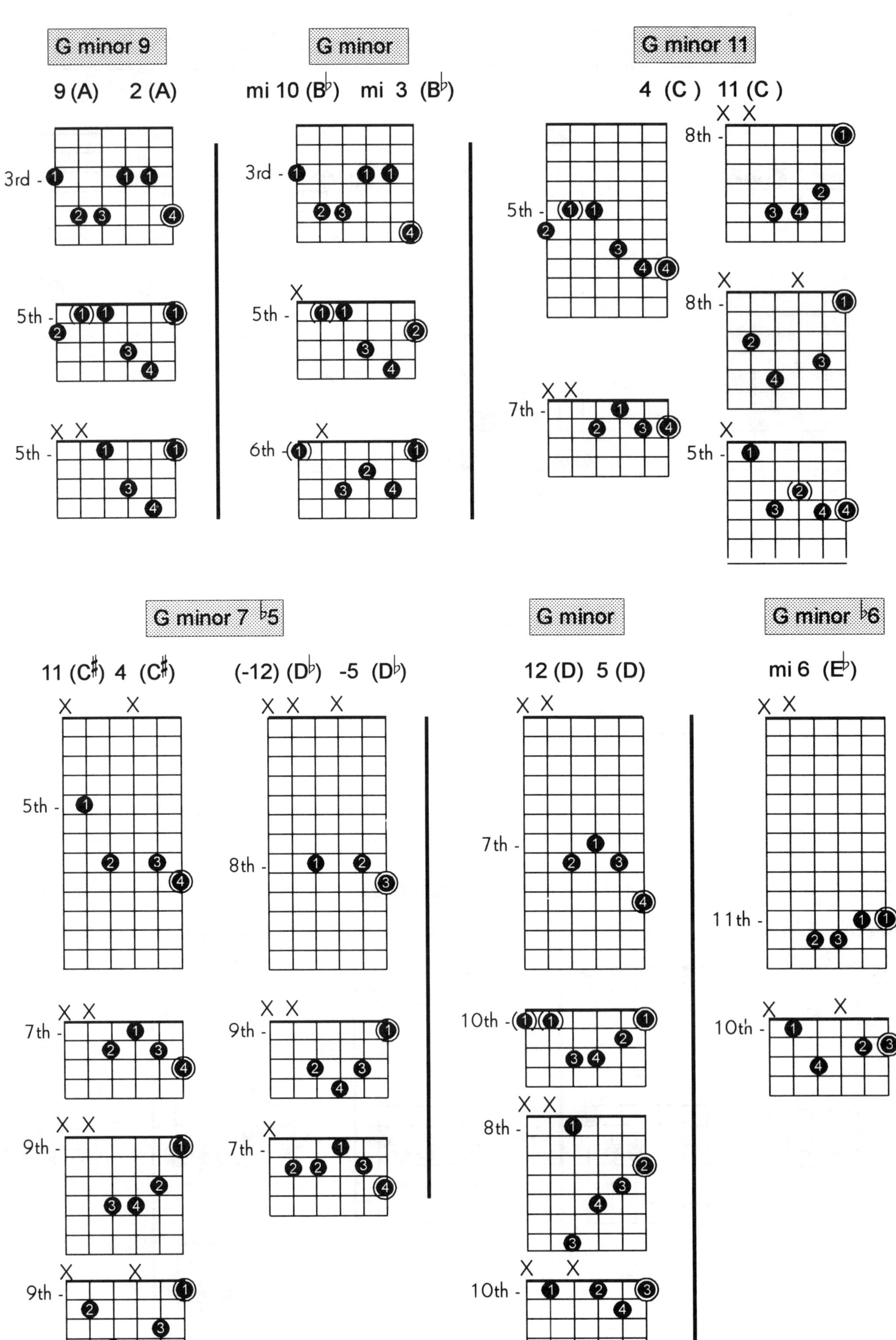
G minor 9
9 (A) 2 (A)
3rd -
5th -
5th -
G minor
mi 10 (B♭) mi 3 (B♭)
3rd -
5th -
6th -
G minor 11
4 (C) 11 (C)
5th -
7th -
8th -
8th -
5th -
G minor 7 ♭5
11 (C♯) 4 (C♯)
5th -
7th -
9th -
9th -
(-12) (D♭) -5 (D♭)
8th -
9th -
7th -
G minor
12 (D) 5 (D)
7th -
10th -
8th -
10th -
G minor ♭6
mi 6 (E♭)
11th -
10th -

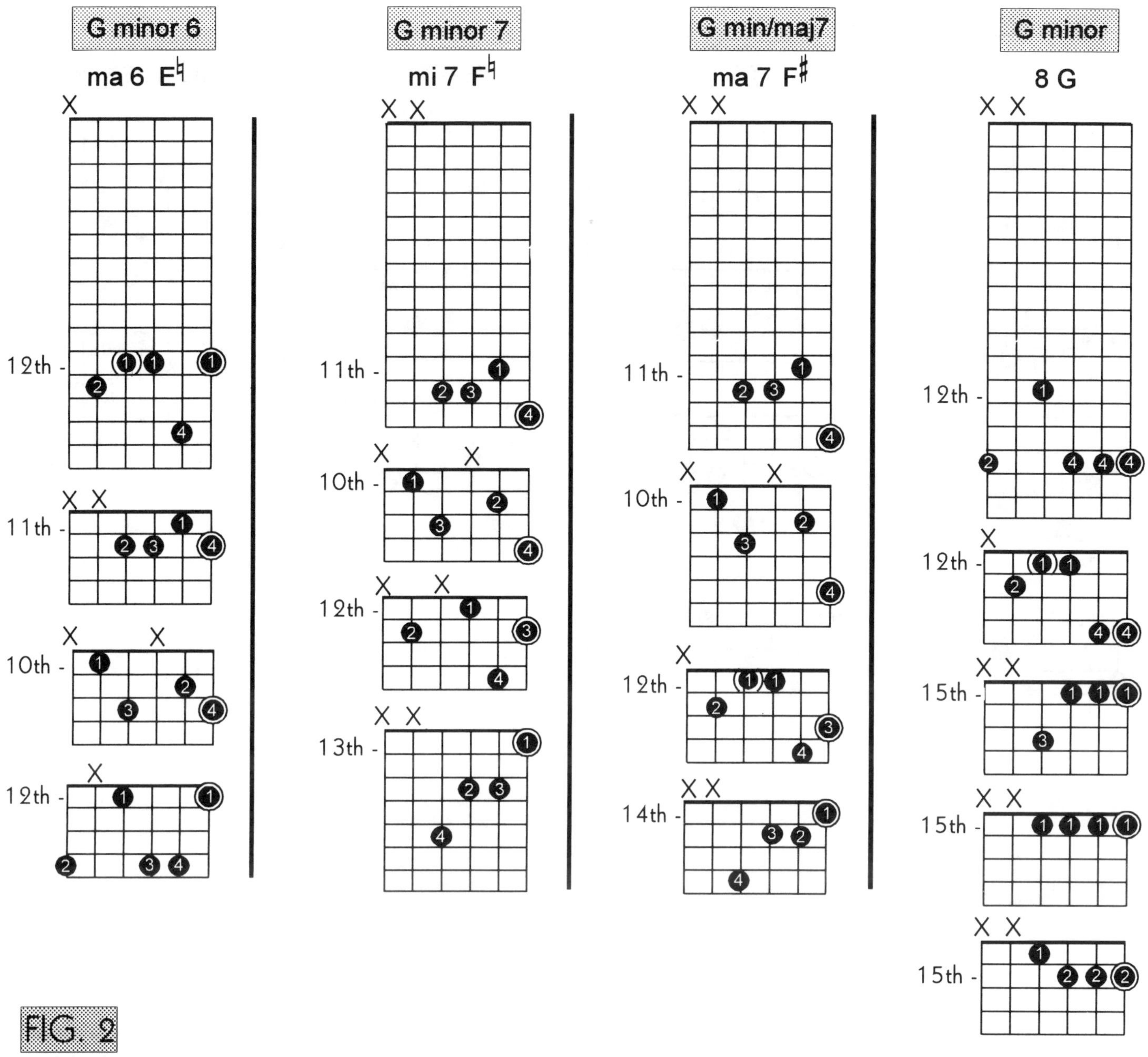

G minor 6
ma 6 E♮
12th -
11th -
10th -
12th -
G minor 7
mi 7 F♮
11th -
10th -
12th -
13th -
G min/maj7
ma 7 F♯
11th -
10th -
12th -
14th -
G minor
8 G
12th -
12th -
15th -
15th -
15th -

FIG. 2

Scale notes and altered scale notes on the second string, commencing with the 4th or 11th, scale note of G minor.

G minor 11
11 (C) 4 (C)
1st -
G minor +11
+11(C♯) +4(C♯)
2nd -

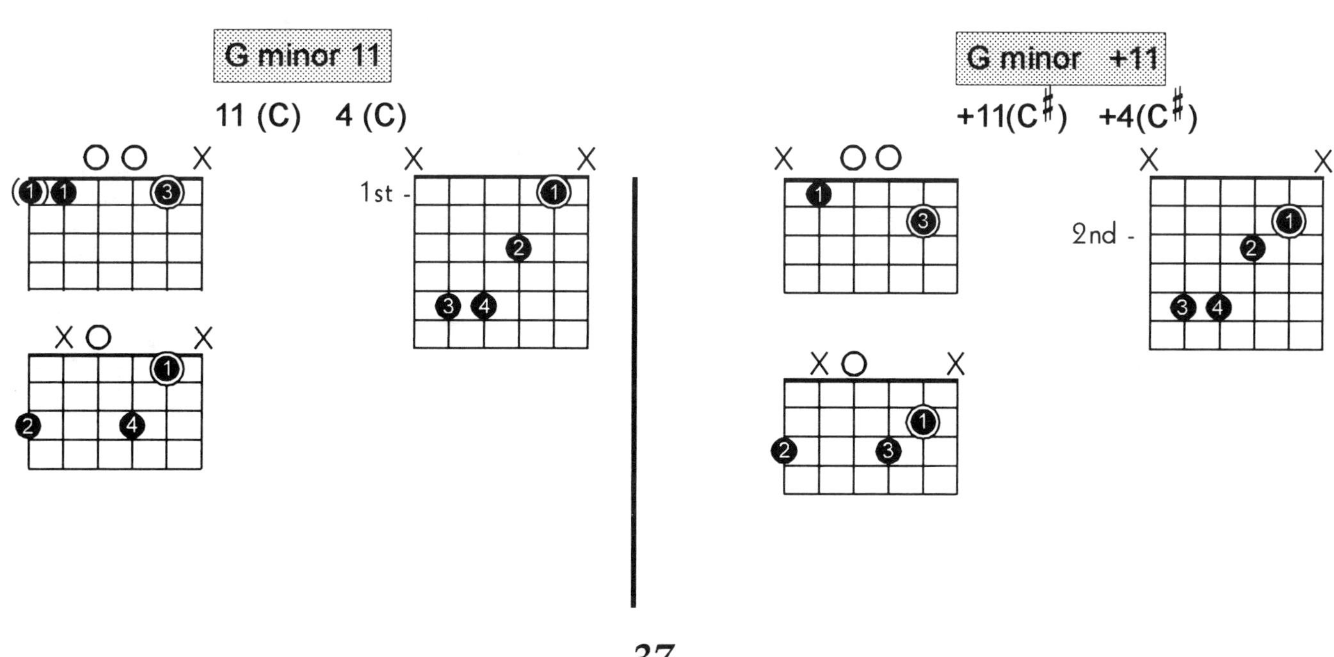

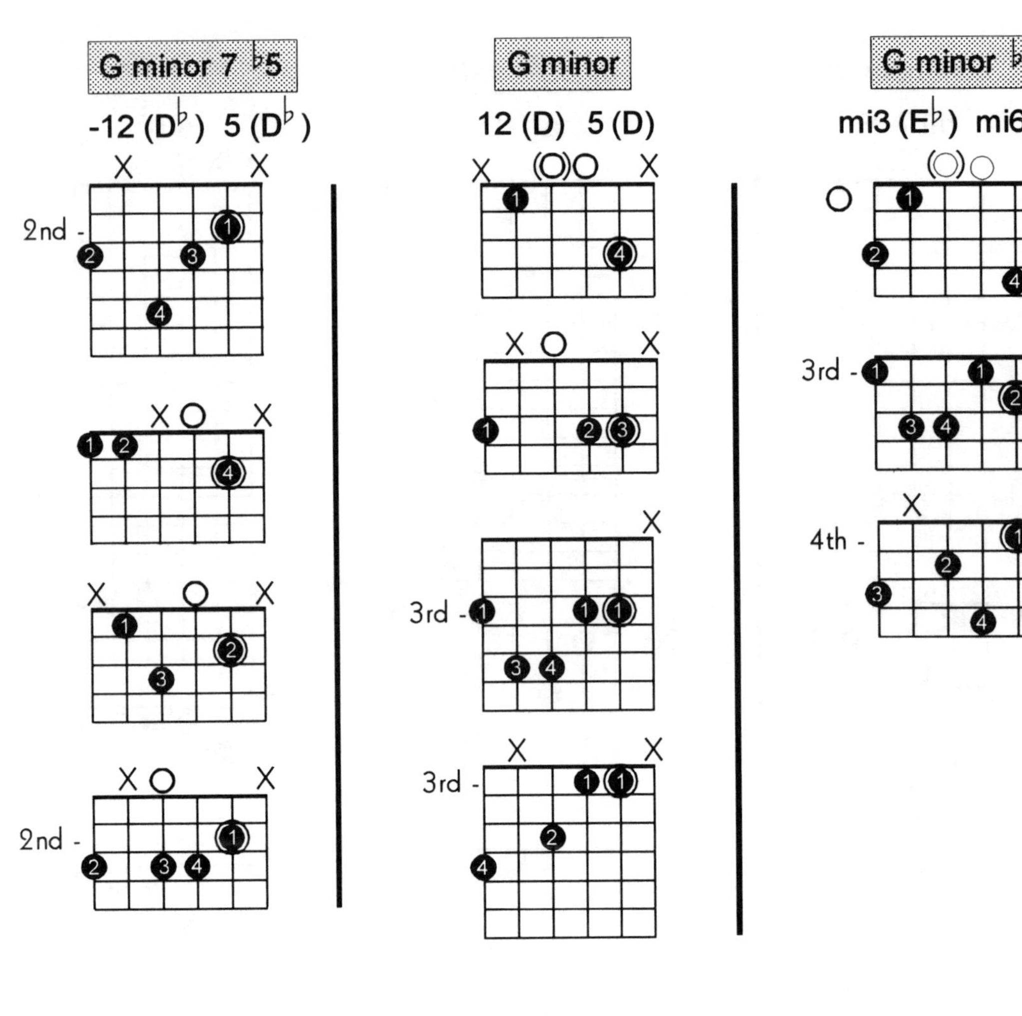
G minor 7 ♭5
-12 (D♭) 5 (D♭)
2nd -
2nd -
G minor
12 (D) 5 (D)
3rd -
3rd -

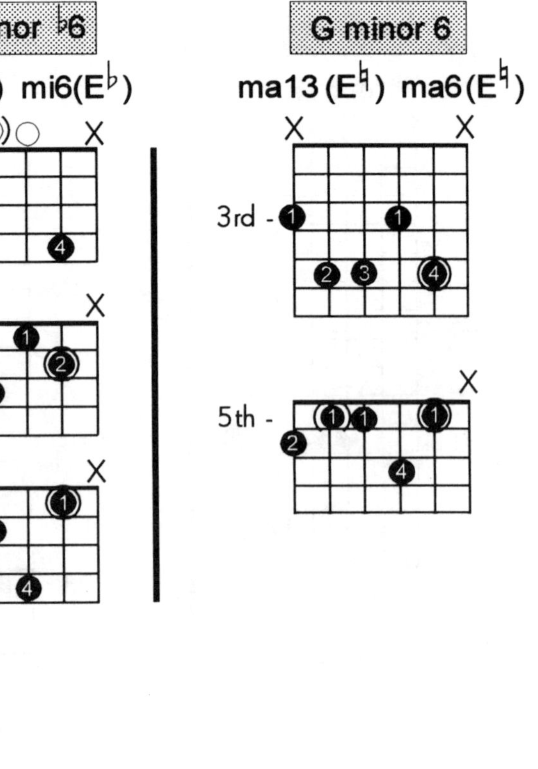
G minor ♭6
mi3 (E♭) mi6(E♭)
3rd -
4th -
G minor 6
ma13 (E♮) ma6(E♮)
3rd -
5th -

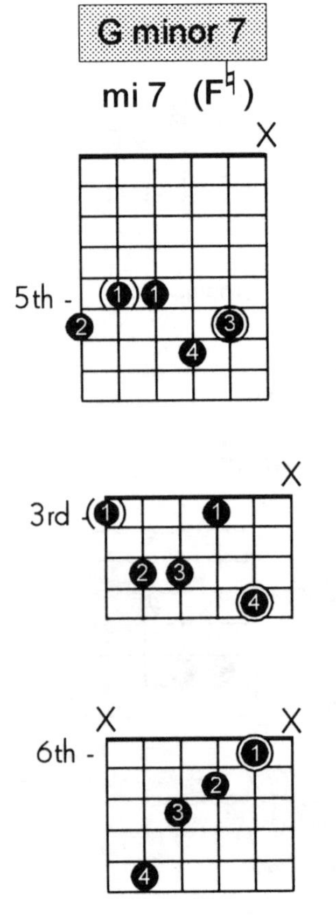
G minor 7
mi 7 (F♮)
5th -
3rd -
6th -

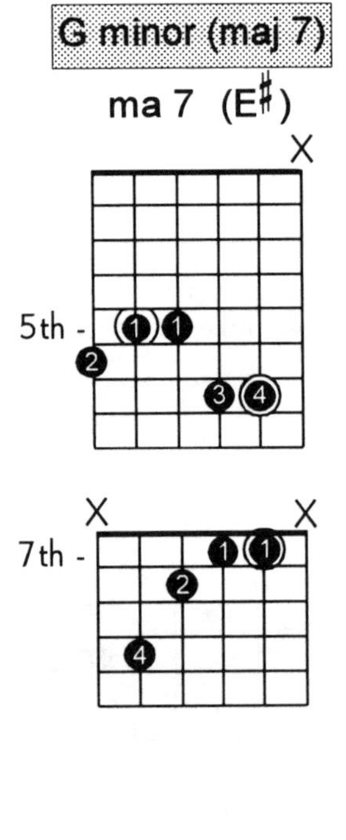
G minor (maj 7)
ma 7 (E♯)
5th -
7th -

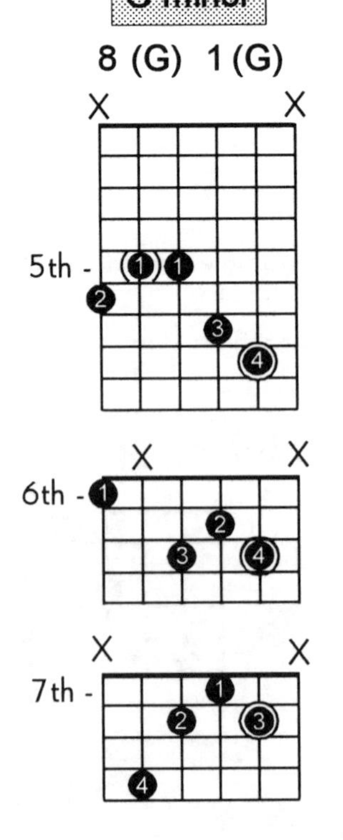
G minor
8 (G) 1 (G)
5th -
6th -
7th -

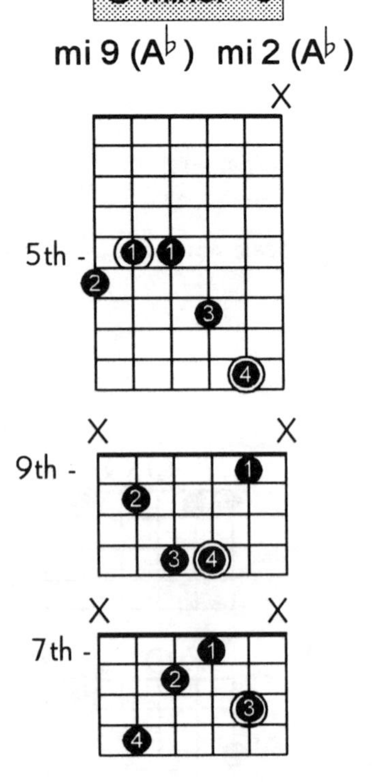
G minor ♭9
mi 9 (A♭) mi 2 (A♭)
5th -
9th -
7th -

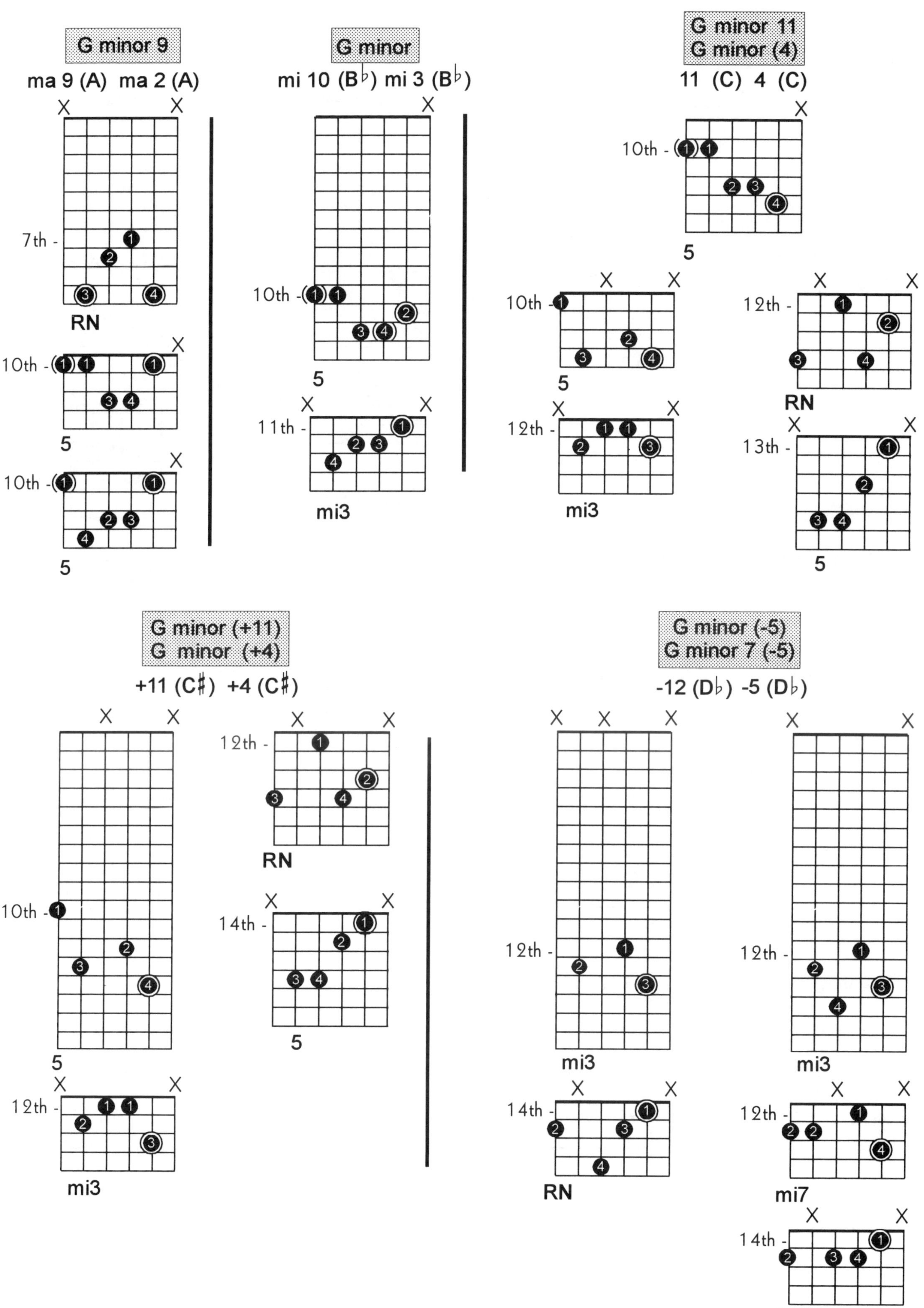

G minor 9
ma 9 (A) ma 2 (A)
7th -
RN
10th -
5
10th -
5
G minor
mi 10 (B♭) mi 3 (B♭)
10th -
5
11th -
mi3
G minor 11
G minor (4)
11 (C) 4 (C)
10th -
5
10th -
5
12th -
RN
12th -
mi3
13th -
5
G minor (+11)
G minor (+4)
+11 (C♯) +4 (C♯)
12th -
RN
10th -
14th -
5
5
12th -
mi3
G minor (-5)
G minor 7 (-5)
-12 (D♭) -5 (D♭)
12th -
12th -
mi3
mi3
14th -
RN
12th -
mi7
14th -
RN

FIG. 3

Scale notes and "**altered**" scale notes on the third string, commencing with the root note, G, on the open string position.

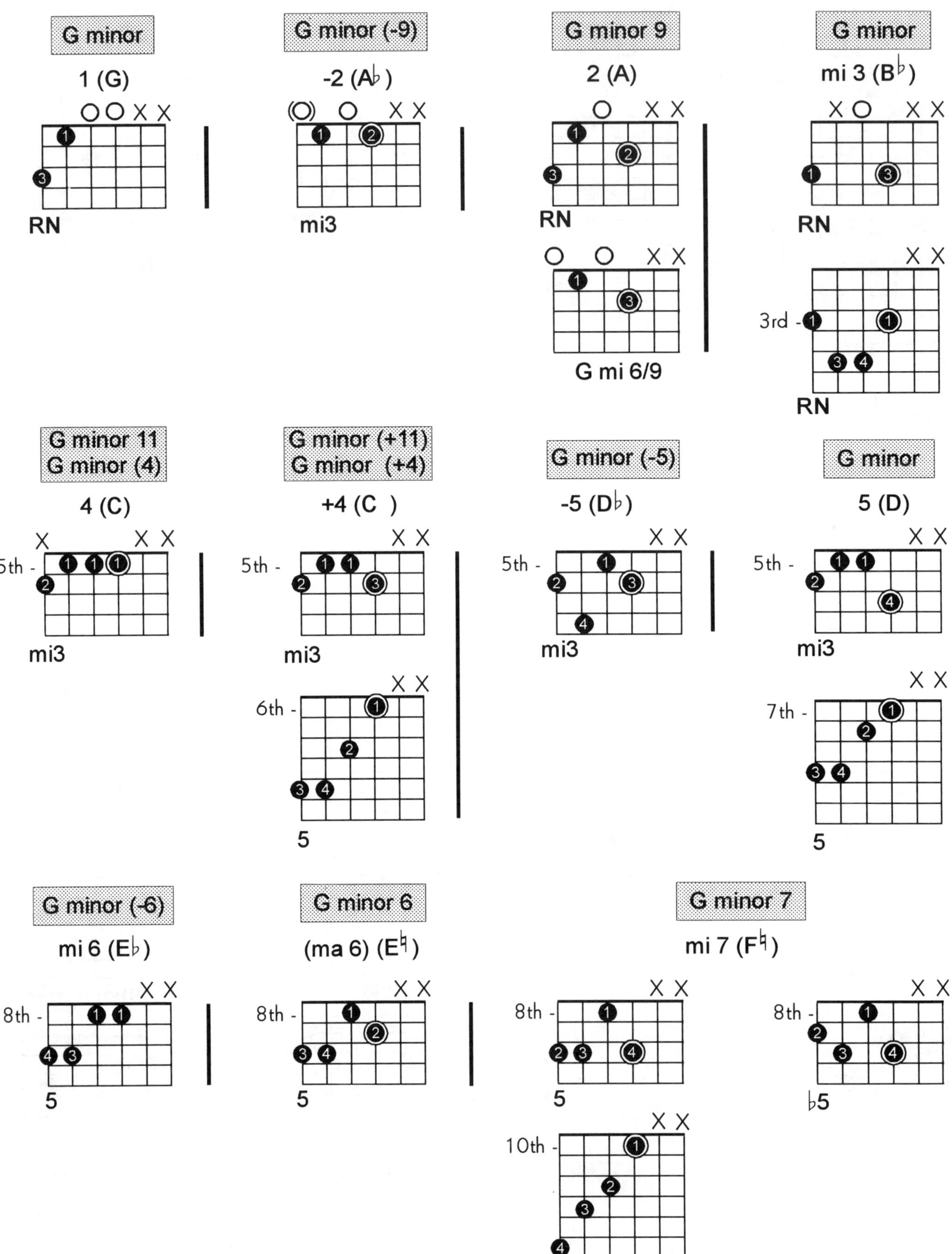

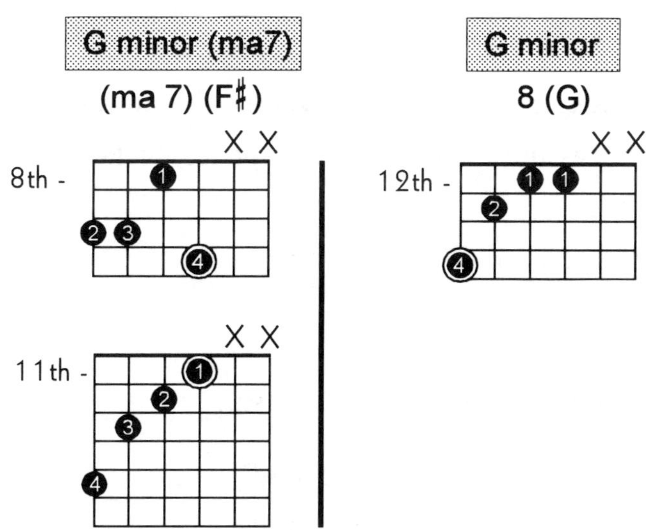

To produce the scale notes and altered scale notes in any key, refer to the tables of scale notes on pages 43 to 45. In all minor keys, each of the twelve tables show the positions of the scale notes on the first frets of each string. The chord forms given in figures 1, 2, and 3 on the preceding pages will be applied to the scale notes on the first, second and third strings.

See the directions given on pages 10 to 13 for adjusting chord diagrams so as to include added or altered notes in the harmony parts whenever these notes are called in chord symbols. Additionally, the "Experiments with chord forms" can be applied to minor chords.

Reference Tables For Minor Keys

Scale notes, in all minor keys, and their positions on the fingerboard. Directions are the same as those given on page 33. For scale notes and "altered" scale notes of key G minor see page 34.

Cycle of minor keys with flat key signatures:

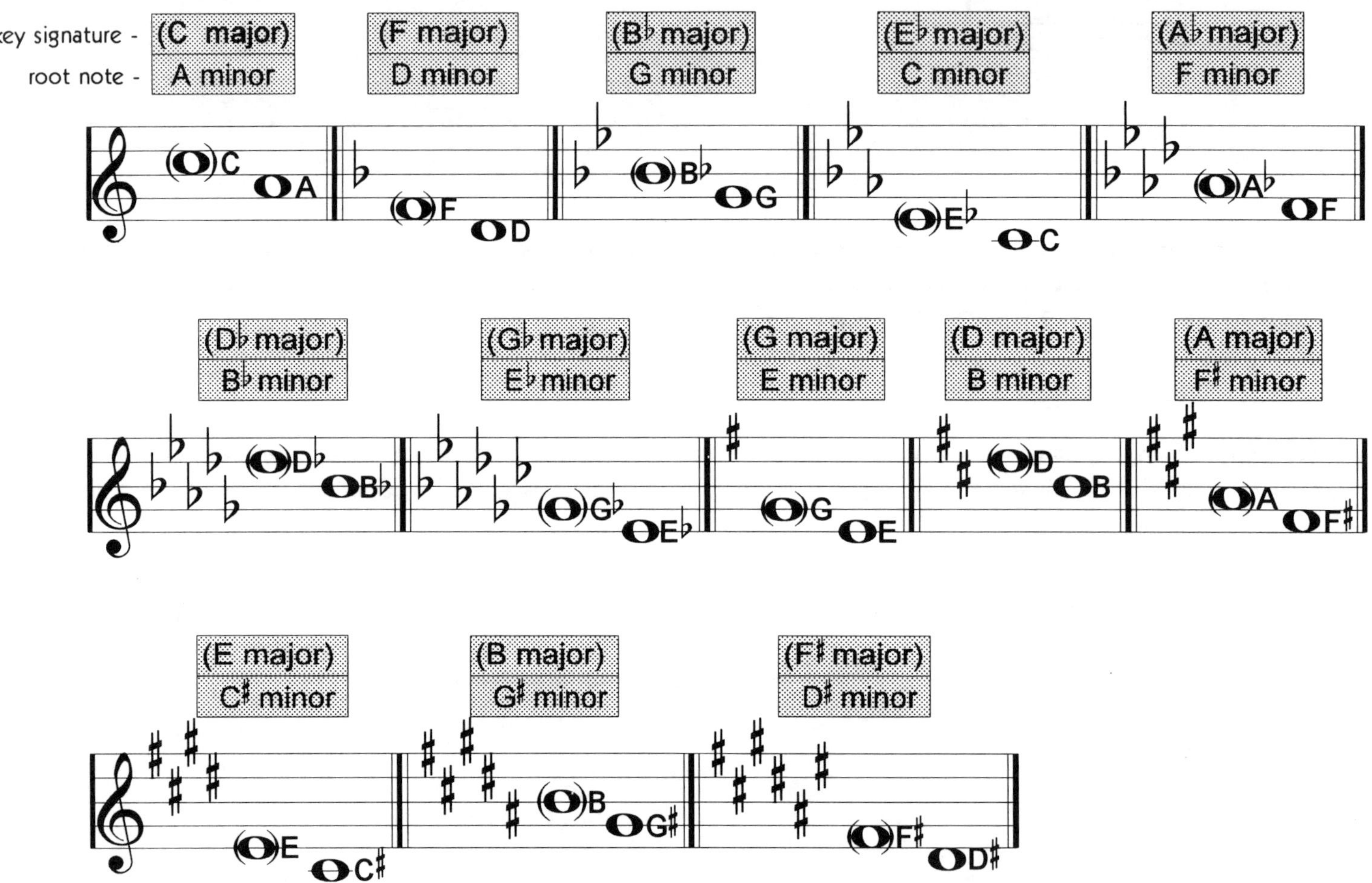

Symbol Terms

X = major third(a note that is foreign to the minor key)

O = the notes of the minor triad

( ) = the "raised sixth" and "raised seventh" scale notes are shown in brackets

R = root note

key signature: F major
root note: D minor

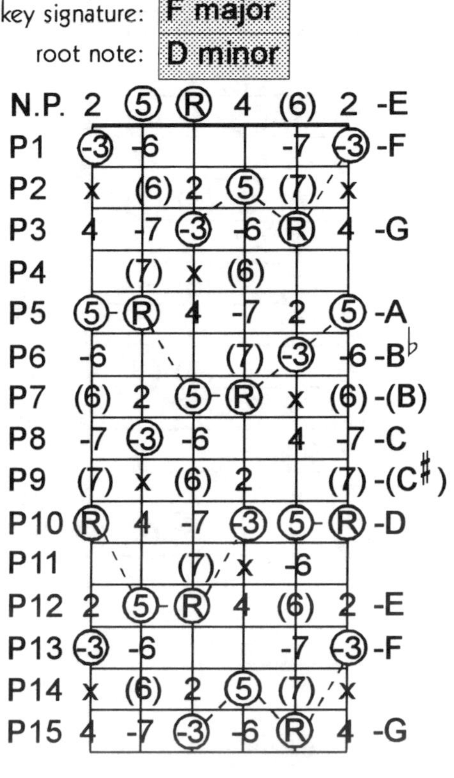

B♭ major
G minor

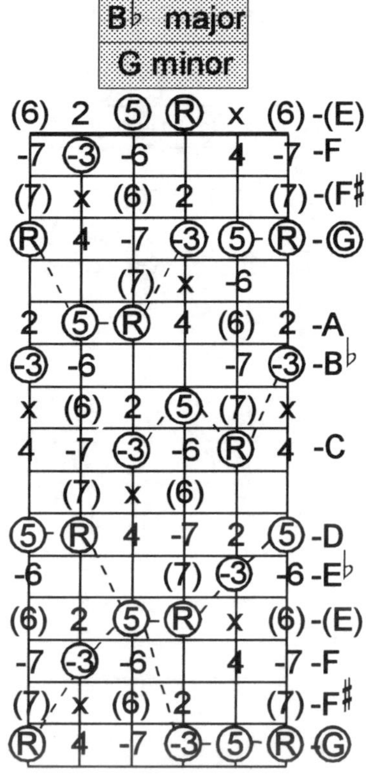

(E minor)
C minor

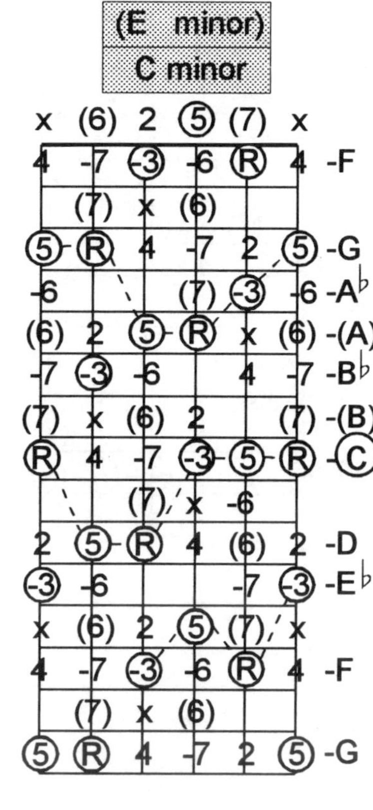

key signature: (A major)
root note: F minor

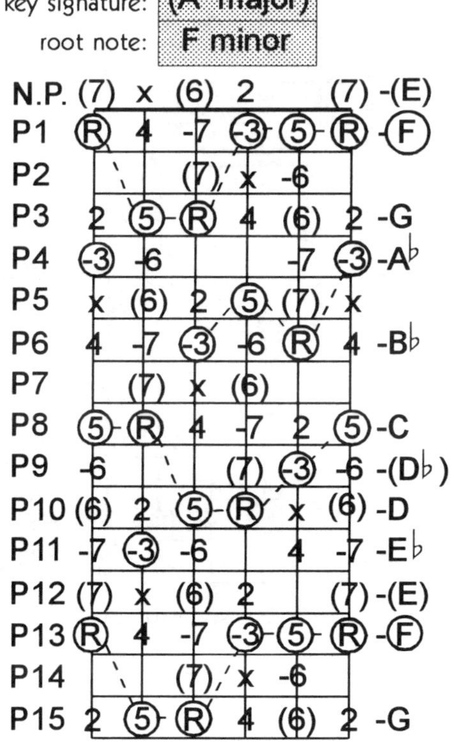

(D♭ major)
B♭ minor

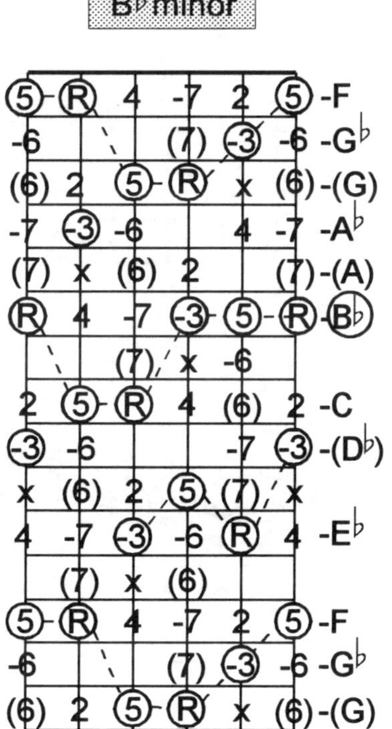

(G♭ major)
E♭ minor

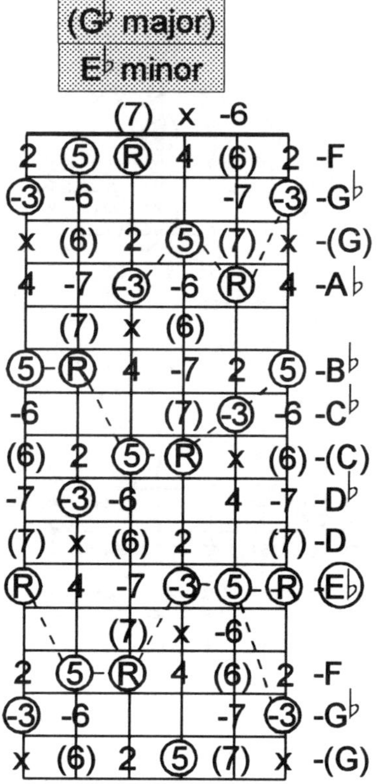

Cycle of keys with sharp key signatures and the "open key" signature:

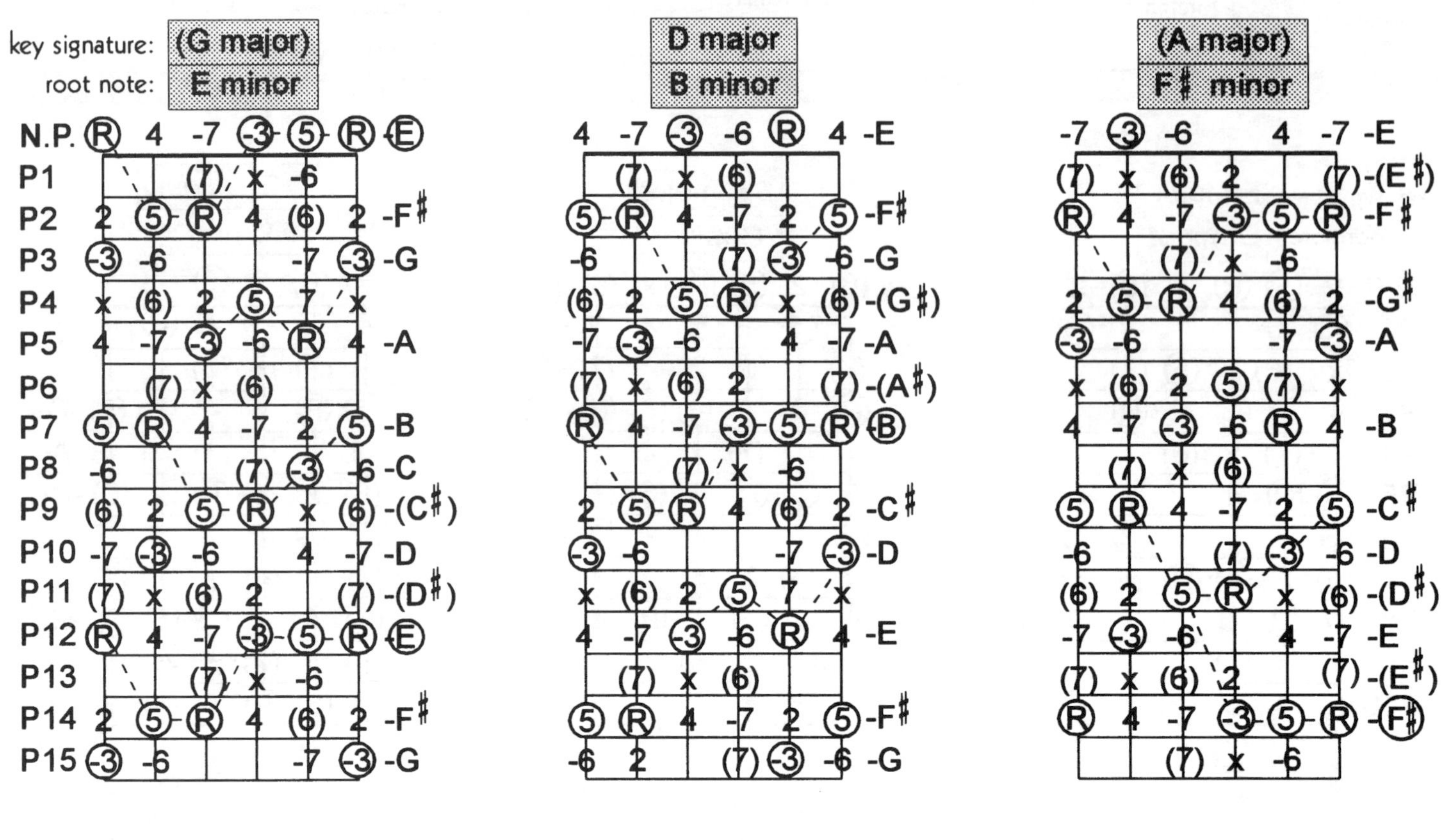

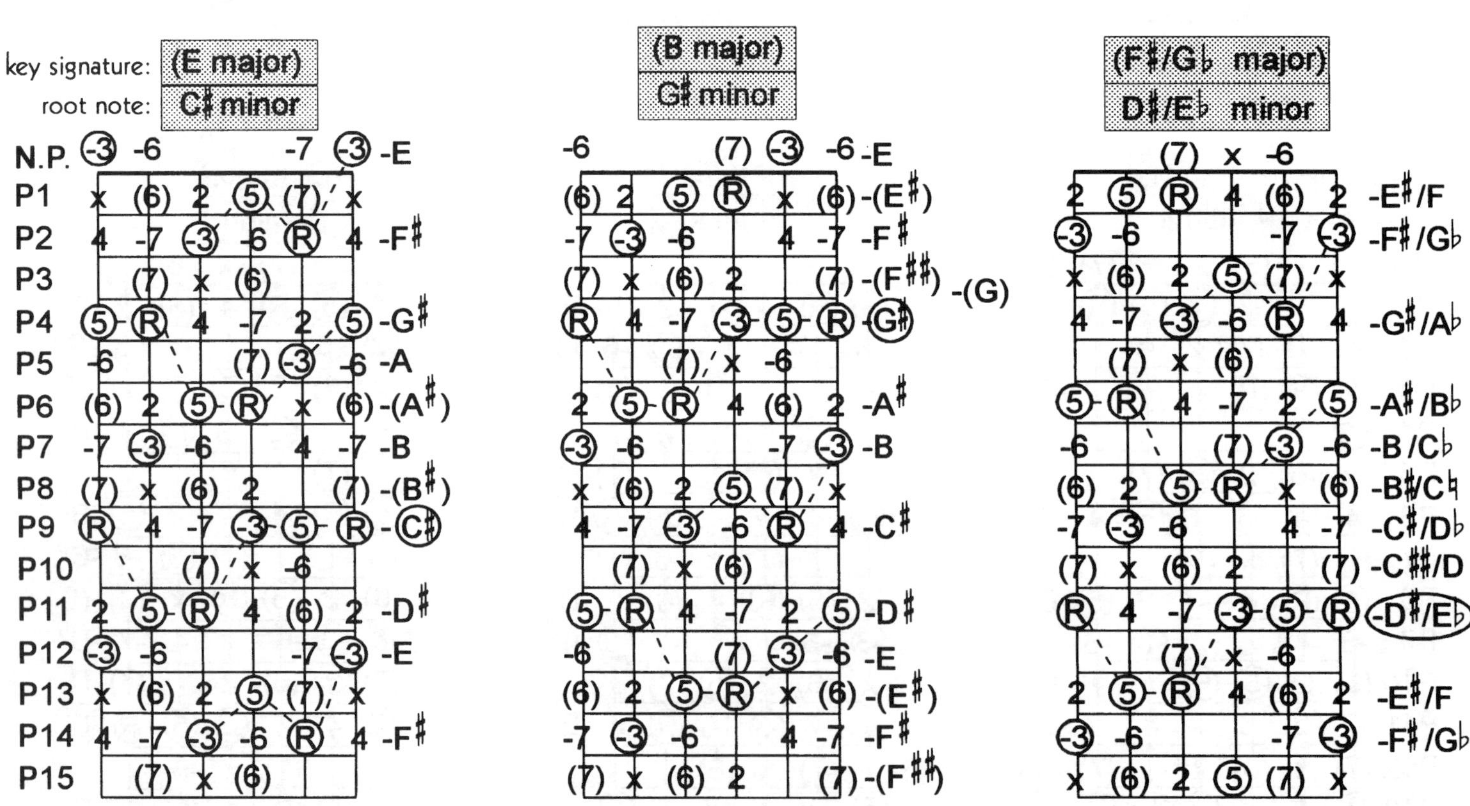

In chord symbol sequences A minor is invariably used instead of G minor, but in music notation the key signature for G minor is preferred instead of C minor.

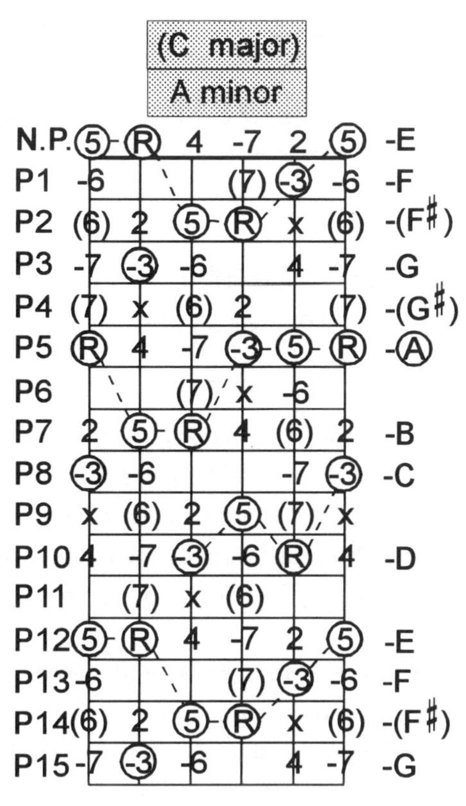

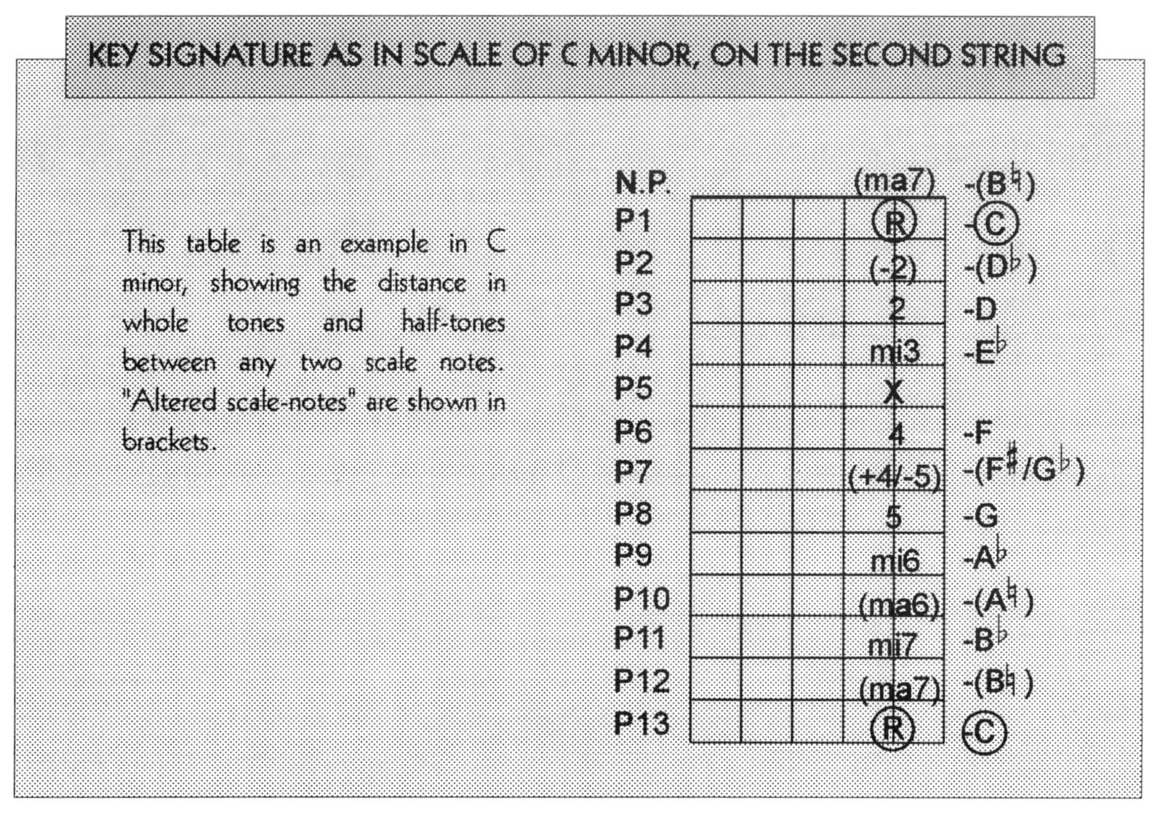

KEY SIGNATURE AS IN SCALE OF C MINOR, ON THE SECOND STRING

This table is an example in C minor, showing the distance in whole tones and half-tones between any two scale notes. "Altered scale-notes" are shown in brackets.

Part Three

"Dominant" Scale Notes In Chord Form

The dominant scale in any key commences on the fifth scale-note of the key and takes its name from that of the fifth scale-note just mentioned. The keynote is commonly referred to as the "tonic" while the fifth note of the scale is known as the "dominant" or "V" note.

Both tonic and dominant scales are in accordance with the key signature for the tonic, or root note, the only difference between the two scales is in the numbering of the notes, viz., those in the scale of the tonic are numbered as counting from the tonic, (called number one), while those in the scale of the dominant are numbered as counted from the dominant, (also called number one in the scale ascending from it). Thus, D the fifth note of key G major and G minor is the first, (or root), note of the dominant scale in these two keys.

The notes of "the chord of the dominant seventh" on root D are shown in a circle in the diagram below and on the next page. The chord is represented, in chord symbol form, by the name of the root note, suffixed with a figure 7, e.g., D7 means "the chord of D dominant seventh"; similarly , D9 means "D7th with a major 9th added". Remember that, in chord symbols, the 2nd is always indicated as the 9th, (the "compound" interval equivalent).

"Dominant" or "V" scale							(1)	2	(3)	4	(5)	6	(♭7)	8
(D)	E	(F♯)	G	(A)	B	(C)	(D)	E	(F♯)	(A)	G	B	(C)	D
(1)	2	(3)	4	(5)	6	♭7	8	9	10	11	12	13	♭14	15

Note that C, the 7th above V (D), is a half-tone less than the "major 7th"(C#) in the key of D major, thus it is a "minor 7th".

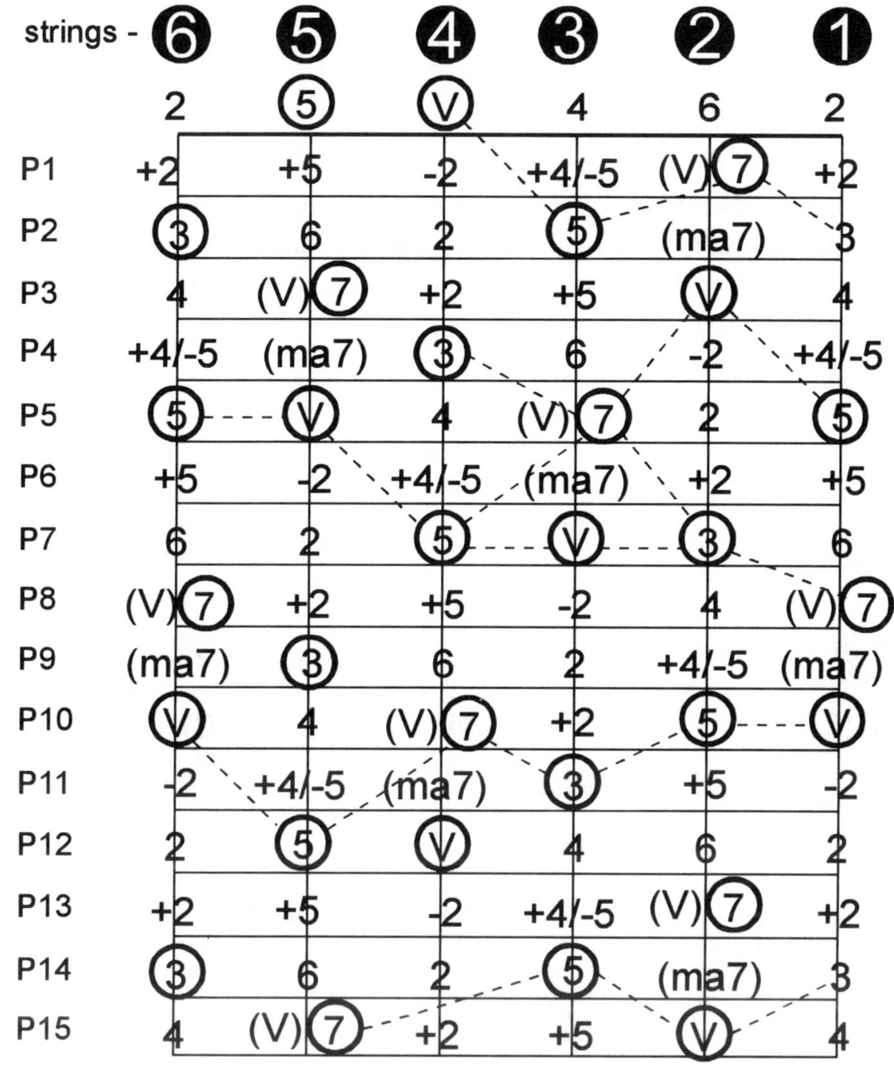

V represents D, the root note of the scale of the dominant and of the chord of the dominant seventh; (the four notes of the dominant 7th chord are shown in a circle). These are the notes used in the harmony parts of the chords given in Figs. 1, 2 and 3 for "dominant scale notes in chord form".

To adjust the chords so as to allow for including "added" and/or "altered" scale-notes in the harmony parts see pages 10 and 13; also see "experiments with chord forms", page 23.

(V)7 stands for the seventh interval above the root of the dominant chord standard forms.

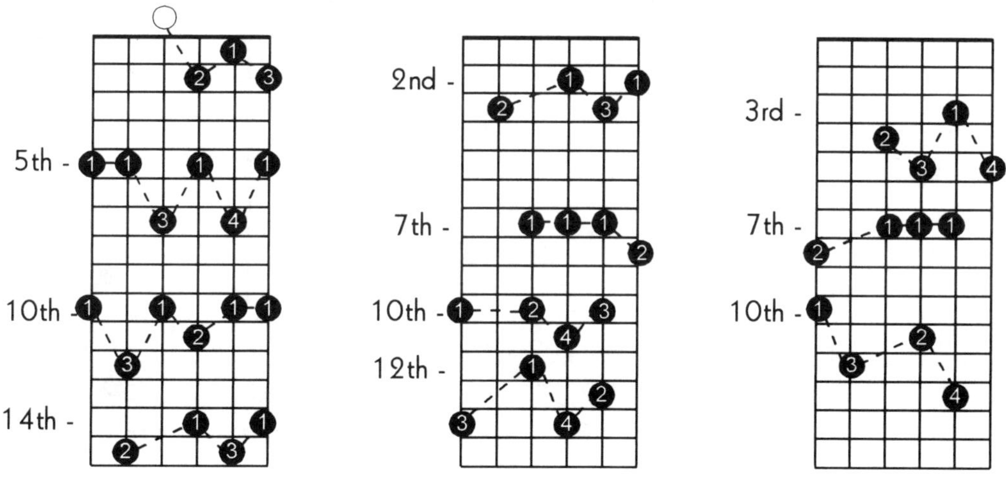

"Standard" Forms for the Chord of the Dominant Seventh

The examples, in figs. 1, 2 and 3, following, show the scale notes and "altered" scale-notes, of the dominant scale on D, in chord form. To produce the same chord forms in all other dominant scales simply move them up or down the fingerboard. Refer to the reference tables, starting on page 56 for any required dominant scale-note. Select the chord-form for that scale-note from Fig. 1, 2 or 3, whichever, and then place the finger given, in chord form, for the "lead" note, directly on the new dominant scale note.

FIG. 1

Scale notes and "**altered**" scale notes on the first string, commencing with open-string note E,(the 2nd and the 9th), in the dominant scale on the root note D.

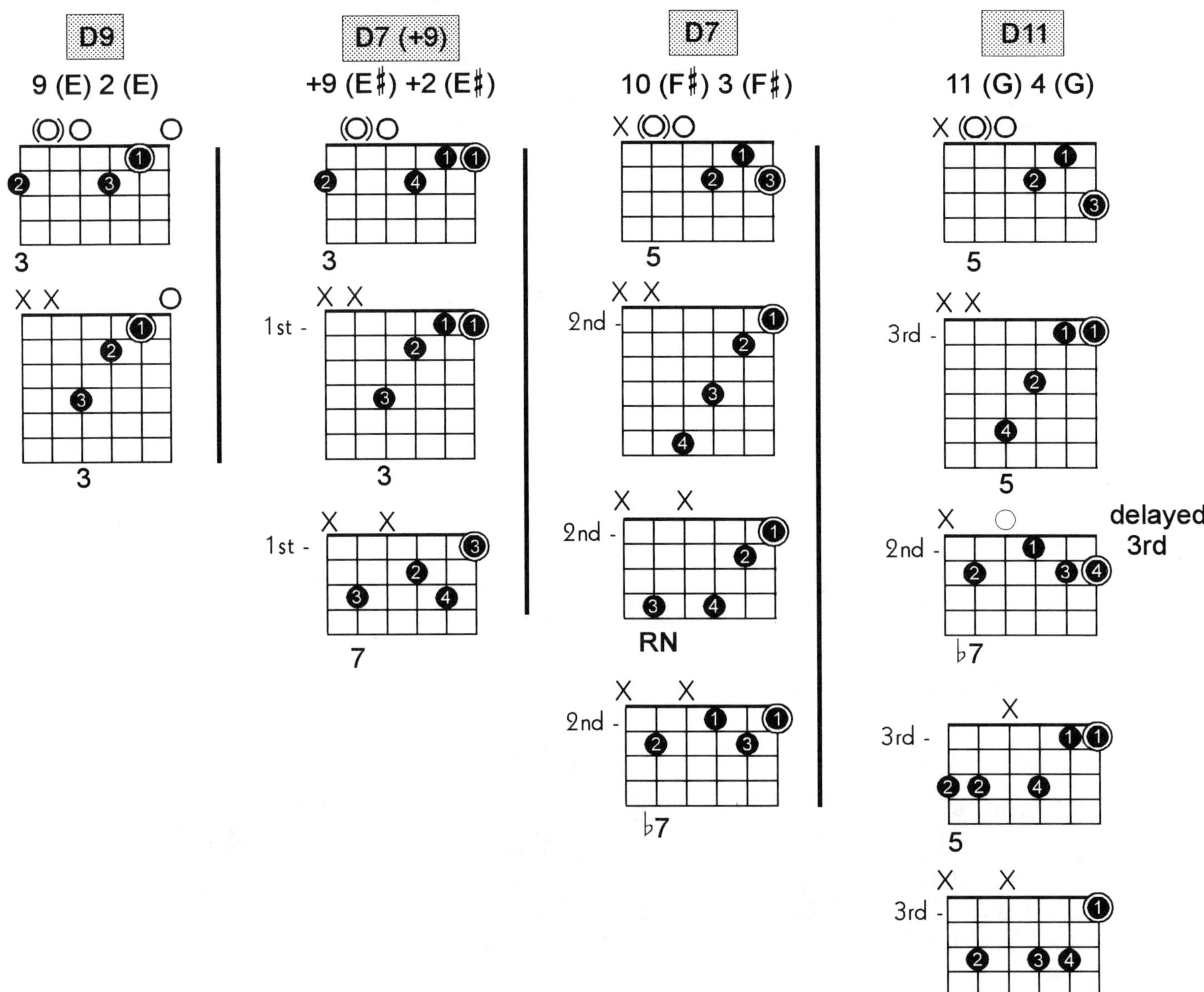

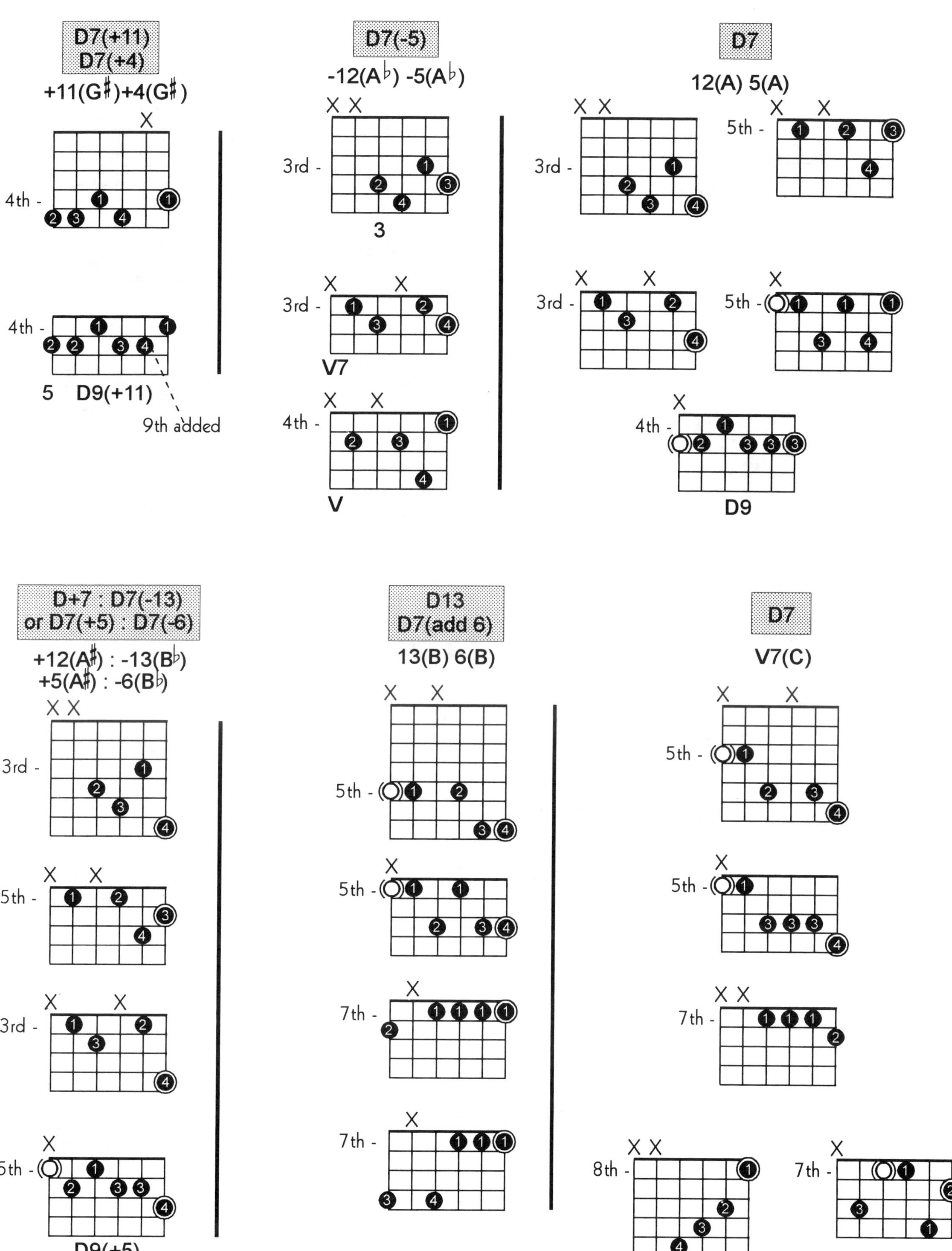
D7(+11)
D7(+4)
+11(G♯)+4(G♯)
4th -
4th -
5 D9(+11)
9th added
D7(-5)
-12(A♭) -5(A♭)
3rd -
3
3rd -
V7
4th -
V
D7
12(A) 5(A)
3rd -
5th -
3rd -
5th -
4th -
D9
D+7 : D7(-13)
or D7(+5) : D7(-6)
+12(A♯) : -13(B♭)
+5(A♯) : -6(B♭)
3rd -
5th -
3rd -
5th -
D9(+5)
D13
D7(add 6)
13(B) 6(B)
5th -
5th -
7th -
7th -
D7
V7(C)
5th -
5th -
7th -
8th -
7th -

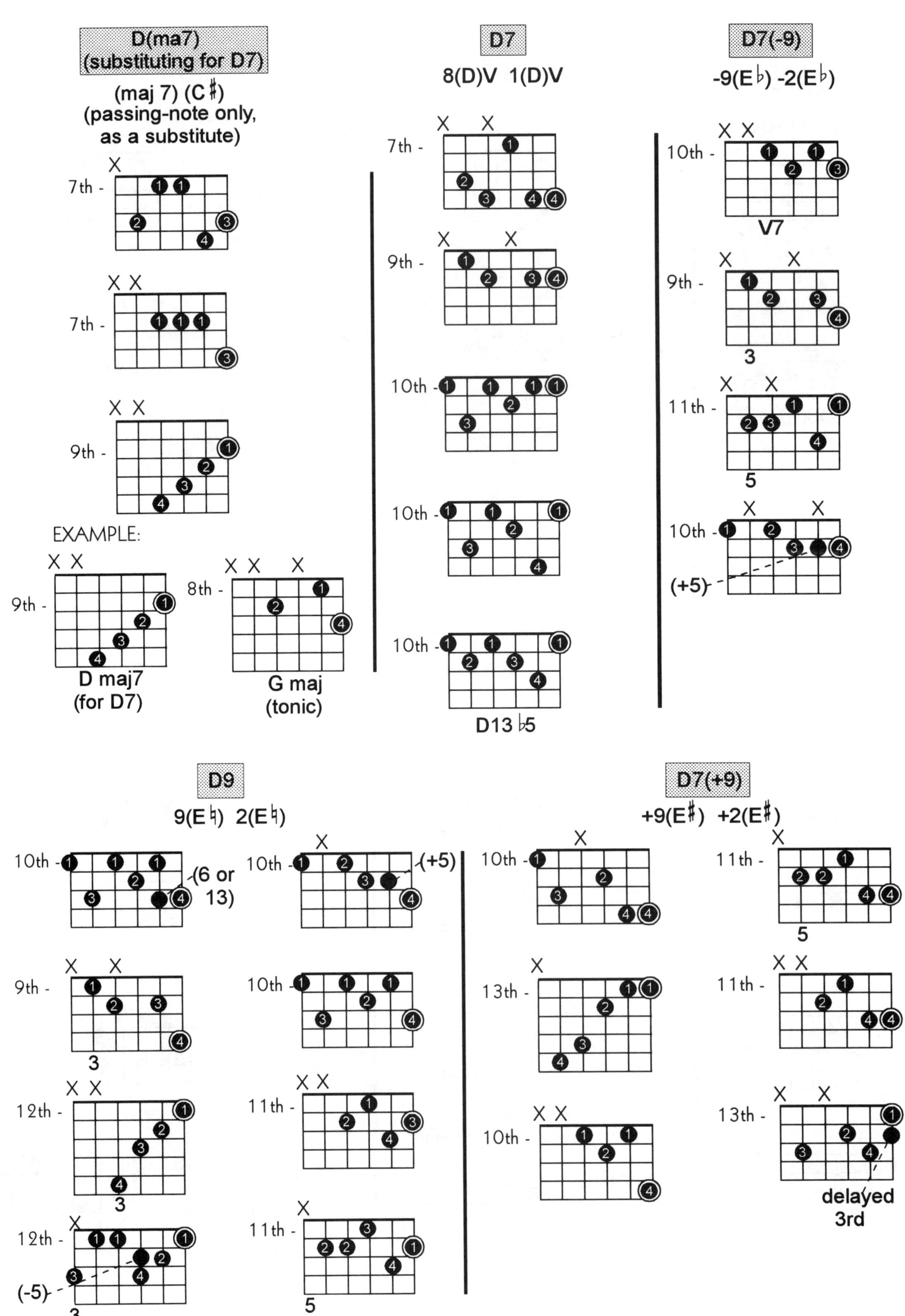

D(ma7)
(substituting for D7)
(maj 7) (C♯)
(passing-note only,
as a substitute)
7th -
7th -
9th -
EXAMPLE:
9th -
D maj7
(for D7)
8th -
G maj
(tonic)
D7
8(D)V 1(D)V
7th -
9th -
10th -
10th -
10th -
D13 ♭5
D7(-9)
-9(E♭) -2(E♭)
10th -
V7
9th -
3
11th -
5
10th -
(+5)
D9
9(E♮) 2(E♮)
10th -
(6 or
13)
10th -
(+5)
9th -
3
10th -
12th -
3
11th -
12th -
(-5)
3
11th -
5
D7(+9)
+9(E♯) +2(E♯)
10th -
11th -
5
13th -
11th -
10th -
13th -
delayed
3rd

FIG. 2 As for Fig.1 but with the scale notes and "altered" notes on the second string, commencing with the 6th note of the dominant scale on D.

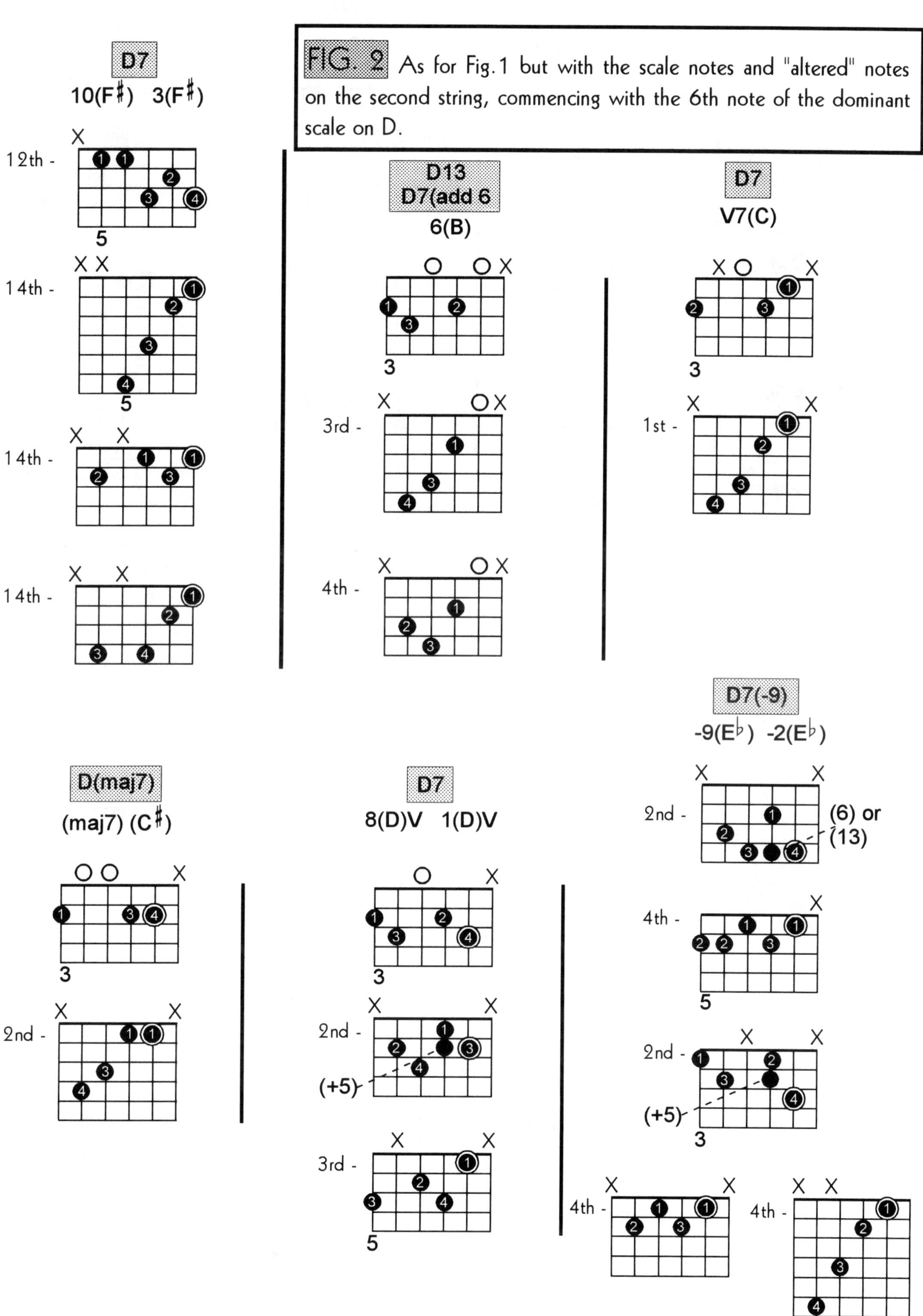

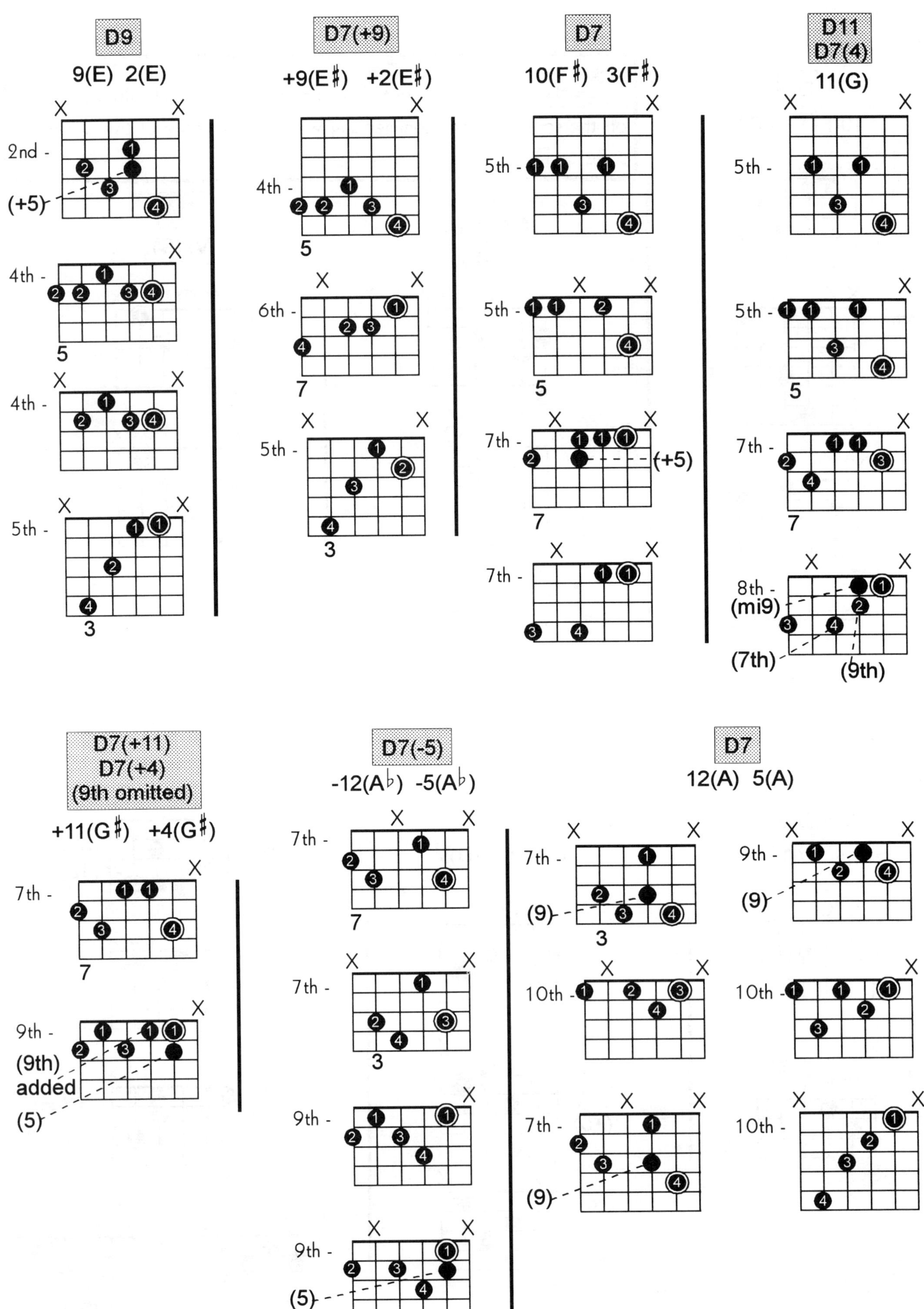
D9
9(E) 2(E)
2nd -
(+5)
4th -
5
4th -
5th -
3
D7(+9)
+9(E♯) +2(E♯)
4th -
5
6th -
7
5th -
3
D7
10(F♯) 3(F♯)
5th -
5th -
5
7th -
(+5)
7
7th -
D11
D7(4)
11(G)
5th -
5th -
5
7th -
7
8th -
(mi9)
(7th)
(9th)
D7(+11)
D7(+4)
(9th omitted)
+11(G♯) +4(G♯)
7th -
7
9th -
(9th)
added
(5)
D7(-5)
-12(A♭) -5(A♭)
7th -
7
7th -
3
9th -
9th -
(5)
D7
12(A) 5(A)
7th -
(9)
3
9th -
(9)
10th -
10th -
7th -
(9)
10th -

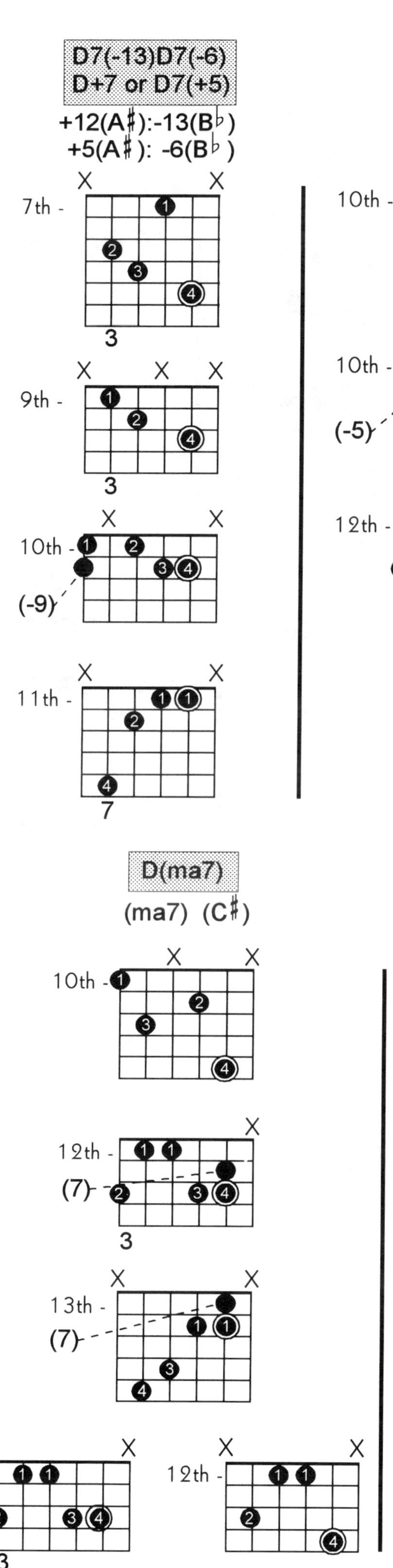

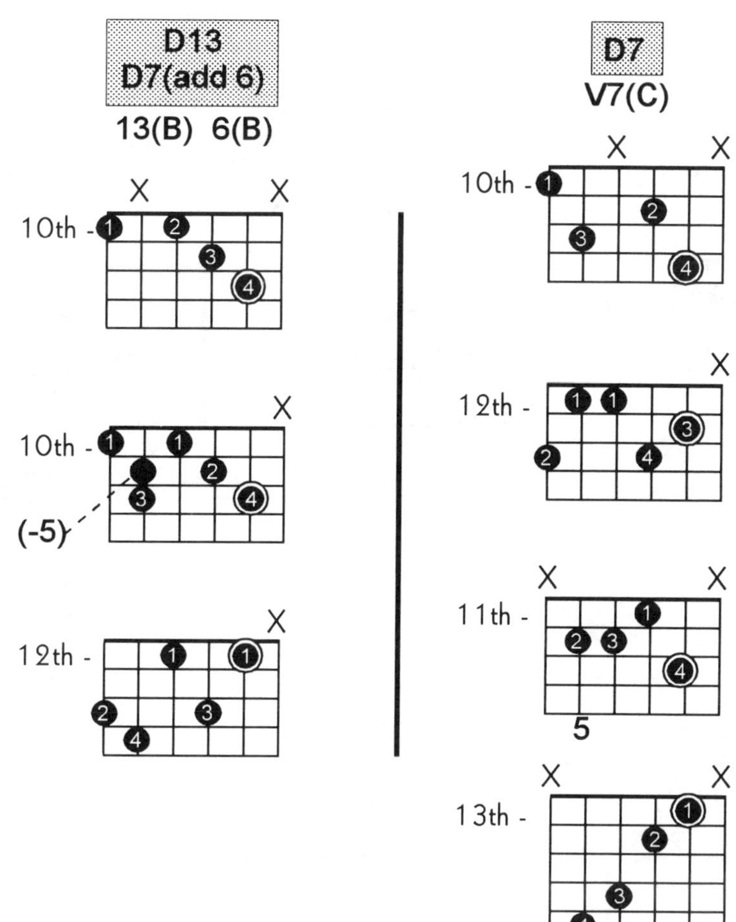

FIG. 3 As for Fig.1 and 2 but with the same notes on the third string, commencing with the 4th(or 11th), on the open string(G).

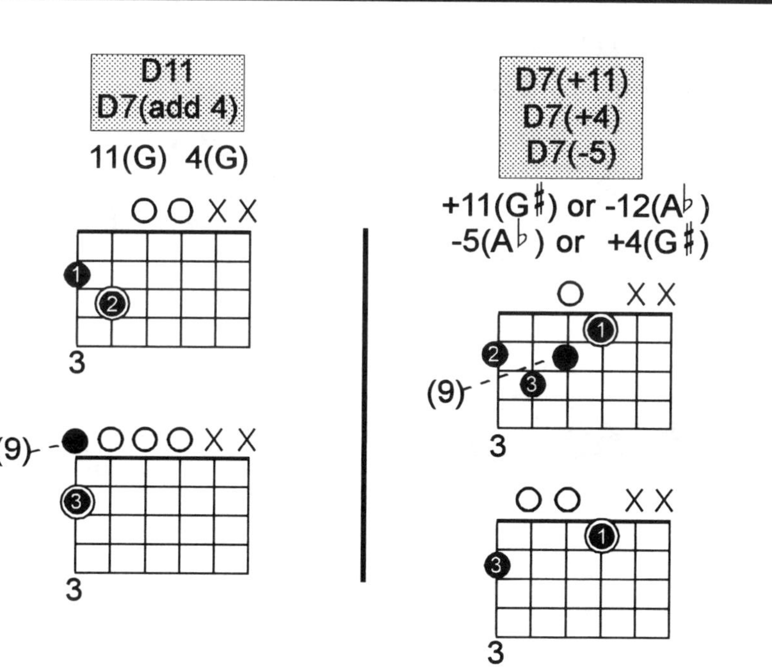

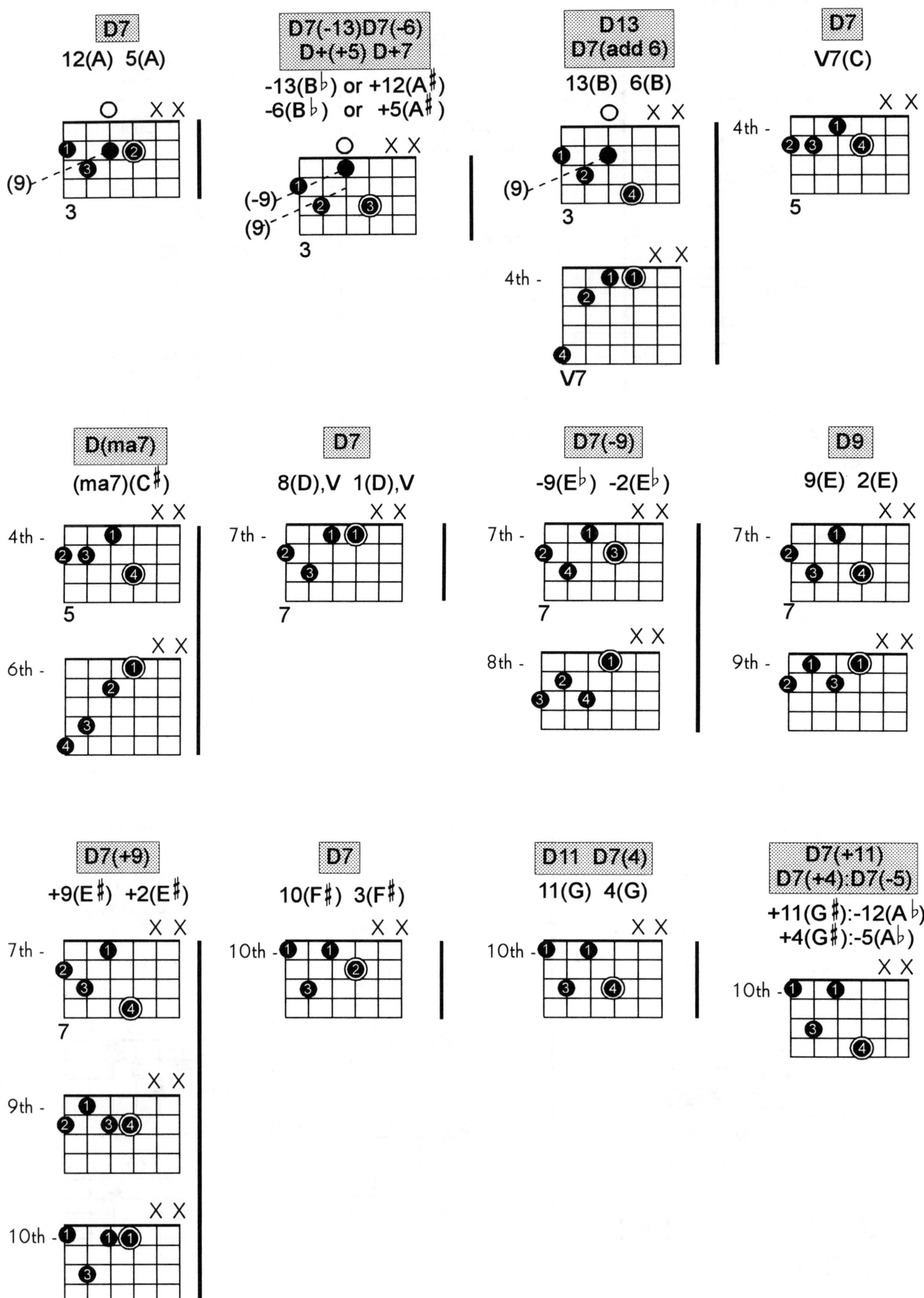

D7
12(A) 5(A)
(9)
3
D7(-13)D7(-6)
D+(+5) D+7
-13(B♭) or +12(A♯)
-6(B♭) or +5(A♯)
(-9)
(9)
3
D13
D7(add 6)
13(B) 6(B)
(9)
3
4th -
V7
D7
V7(C)
4th -
5
D(ma7)
(ma7)(C♯)
4th -
5
6th -
D7
8(D),V 1(D),V
7th -
7
D7(-9)
-9(E♭) -2(E♭)
7th -
7
8th -
D9
9(E) 2(E)
7th -
7
9th -
D7(+9)
+9(E♯) +2(E♯)
7th -
7
9th -
10th -
D7
10(F♯) 3(F♯)
10th -
D11 D7(4)
11(G) 4(G)
10th -
D7(+11)
D7(+4):D7(-5)
+11(G♯):-12(A♭)
+4(G♯):-5(A♭)
10th -

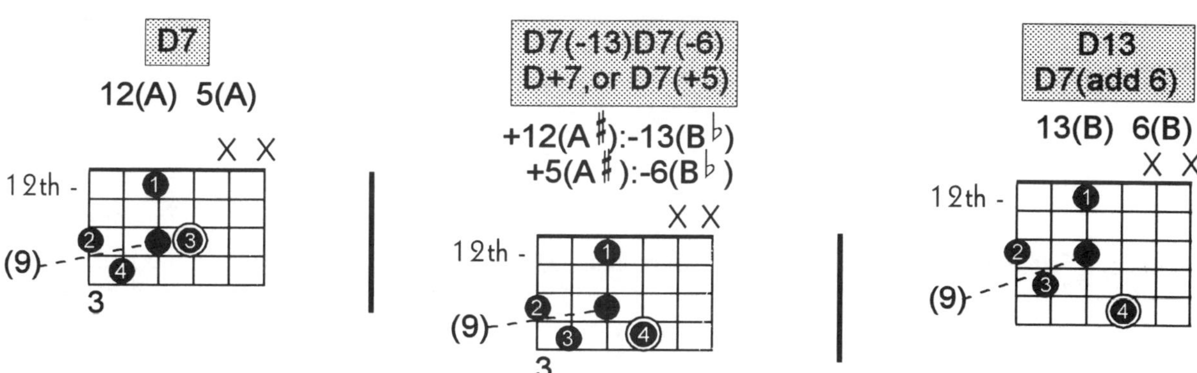

The complete range of chord forms for scale notes and altered scale-notes of the dominant scale on 'D' can readily be produced in all other dominant scales whenever they should be required.

Reference tables starting on the next page show the positions on the fingerboard of the scale notes in all dominant scales. A simple method for producing the chord form, for any particular scale note in the "lead" position, is as follows: - select the particular scale note of any chosen dominant scale, and note, on the appropriate table, the position on the fingerboard on which the particular scale note occurs - (including alternative positions). Now choose a chord form (the chord tones connected by dotted lines) given for the particular scale note and notice which finger is allotted to the "lead" note; place this finger directly on the previously selected scale note's position and then form the chord by placing the other fingers as shown in the chord diagram which you selected.

Allan testing one of his signature model guitars at Carvin factory, San Diego, CA
Courtesy of Carvin Guitar

Reference Tables Dominant Scales

Scale notes and "altered" scale-notes of dominant scales in all major keys directions are similar to those given on page.

(Note - the root positions are indicated with lines and arrows; a useful preparatory exercise is to play the roots in "octave-form" so as to quickly fix the positions in mind; chord-forms are then readily formed around the roots): 'V' means "foot note" of the dominant scale; v7 stands for the seventh intervals counted from the root note V).

Note that the "major seventh" interval, (given in brackets) is really a "foreign" note in the scale of the dominant and belongs to the major scale which shares the same note as the root nevertheless, it is sometimes used as a "passing note" or a "substitute" for the 'dominant seventh' scale note.

*(minor scales which share the same keynote also share the same dominant seventh chord).

(KS) means "key signature". V stands for root note of the dominate scale (Dotted lines outline the "shapes" of chord-forms for the dominant 7th).

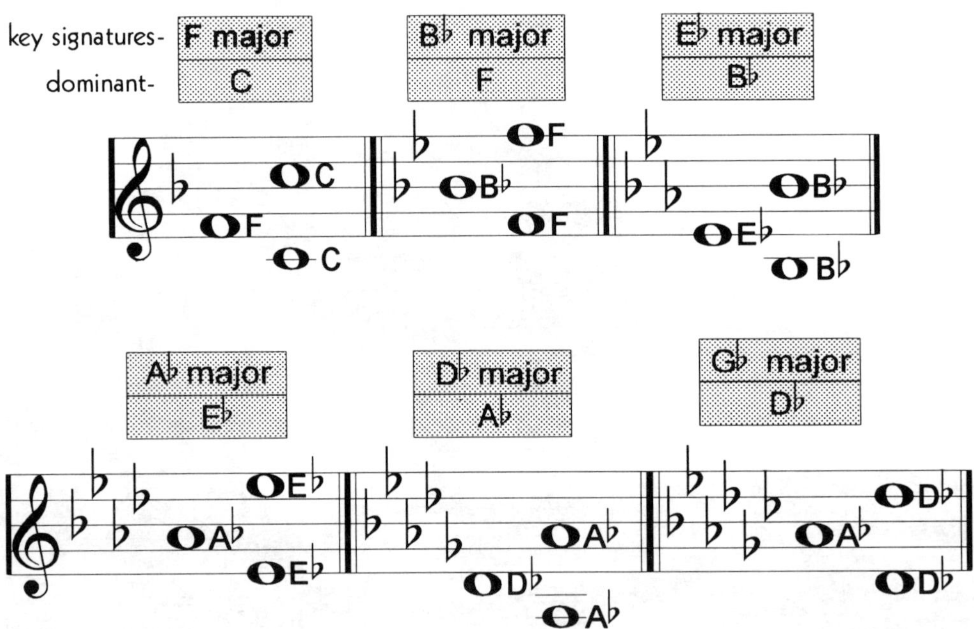

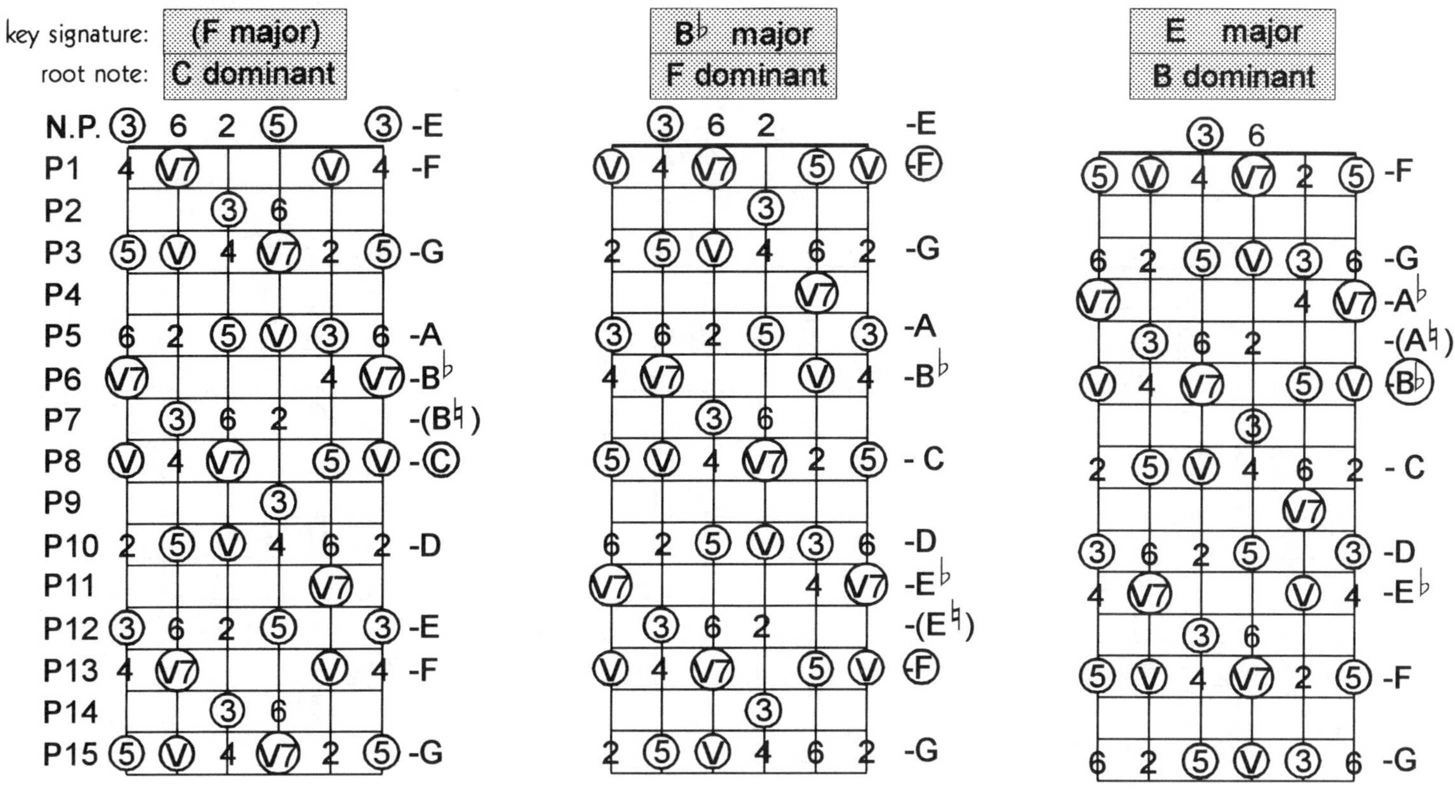
key signature:
root note:
(F major)
C dominant
B♭ major
F dominant
E major
B dominant
N.P.
P1
P2
P3
P4
P5
P6
P7
P8
P9
P10
P11
P12
P13
P14
P15
-E
-F
-G
-A
-B♭
-(B♮)
-C
-D
-E
-F
-G
-E
-F
-G
-A
-B♭
- C
-D
-E♭
-(E♮)
-F
-G
-F
-G
-A♭
-(A♮)
-B♭
- C
-D
-E♭
-F
-G

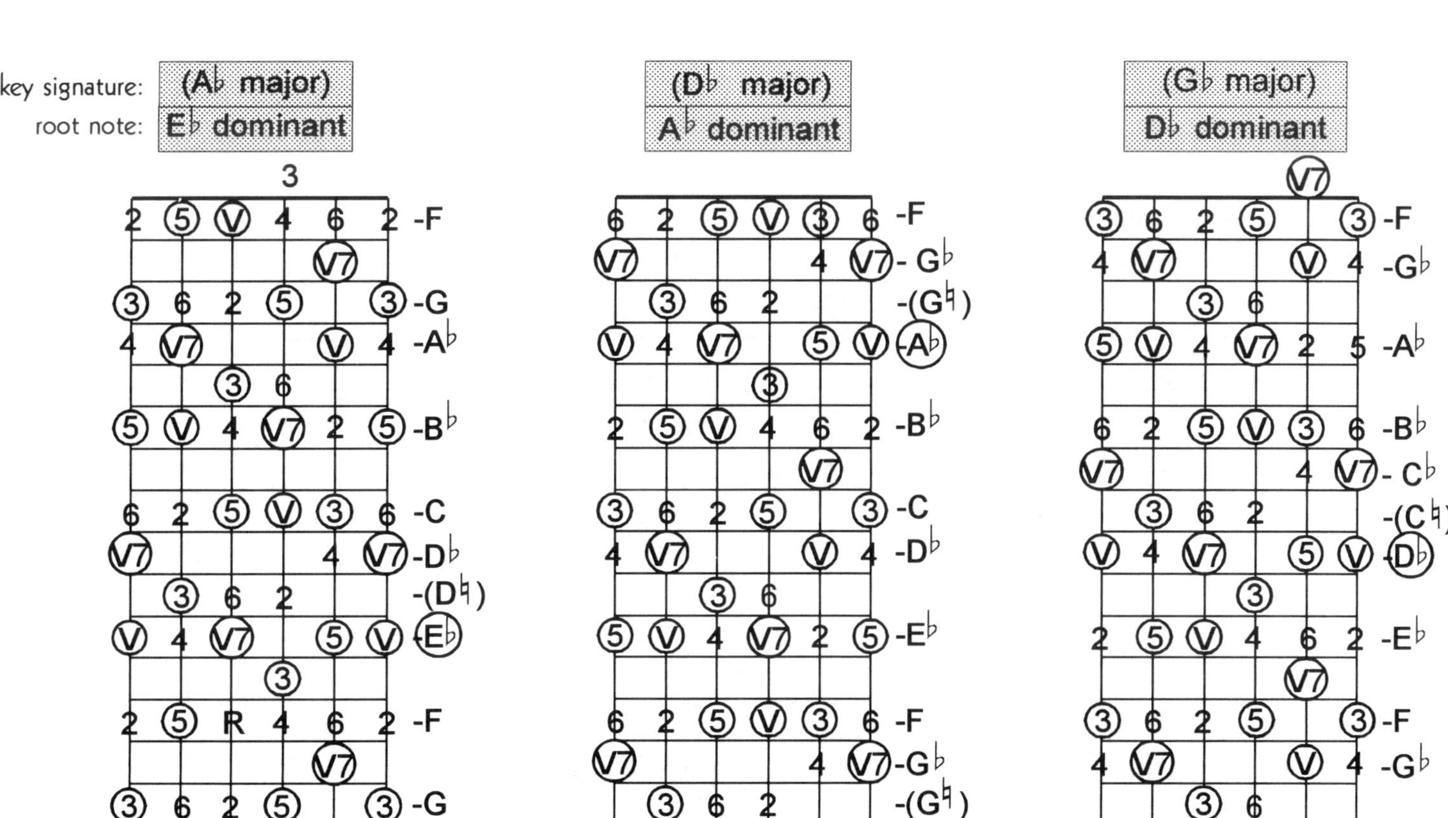
key signature:
root note:
(A♭ major)
E♭ dominant
(D♭ major)
A♭ dominant
(G♭ major)
D♭ dominant
-F
-G
-A♭
-B♭
-C
-D♭
-(D♮)
-E♭
-F
-G
-F
- G♭
-(G♮)
-A♭
-B♭
-C
-D♭
-E♭
-F
-G♭
-(G♮)
-F
-G♭
-A♭
-B♭
- C♭
-(C♮)
-D♭
-E♭
-F
-G♭

Cycle of keys with sharp key signatures and the 'open' key.

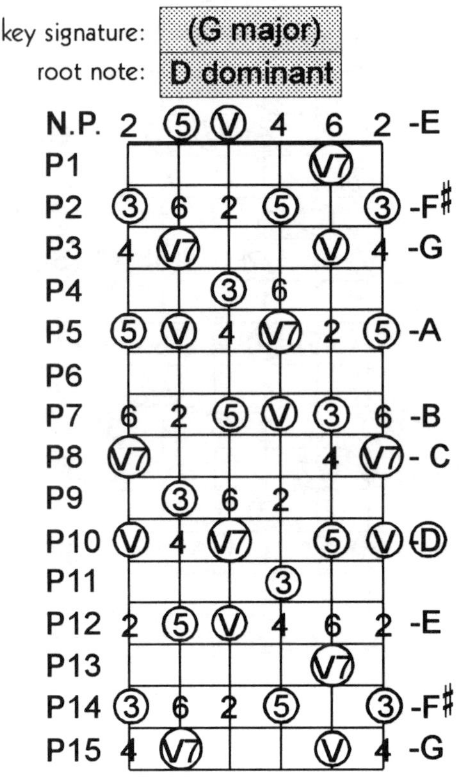

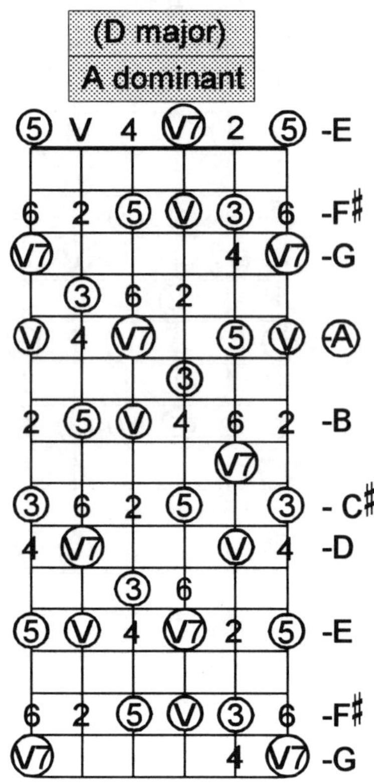

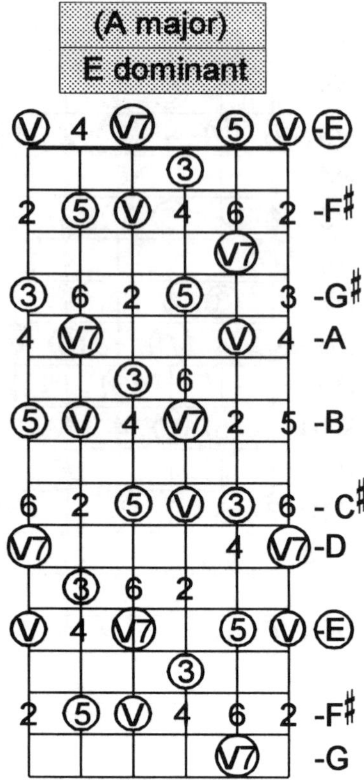

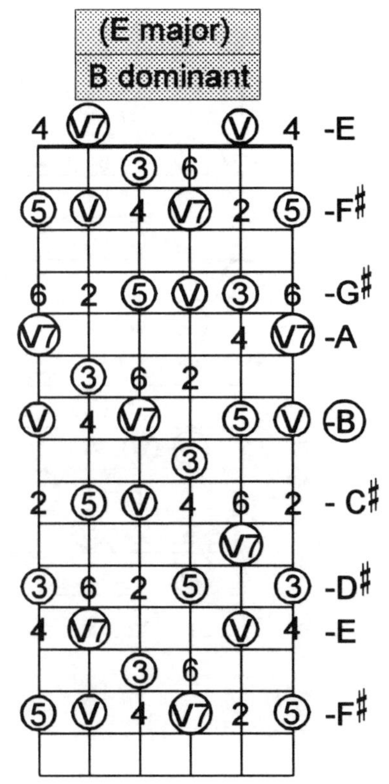

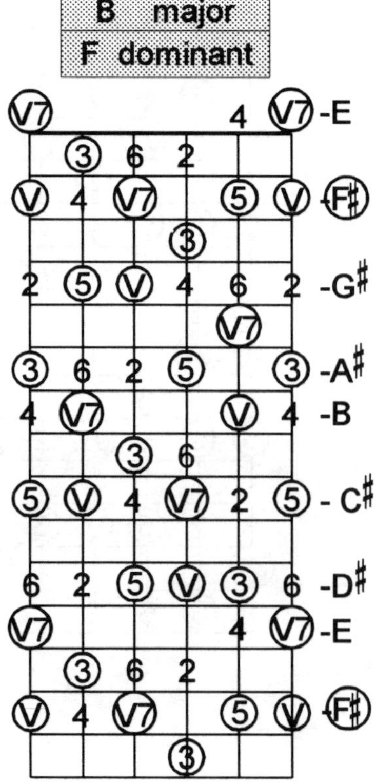

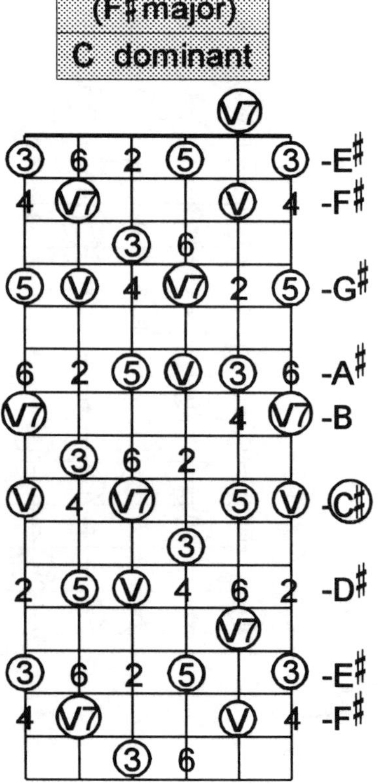

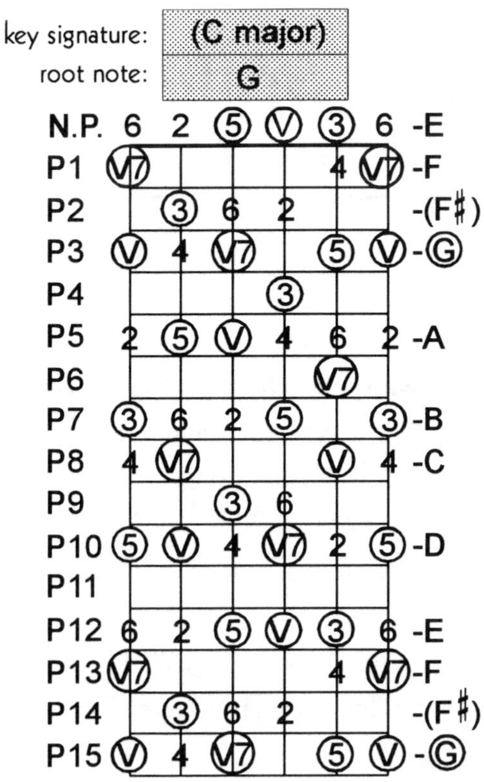
key signature: (C major)
root note: G
N.P. 6 2 5 V 3 6 -E
P1 V7 4 V7 -F
P2 3 6 2 -(F♯)
P3 V 4 V7 5 V -G
P4 3
P5 2 5 V 4 6 2 -A
P6 V7
P7 3 6 2 5 3 -B
P8 4 V7 V 4 -C
P9 3 6
P10 5 V 4 V7 2 5 -D
P11
P12 6 2 5 V 3 6 -E
P13 V7 4 V7 -F
P14 3 6 2 -(F♯)
P15 V 4 V7 5 V -G

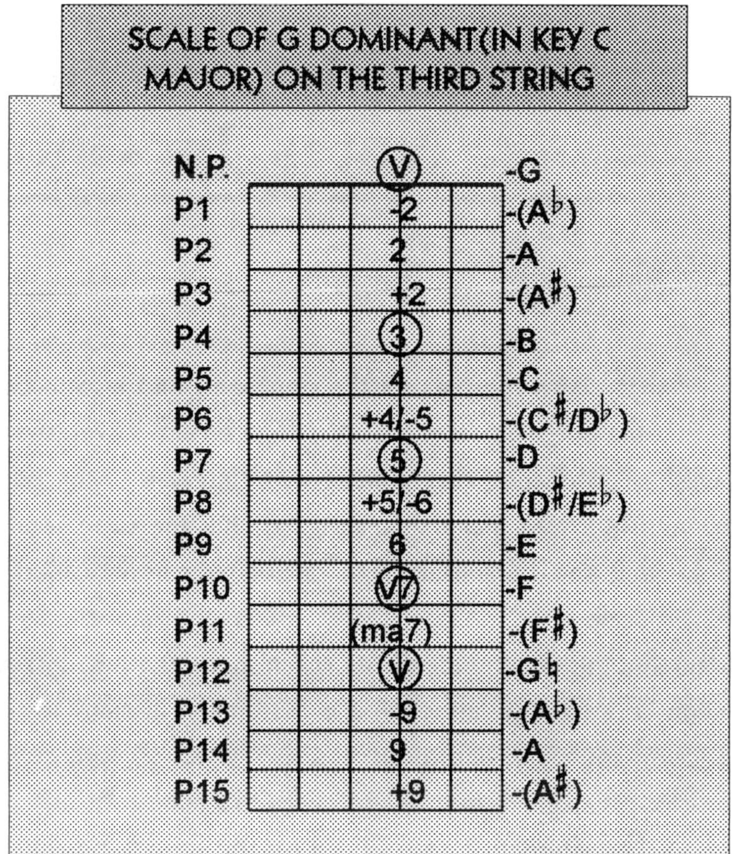
SCALE OF G DOMINANT(IN KEY C MAJOR) ON THE THIRD STRING
N.P. V -G
P1 -2 -(A♭)
P2 2 -A
P3 +2 -(A♯)
P4 3 -B
P5 4 -C
P6 +4/-5 -(C♯/D♭)
P7 5 -D
P8 +5/-6 -(D♯/E♭)
P9 6 -E
P10 V7 -F
P11 (ma7) -(F♯)
P12 V -G♮
P13 -9 -(A♭)
P14 9 -A
P15 +9 -(A♯)

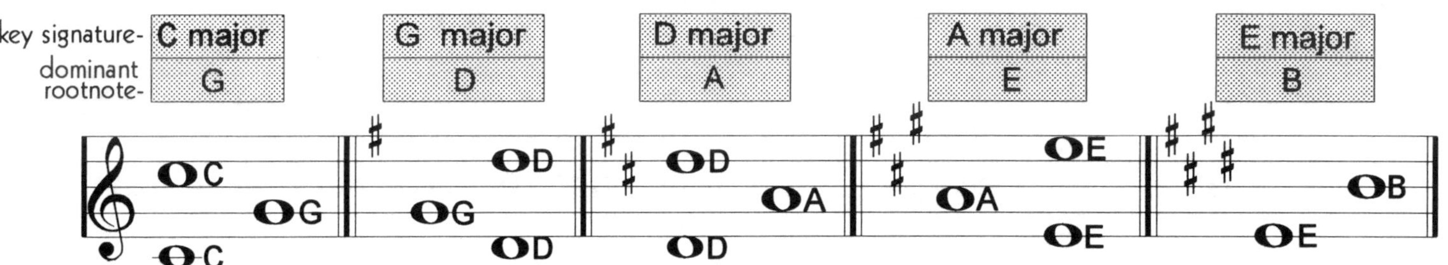
key signature- C major
dominant rootnote- G
G major
D
D major
A
A major
E
E major
B
C G C
G D D
D A D
A E E
E B

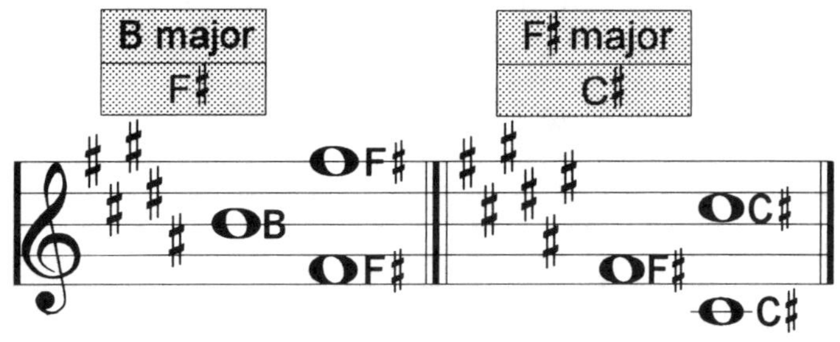
B major
F♯
F♯ major
C♯
F♯ B F♯
C♯ F♯ C♯

Part Four

"Diminished" Dominant Scale Notes In Chord Form

In comparison with the scale of the dominant, and also in comparison with "the chord of the dominant seventh", the 3rd, 5th and the "V7th" are each lowered a half-tone to become the "minor 3rd", "diminished 5th" and "diminished" V7th intervals in the dominant scale. The root note, V, remains unchanged but note that the "minor 3rd" has the same sound as the "augmented 9th", (or "augmented 2nd"), while the "diminished 7th" as it is commonly called, has the same sound as the "6th" of the dominant scale.

Incidentally, the occurrence of the diminished intervals, in keys in the cycle of flat keys, calls for the use of the term "double-flat" although it is customary, in many instances, to employ alternative terms which are identical in sound; example: the chord of E flat seventh consists of the notes E♭, G, B♭ and D♭ , therefore to produce the diminished seventh with the same root note, the latter three notes would become G♭, B♭♭ and D♭♭. The alternative names used for the sounds produced by B♭♭ and D♭♭ are A♮ and C♮, the names used for the "aug4th" and the "6th" of the same scale.

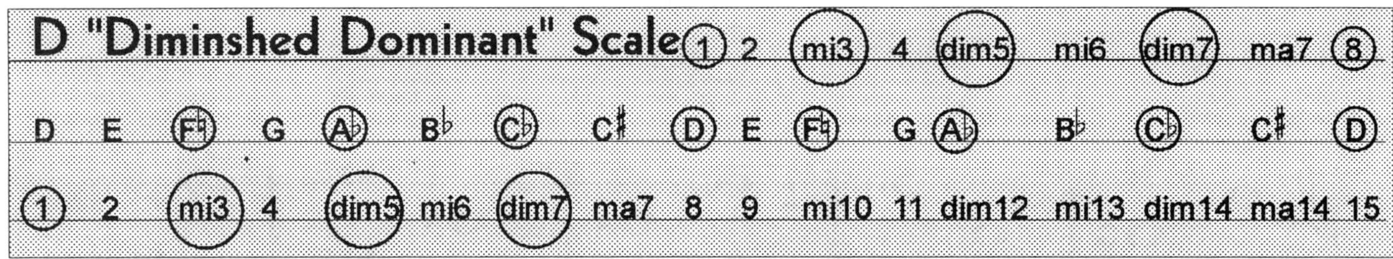

Standard chord forms for guitar(D dim7 or D°, means diminshed)

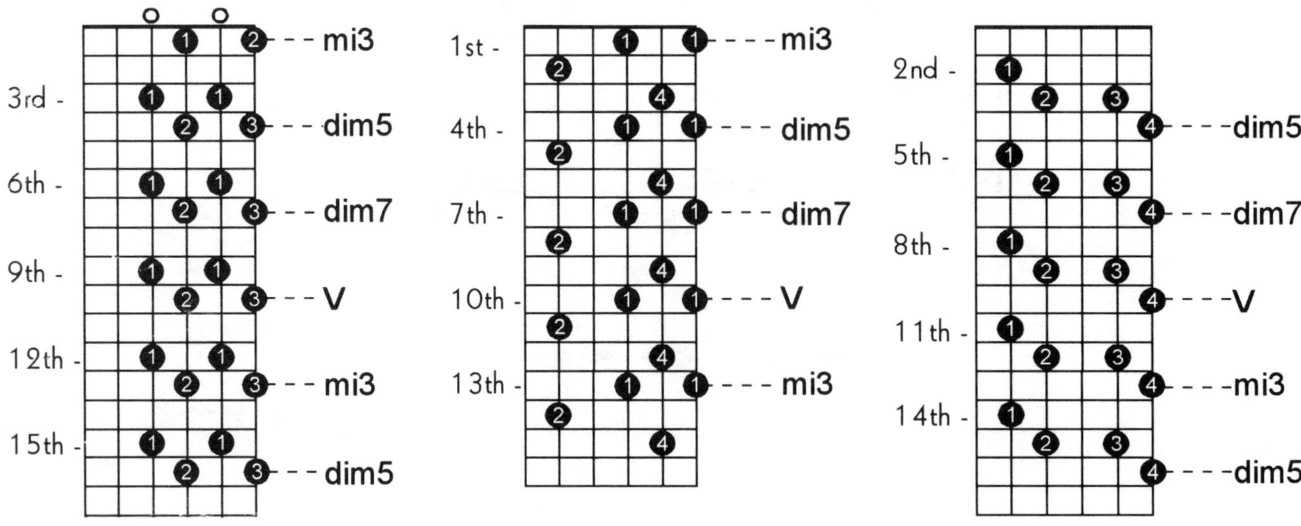

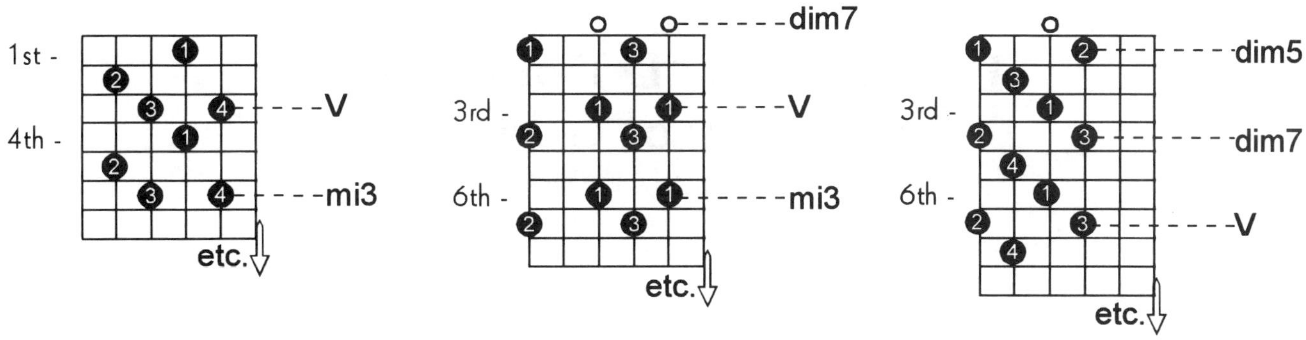

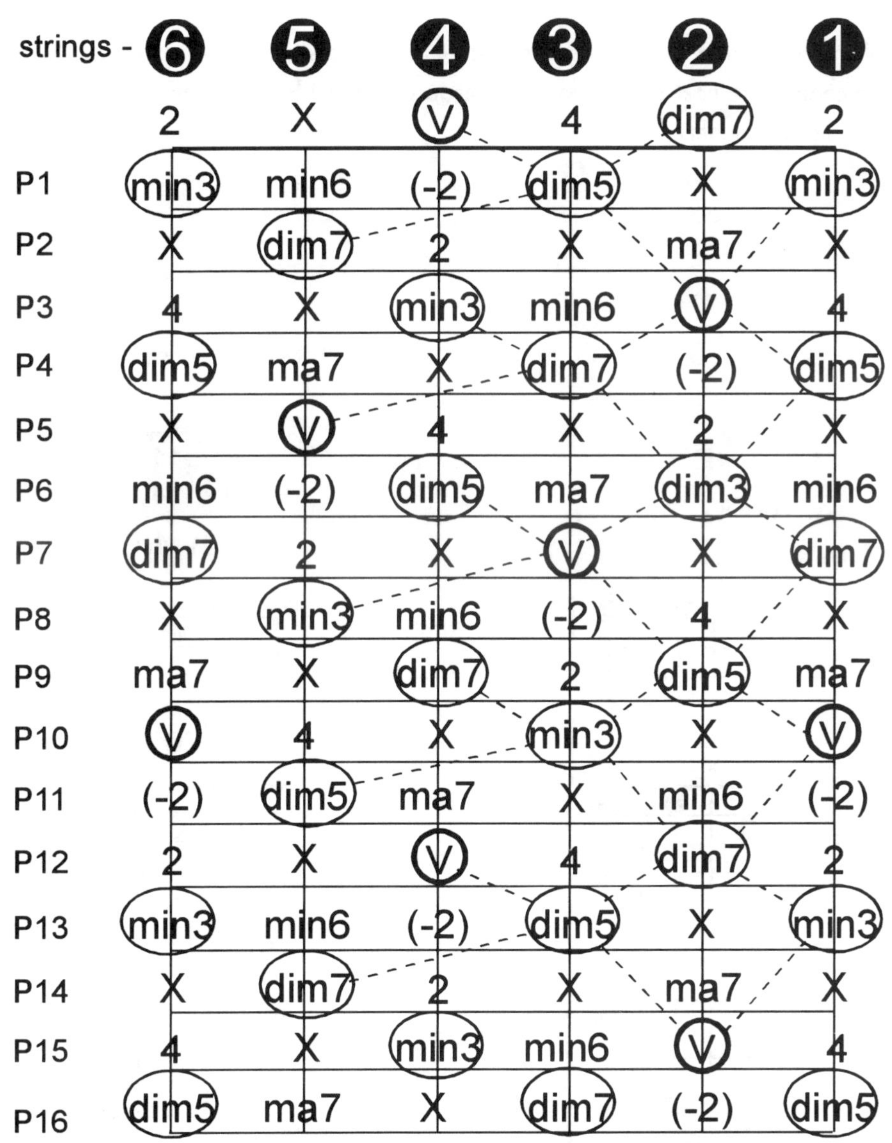

X indicates the notes which were lowered a half-tone, (or fret), to convert the chord of the dominant seventh" to the "chord of the diminished dominant seventh".

The 2nd, (or 9th); 4th (or 11th); minor 6th, (or minor 13th) and the 'major or 7th' often occur as "passing" or as "substitute" notes for the root, minor 3rd; dim. 5th and dim. 7th.

V stands for "root".

Scales In Chord Form
"Diminished Dominant" Scales

Examples In "D Dominant"
In the Key of G Major

Directions for producing the chord forms for scale notes in all other diminished dominant seventh scales are the same as described for producing major, minor and dominant scales in chord form.

The four different notes of the chord of the diminished dominant seventh are each at a distance of a "minor 3rd" from the chord-note next above and the chord note next below; for this reason the chord forms for each chord-note are identical in the "pattern" of the chord diagrams

FIG. 1 Scale-notes and "passing-notes", in the order in which they occur on the first string, in chord form.

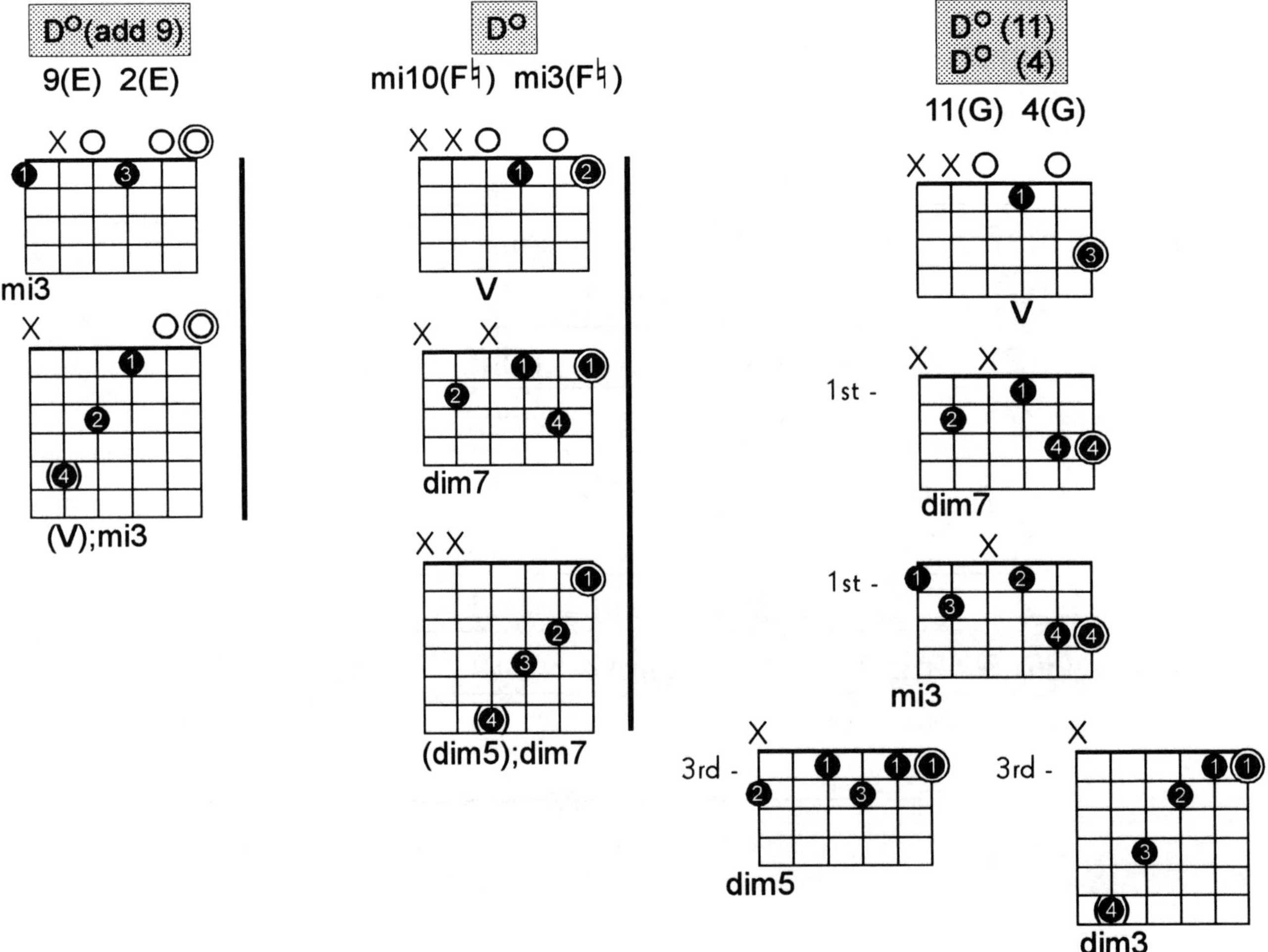

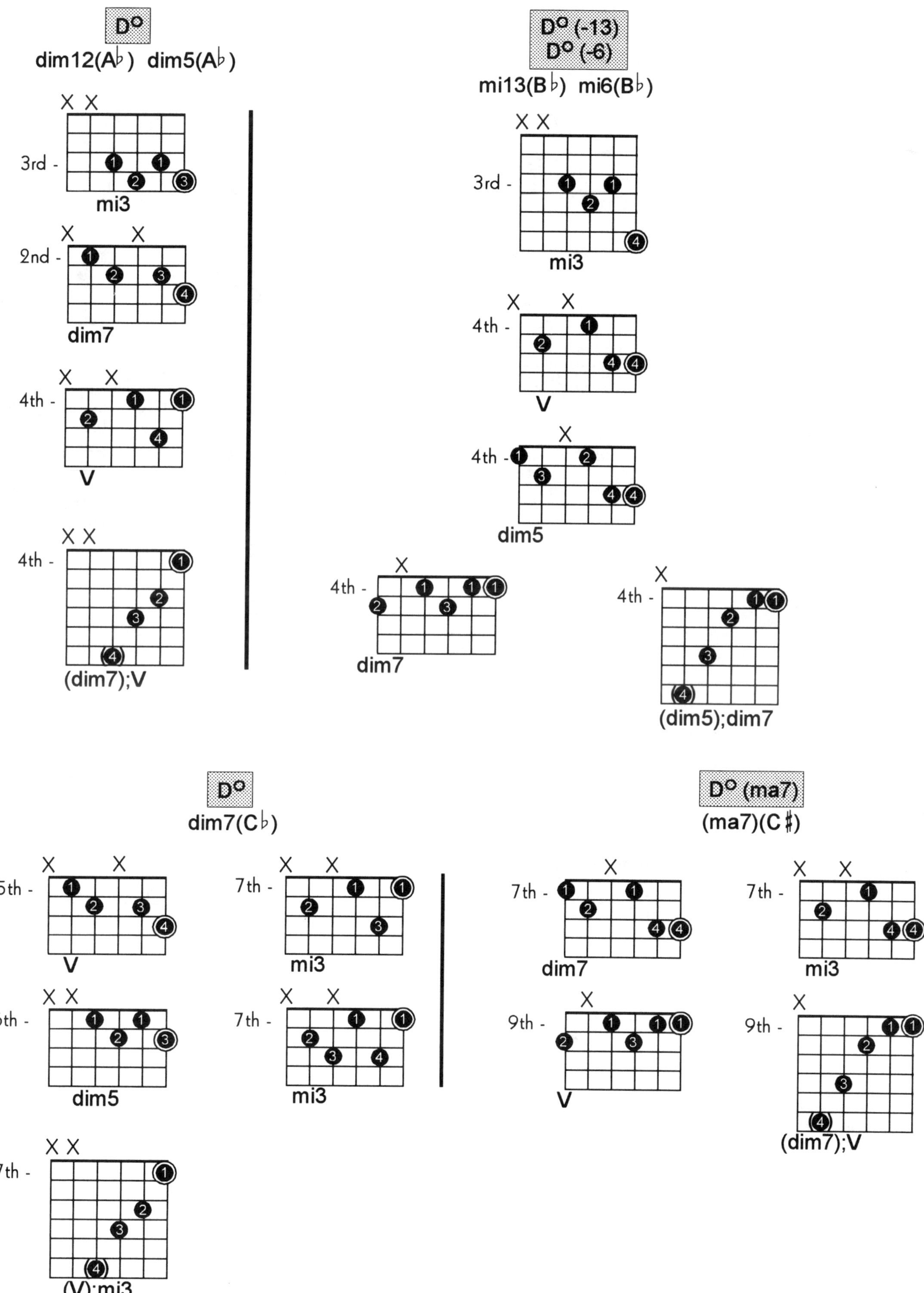
D°
dim12(A♭) dim5(A♭)
3rd -
mi3
2nd -
dim7
4th -
V
4th -
(dim7);V
D° (-13)
D° (-6)
mi13(B♭) mi6(B♭)
3rd -
mi3
4th -
V
4th -
dim5
4th -
dim7
4th -
(dim5);dim7
D°
dim7(C♭)
5th -
V
7th -
mi3
6th -
dim5
7th -
mi3
7th -
(V);mi3
D° (ma7)
(ma7)(C♯)
7th -
dim7
7th -
mi3
9th -
V
9th -
(dim7);V

D°

8(D)"V" 1(D)"V"

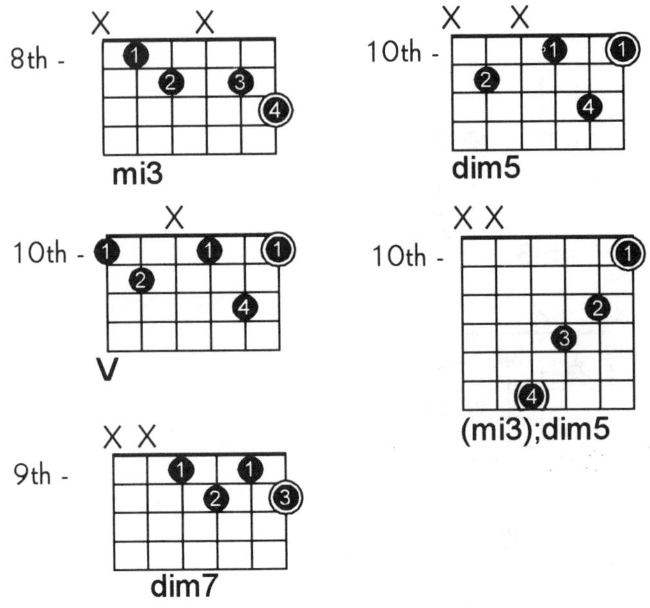

8th - mi3

10th - dim5

10th - V

10th - (mi3);dim5

9th - dim7

D° (add 9)

9(E) 2(E)

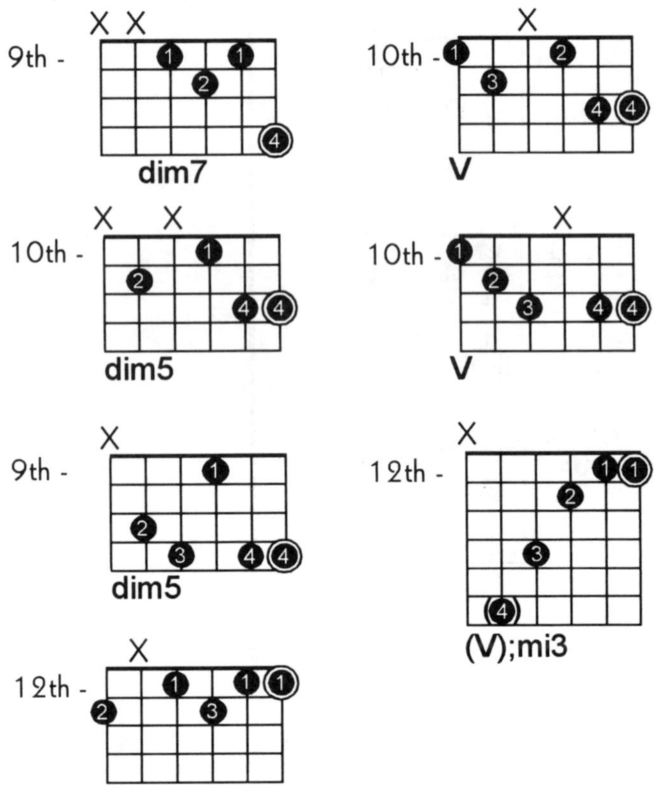

9th - dim7

10th - V

10th - dim5

10th - V

9th - dim5

12th - (V);mi3

12th -

D°

mi10(F♮) mi3(F♮)

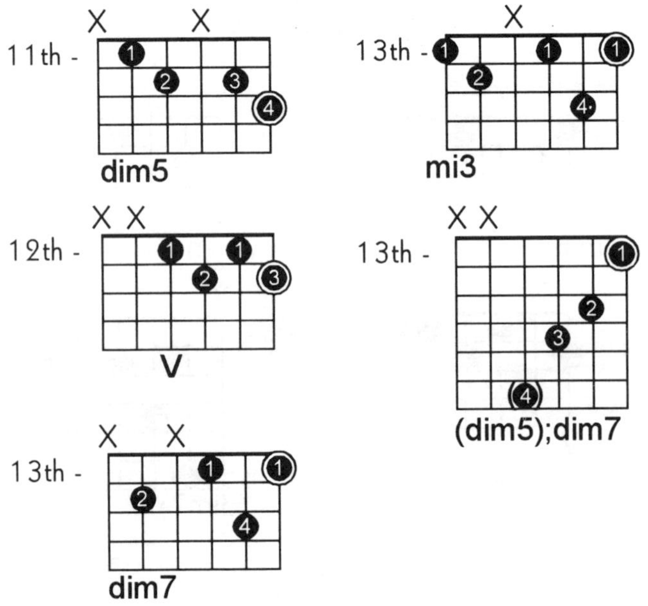

11th - dim5

13th - mi3

12th - V

13th - (dim5);dim7

13th - dim7

FIG. 2 As for Fig.1 but with the same notes on the second string.

D°

dim7(C♭)

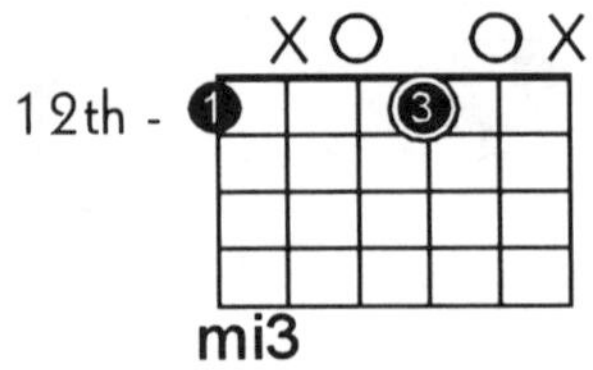

12th - mi3

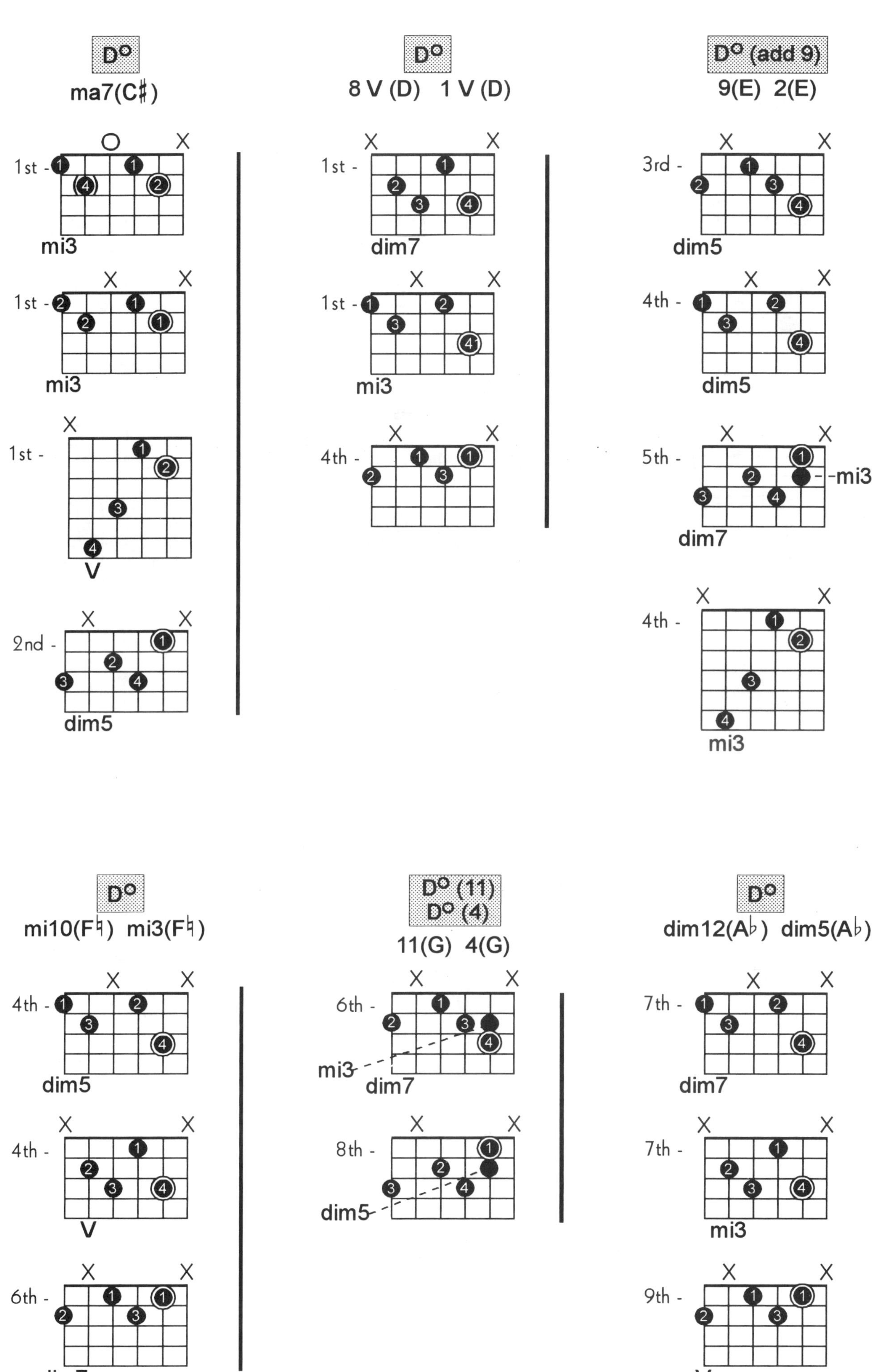
D°
ma7(C♯)
1st -
mi3
1st -
mi3
1st -
V
2nd -
dim5
D°
8 V (D) 1 V (D)
1st -
dim7
1st -
mi3
4th -
D° (add 9)
9(E) 2(E)
3rd -
dim5
4th -
dim5
5th -
mi3
dim7
4th -
mi3
D°
mi10(F♮) mi3(F♮)
4th -
dim5
4th -
V
6th -
dim7
D° (11)
D° (4)
11(G) 4(G)
6th -
mi3
dim7
8th -
dim5
D°
dim12(A♭) dim5(A♭)
7th -
dim7
7th -
mi3
9th -
V

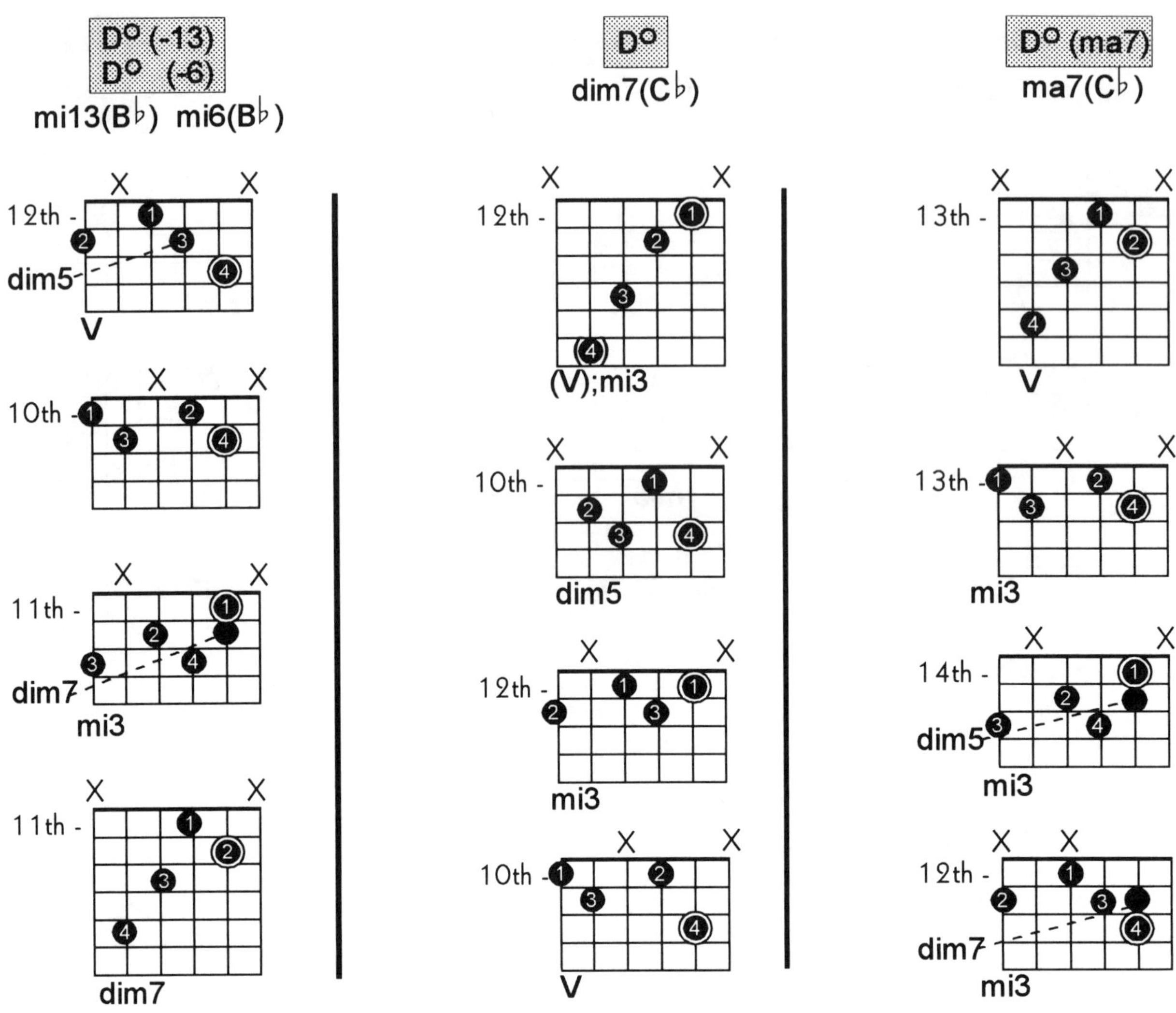

FIG. 3 As for fig. 1 and 2 but with the same notes on the third string.

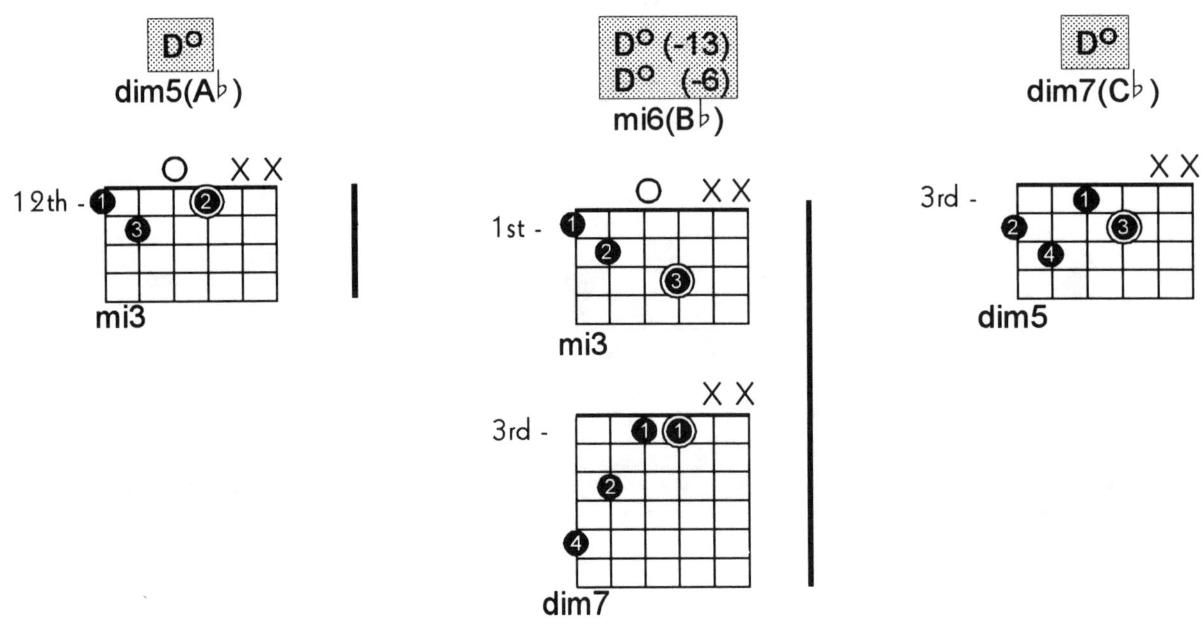

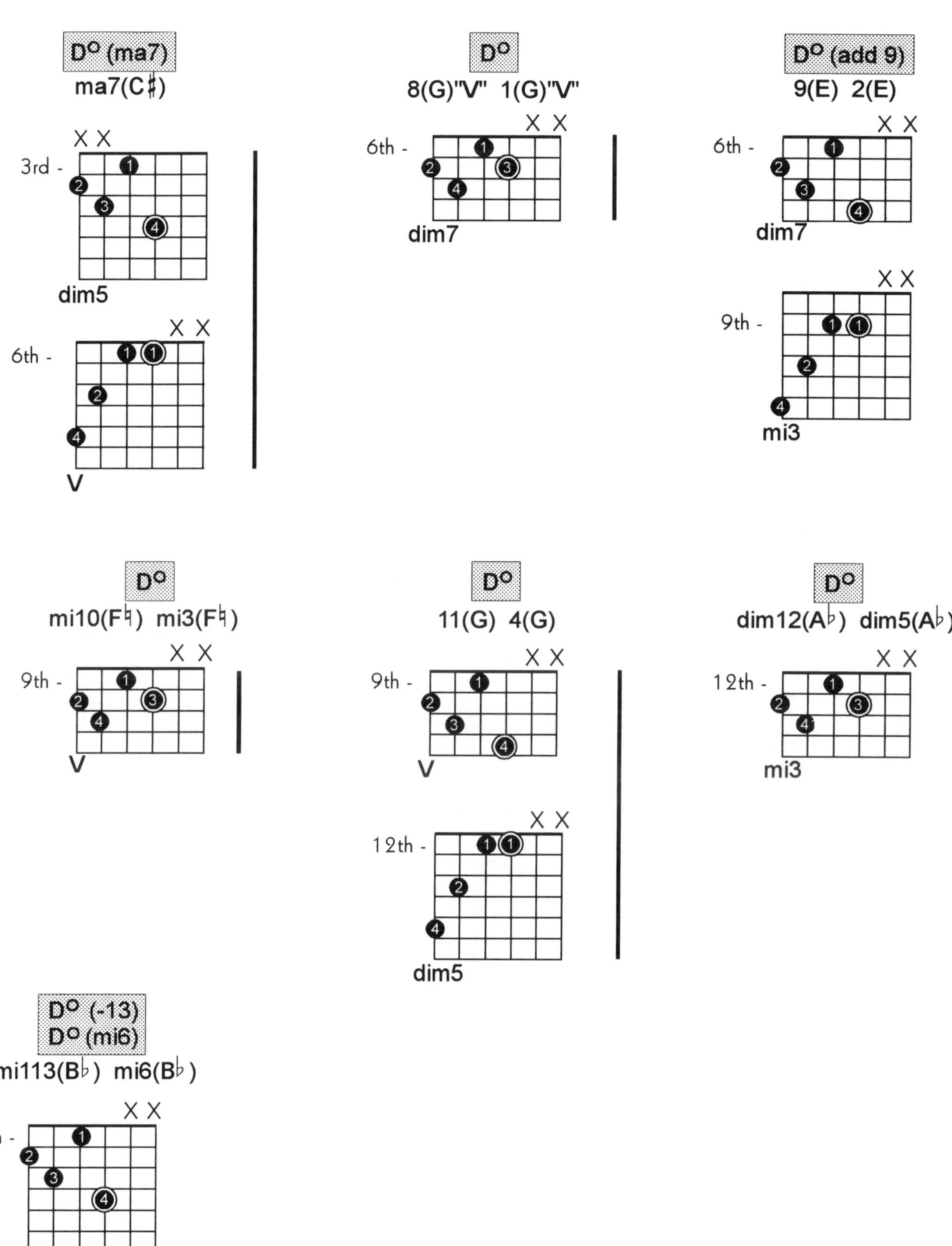
D° (ma7)
ma7(C♯)
3rd -
dim5
6th -
V
D°
8(G)"V" 1(G)"V"
6th -
dim7
D° (add 9)
9(E) 2(E)
6th -
dim7
9th -
mi3
D°
mi10(F♮) mi3(F♮)
9th -
V
D°
11(G) 4(G)
9th -
V
12th -
dim5
D°
dim12(A♭) dim5(A♭)
12th -
mi3
D° (-13)
D° (mi6)
mi113(B♭) mi6(B♭)
12th -
mi3

Reference Tables
"Diminished Dominant" Scales

"Diminished dominant" scales in all major keys, including "passing notes", I.E., major 2nd, (or 9th); 4th, (or 11th); minor 6th, (or minor 13th) and "major 7th".

Cycle Of Keys With Flat Signatures

Terms: - V represents the "root" note of the scale; -3 and -5 stand for the diminished 3rd and diminished 5th; d7 stands for "diminished 7th" while X denotes the "canceled" 3rd., 5th and V7th of the dominant scale (the four notes of the chord of the diminished seventh are give in a circle).

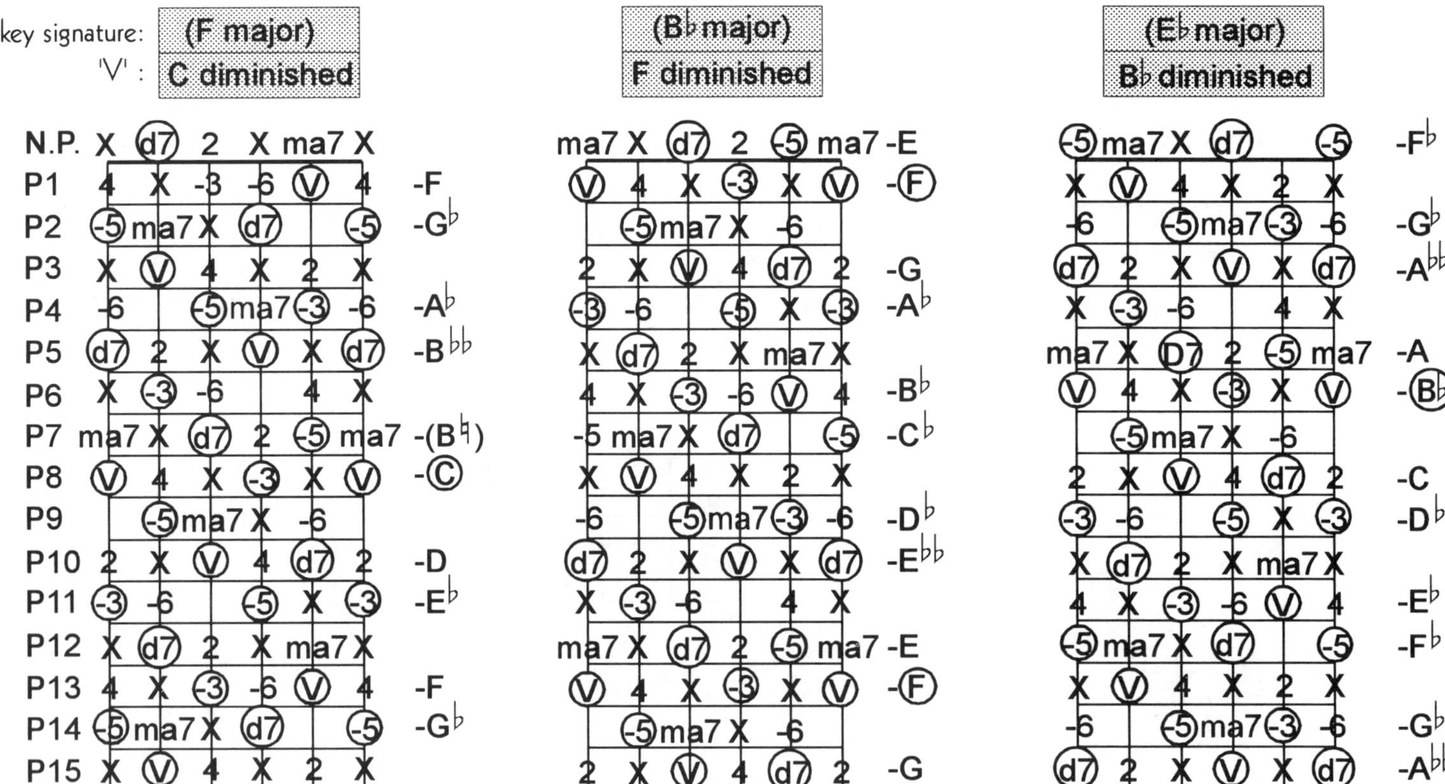

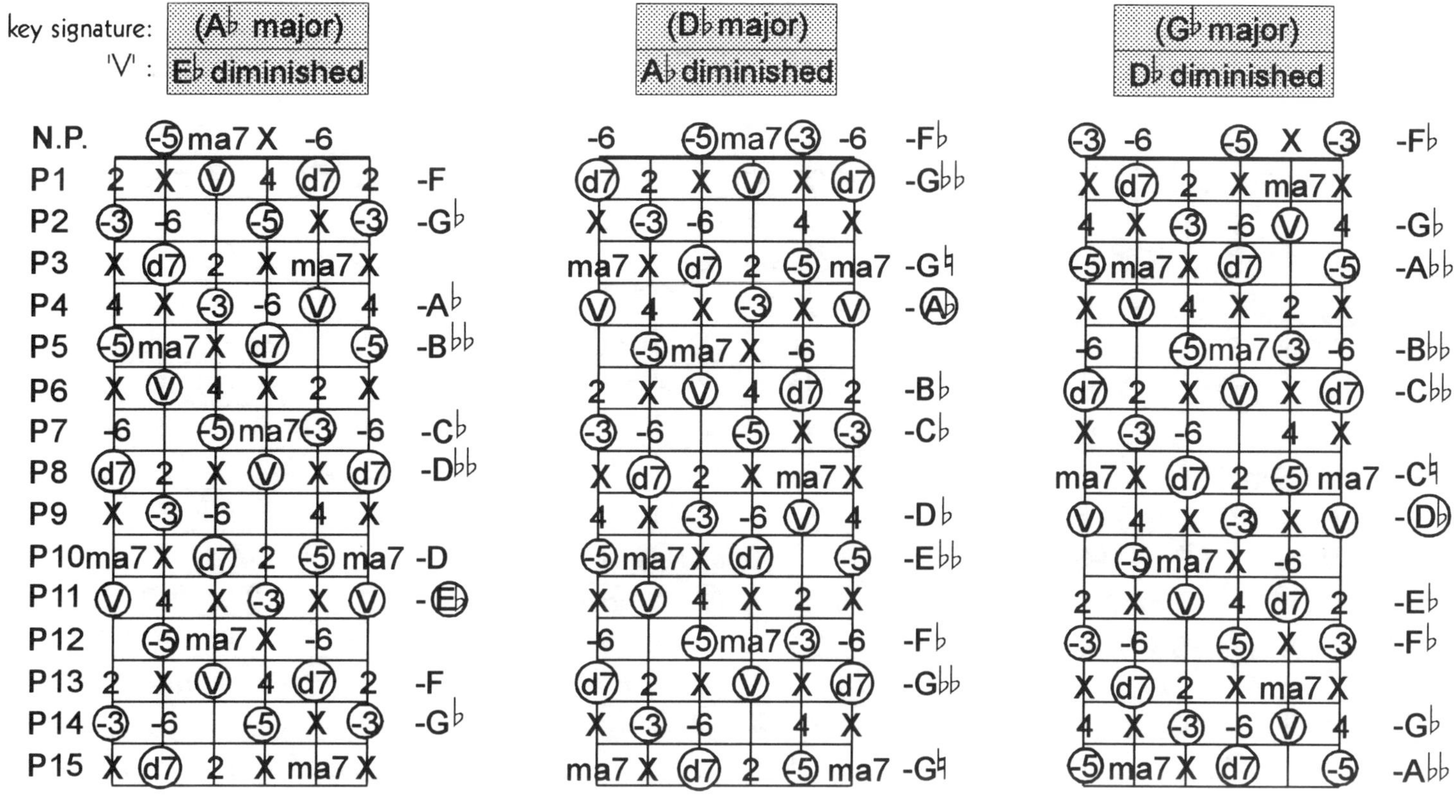

Cycle of keys with sharp signatures and the "open key", C major

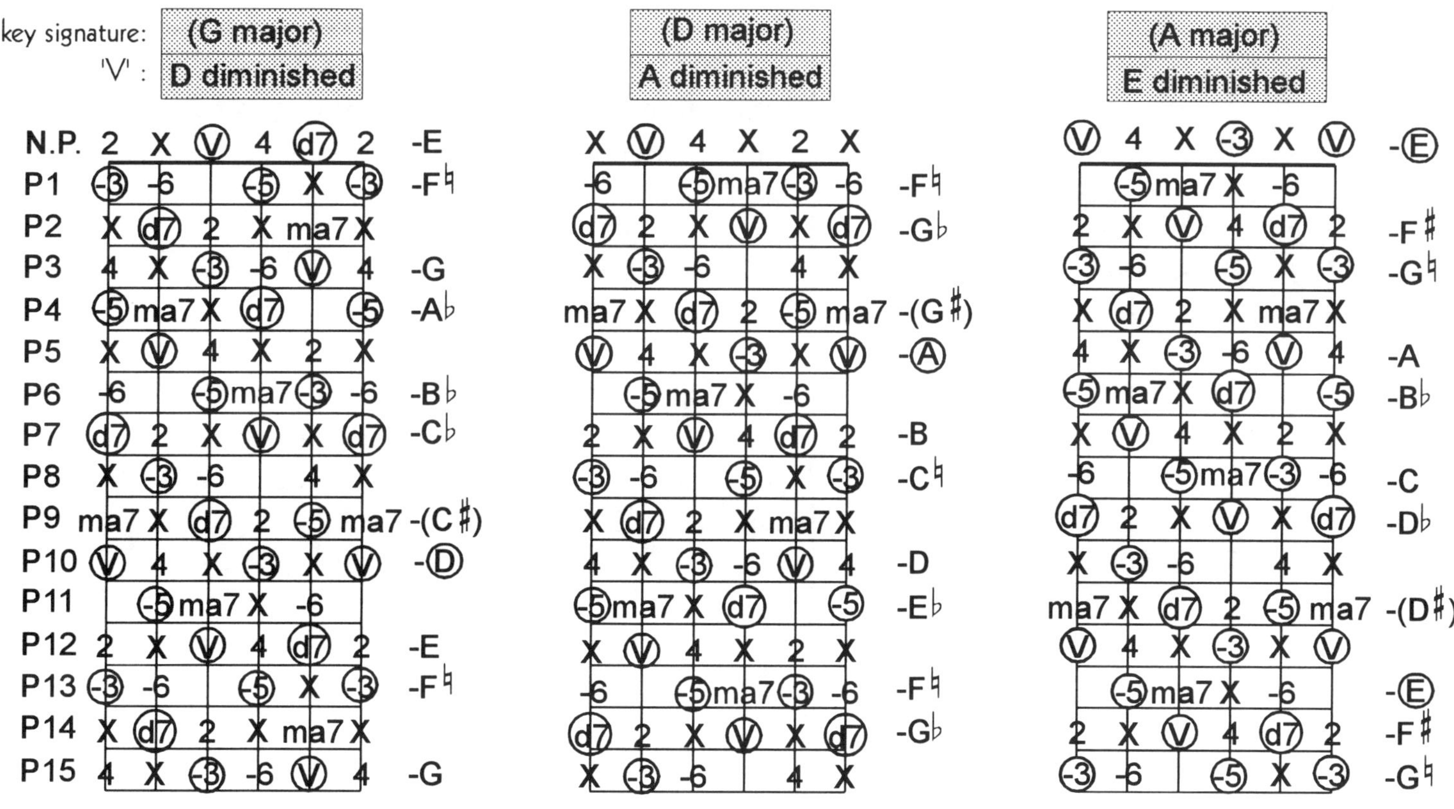

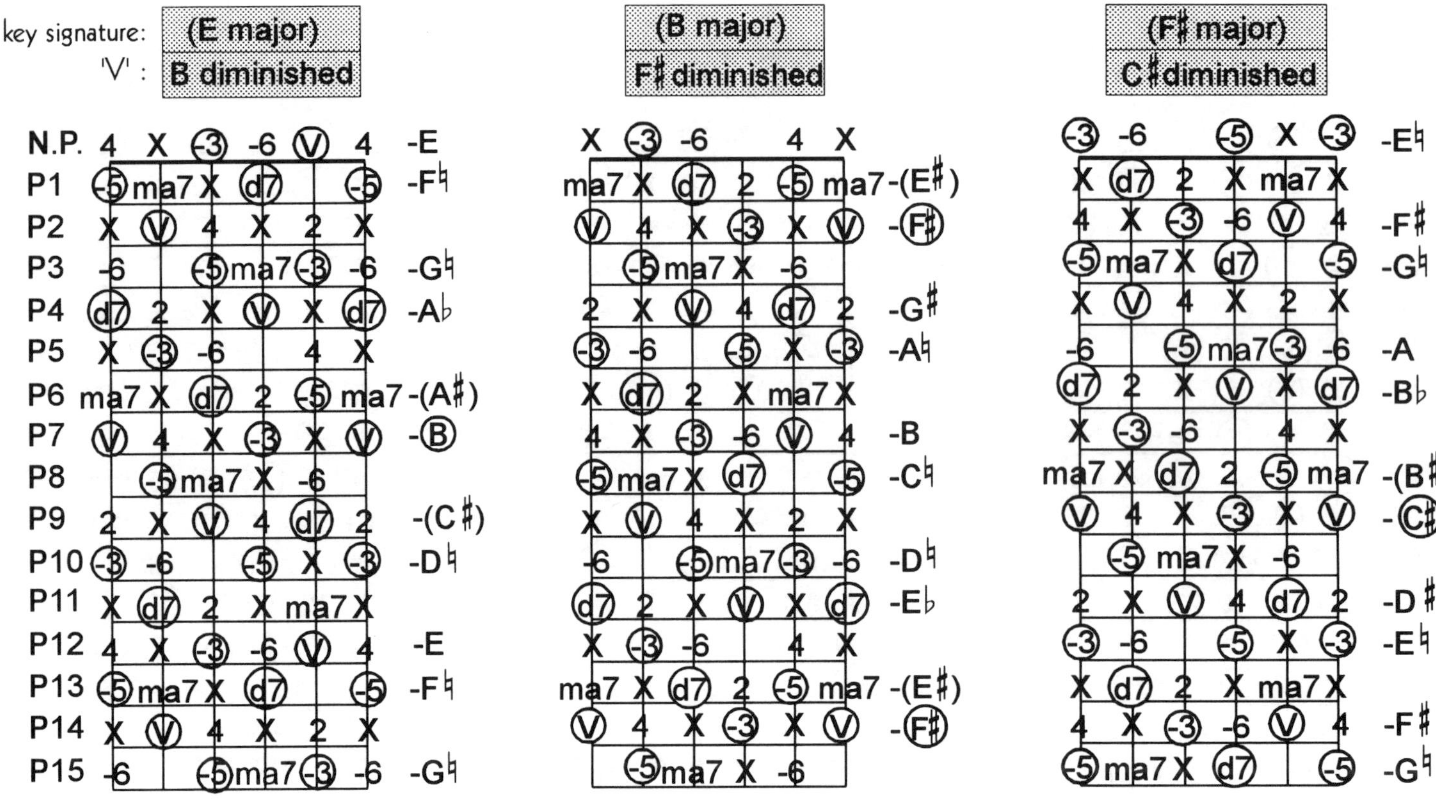

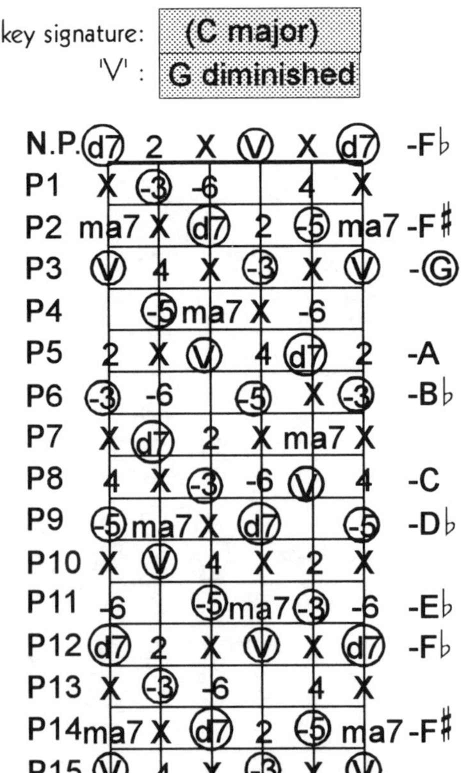

"Diminished seventh" chord symbols, in harmonic accompaniment of popular songs.

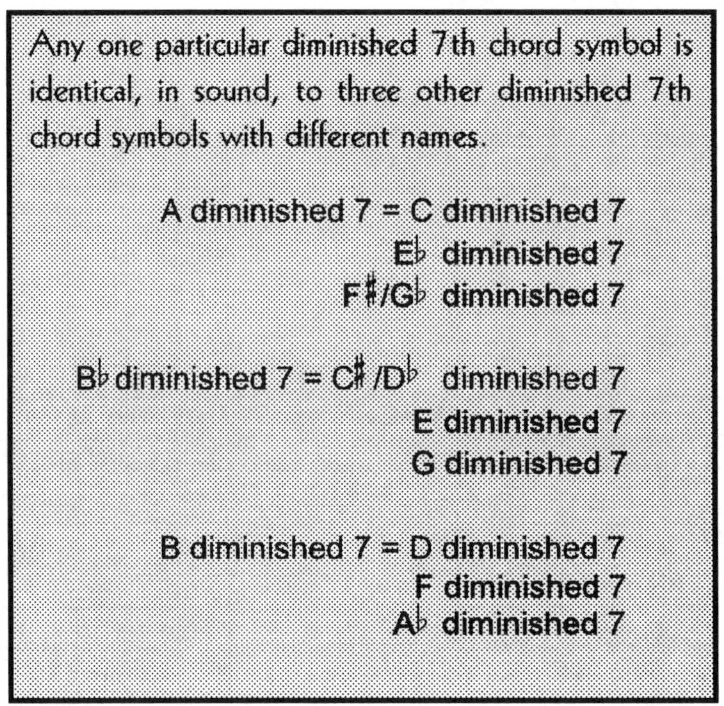

Any one particular diminished 7th chord symbol is identical, in sound, to three other diminished 7th chord symbols with different names.

A diminished 7 = C diminished 7
E♭ diminished 7
F♯/G♭ diminished 7

B♭ diminished 7 = C♯/D♭ diminished 7
E diminished 7
G diminished 7

B diminished 7 = D diminished 7
F diminished 7
A♭ diminished 7

Reference table: Notes produced at each fret.

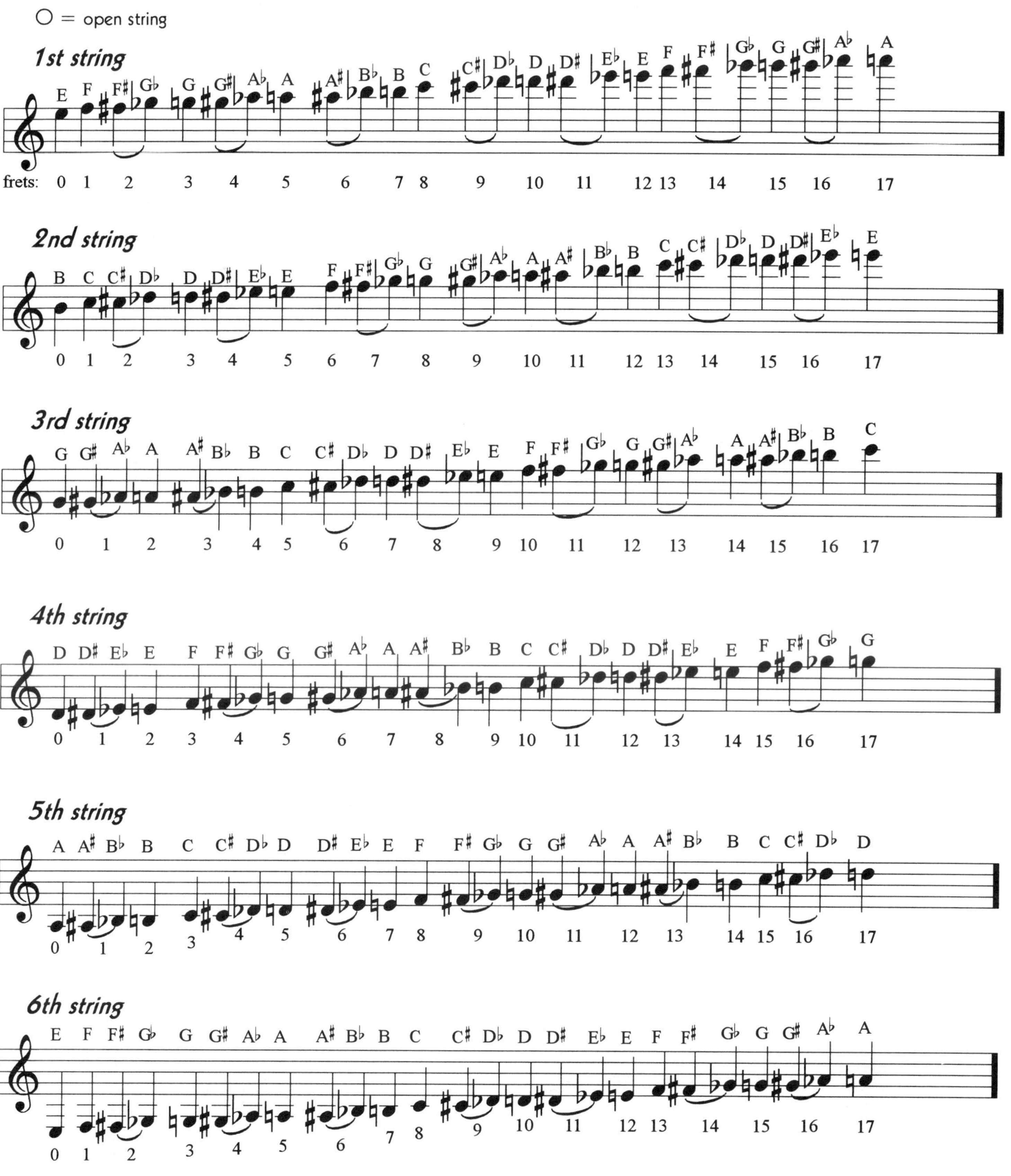

Enharmonics
Different Names For The Same Sound

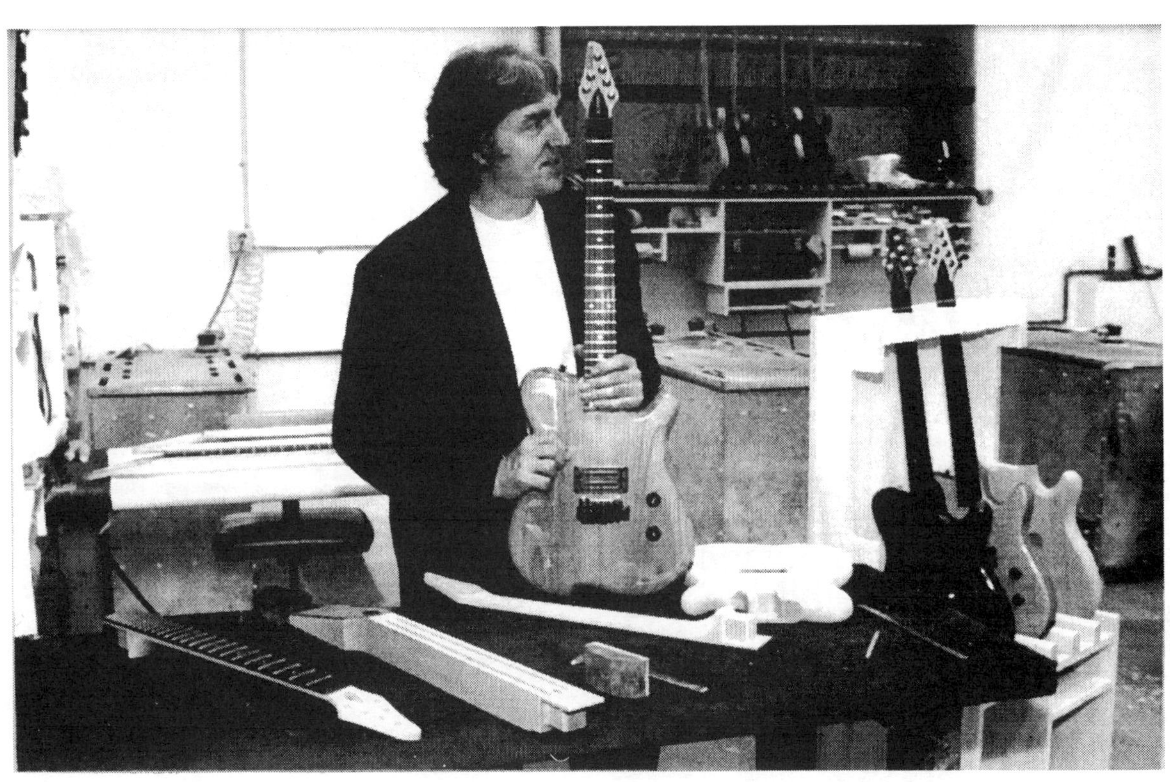

The models passed Allan's inspections!
Courtesy of Carvin Guitar

Chord Sequences In Harmonic Accompaniments

Up to this stage the system has presented the chord diagrams in the order in which they are played when ascending and/or descending the various scales stepwise, and while many readers will be familiar with most of the "standard" chord diagrams for the various chord symbols which form the "chord-connections" in accompaniments to popular songs, there will most likely be a number of readers who would appreciate some guidance in the selecting of chord forms for the purpose of linking them together to provide for good, or at least adequate, accompaniment to solo artists of to ensemble playing. Therefore, the following directions and examples in selecting chord diagrams for use in various chord progressions which occur frequently in accompaniment work are intended to serve as a guide to readers who may find such guidance to be helpful.

The "chord connections" which form the harmonic accompaniment to a popular song consists, as you will know, of a "mixed bag" of major, minor, dominant and diminished chords belonging to the scale of the key indicated by the key signature and also to the scales of the keys into which the notes of the song lead to as they weave their way throughout the song before "homing back" to the key in which they started.

This melody-line, just mentioned, quite often suggests the appropriate harmony and "counter-melody" lines for the accompaniment and is therefore, a sequence of notes belong to the various chord symbols. The latter, according to how many different keys the melody line weaves its way through, may be sparse or plentiful, thus, chord-changes will vary accordingly and in cases where the changes are fairly rapid it is important to choose chord forms which, when linked together to form a chord sequence, call for a minimum of hand and arm movement when moving from one chord to the next one in the sequence . Such chord forms could include those which are fairly easy to execute while other forms could consist of a combination of chords with the "lead" note on the first string, and some with the "lead" note on the second string, (I.E., "inside chords"). Even when the chord-changes are quite rapid it is often possible to group all the various chords within a compass of a few consecutive frets.

As for the "sounds" produced in your selection of chords for use in chord-connections, you ear must be the main guide to producing a satisfactory accompaniment to a given melody. For chord symbols other than those give in the book, choose a chord diagram from Part 1, 2, 3 or 4, whichever is called for as you deal with each chord symbol in a given accompaniment, and simply move the chord "shape" up or down, the fingerboard, as the case may be, to the position required for applying to the given chord symbol.

For chord sequences in which one chord symbol only is given for a section lasting for two bars, or more, the use of the same chord diagram throughout the sequence can sometimes be rather monotonous, so to avoid undue monotony there are two methods available for use, as shown in figs. 1 and 2, following: -

FIG. 1 A "two-bar" harmony phrase with C major chord symbol only. Oblique lines represent the four beats of 4/4 tempo in each bar: a curved line connecting two "beats" means play te chord on the first beat and sustain for beat number two. Any one of the chord diagrams may be used or use a combination of the standard chord shapes.

C Major

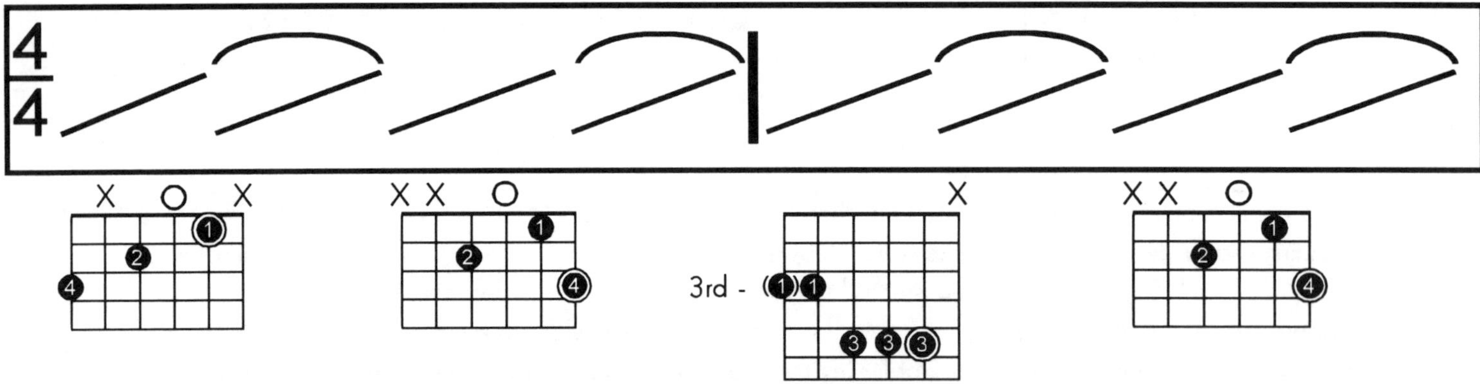

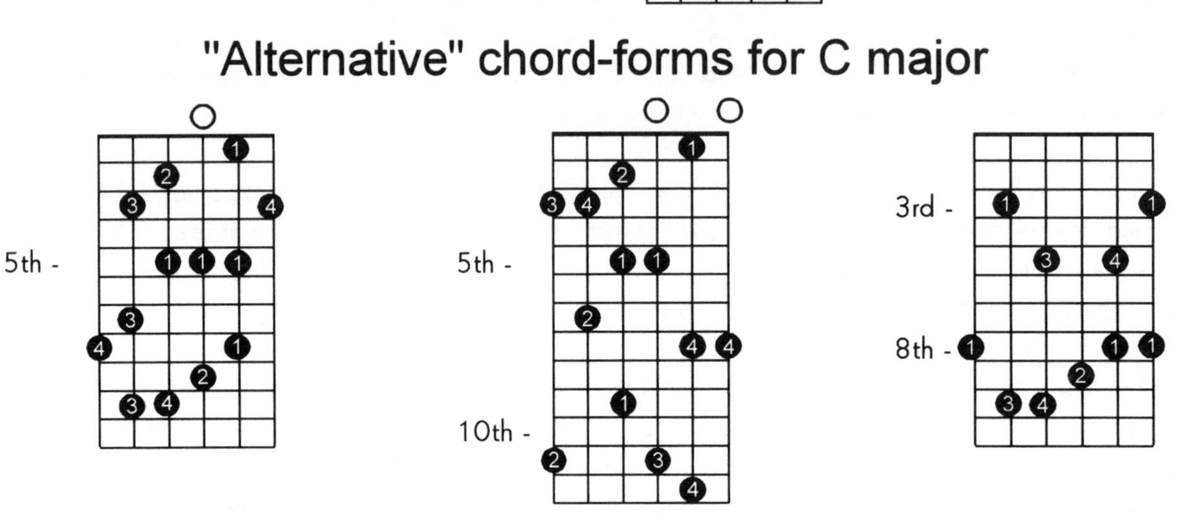

FIG. 2 The same two-bar phrase as in Fig. 1 but this time with the chords of the "major sixth" and "major seventh" used in combination with the "common" major chord. Other "progressive" froms for the same chord may also be included, e.g. "major 6/9", "major 7/9", "major 7th with Aug. 5th", etc.

Standard Chord - C Major

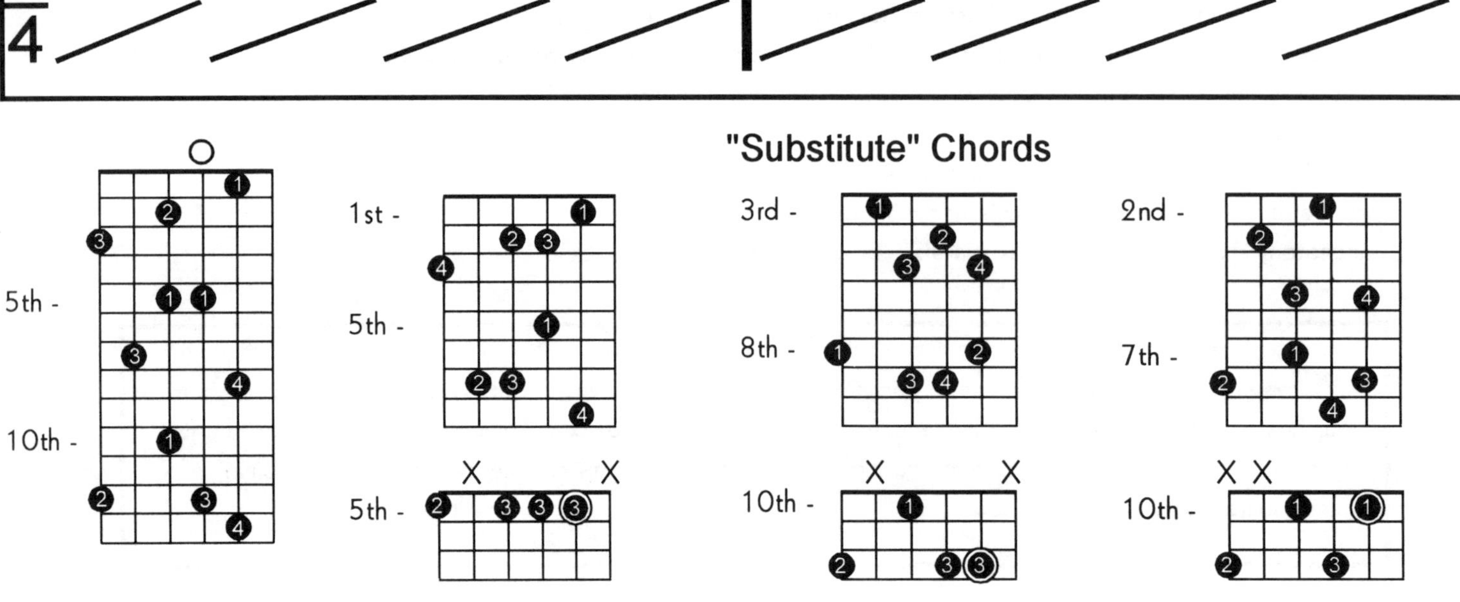

As for Fig. 2 but rhythmically

C Major

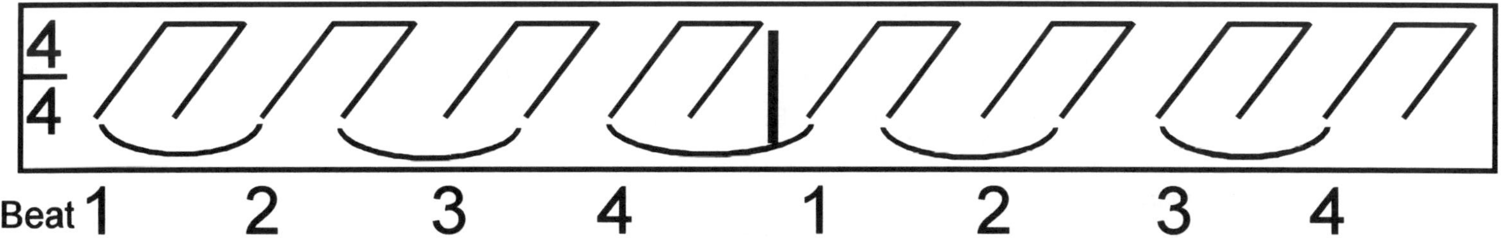

C Major "Progressive" chords C Major 6/9 etc.

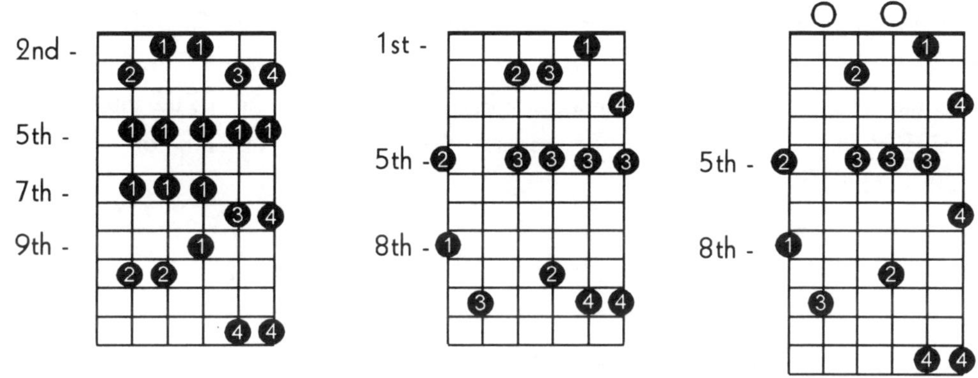

Chord forms on the lower positions on the fingerboard are useful accompaniment to highregister soloists, while chord forms on the higher fingerboard positions are often effective in accompaniments to lower register soloists, especially those forms with "lead" on the first string.

"Substitute" Notes In Chord Forms

The use of 'substitute' notes in place of temporarily-delayed "regular notes" in chord forms is often convenient when playing rhythmic effects and quick chord changes in harmonic sequences.

As a general rule, the note a scale step above, or a half-step below - (and, on some occasions, vice-versa) - can be taken as a substitute note for a chordal note, followed, in the next chord following, by the restoring of the suspended chordal note. In terms of "intervals" the 9th, (two frets above the fundamental note, I.E., the symbol-name note), can substitute for the latter. Also, in dominant chords, the "minor 9th" can deputize for the fundamental, or "root" note. Alternatively, the "major 7th", a fret below the root may be taken as a substitute for the root.

The 4th, (one fret above the "major 3rd"), can substitute for the "delayed 3rd" while the "aug.4th" can replace the 5th, as also can the "aug. 5th". Another substitute note is the "6th", which may stand in for either the 5th or the 7th. Again, when the "chord-connections" are in a major key you can add the "min.7th" interval to minor chord symbols; when, however, they are in a minor key you can add the "maj. 6th", "maj.7th" or "maj.9th" in preference to the "min.7th" interval.

Chord - Bending

The simple adjustments made to any kind of chord diagram in the manner explained and illustrated in the following pages is a most convenient means for interdicting interesting harmonic "coloring" effects in either chord solo passages or in ensemble accompaniments.

The adjustment consists of moving a note, and in some instances moving two or more notes, of a chord diagram up, or down, (according to choice), one fret or two or three frets if you like, and then returning the note(s) to the original position. When applied to a chord for which the "lead" note is to be sustained for several beats,, as with a sustained melody-note in chord solo work, the "lead" note can retain its position throughout the "bending" of notes in the harmony parts; otherwise, the top note of the chord may also be moved in the manner explained above.

FIG.3 To follow, illustrates some examples of "chord-bending" used frequently in sequences in which a given chord symbol lasts for several beats:

FIG. 3a As for Fig. 2 but for the purpose of illustration, using the 'standard' C major chord forms.

C Major

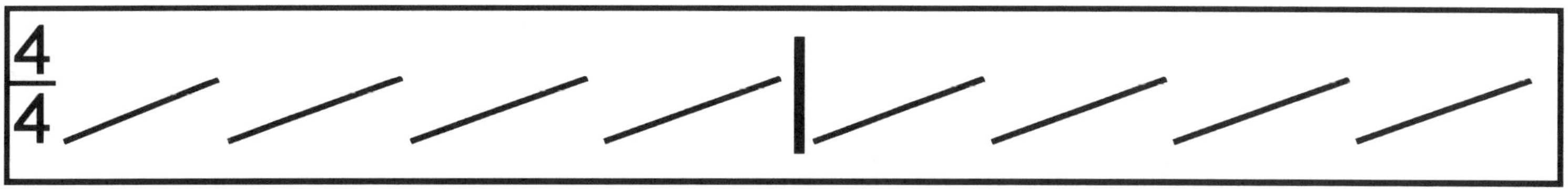

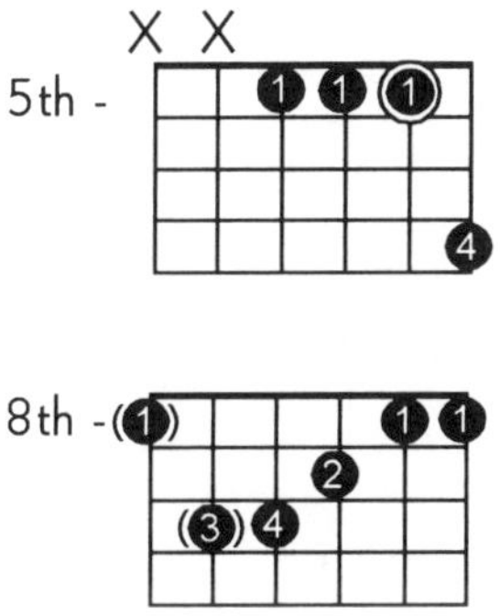

4/4

C maj

X X

5th -

8th -

Standard Forms

FIG. 3b The same two-bar phrase but with substitute chords, similar to those used in Fig. 2.

C Major

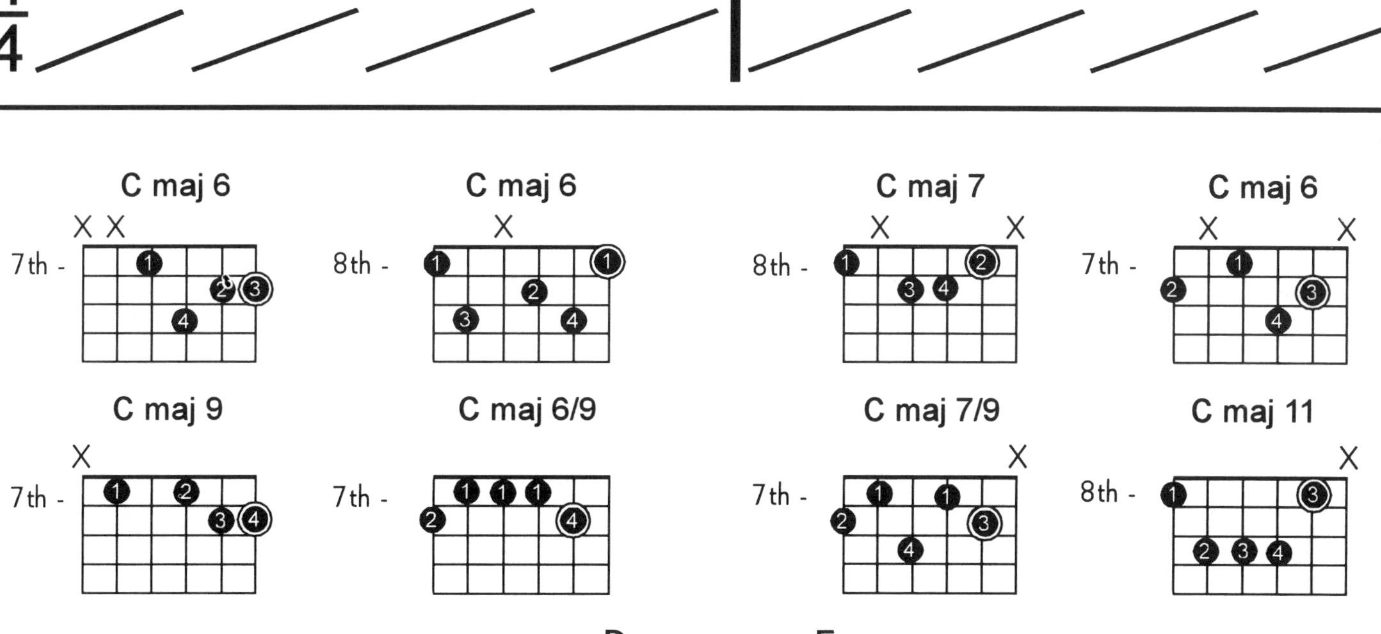

Progressive Forms

You can use any of the chord forms, standard and progressive, having the same chord symbol name. Try them in various orders throughout the two bar phrase. Additionally, you can "bend" any selected chord form in the manner explained overpage and as shown in Fig. 4 , in which the "inner harmony" notes are moved, a fret-at-a-time to two frets up the fingerboard or, alternatively, two frets down, meanwhile keeping the "lead" note unchanged in position. The notes thus moved are subsequently progressed back again to their initial position.

It is necessary, is some instances, to adjust the fingering of the forms produced by the process of "bending". Figs. (c) and (d) are examples of moving the inner-harmony notes to 'two-frets-up' and then moving them to their original position. In both directions the notes are moved "a-fret-at-a-time". Figs. (e) and (f) are similar, except they are in reverse direction to that of figs. (c) and (d).

If the "lead" note is not to be retained in its same position, it may also be treated in the same manner as for the inner harmony notes.

As shown in Fig. (g) the final chord form selected to terminate a phrase can be approached by first playing the same chord form on a position five frets up, and then descending, a fret-at-a-time, to the final chord.

Similarly, Fig. (h) shows the final chord approached by playing the same chord form two frets below and then progressing up to the position of the final chord.

You can, of course, bend only one of the notes of a chord by moving it one fret up, or down - (or two frets up, or down, if you like) - and then return it to its former position. Which notes to choose for the purpose of bending is often a case of trial and error procedure.

(Note - The chord symbols for the "substitute" chords are given in the example, although it is not essential for the reader to work them out.)

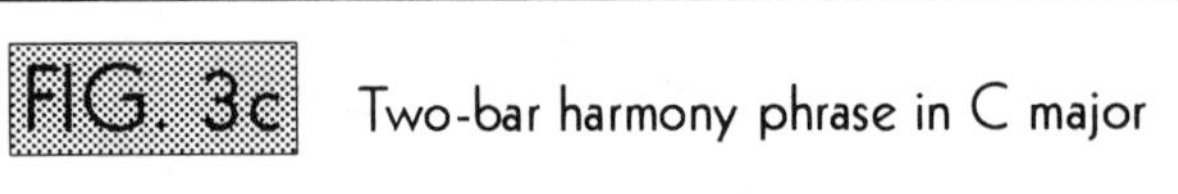

C Major

"Substitute" Chords

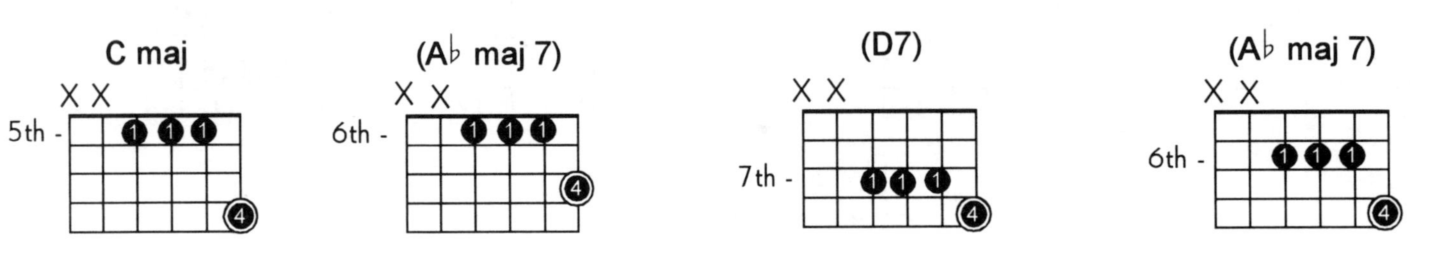

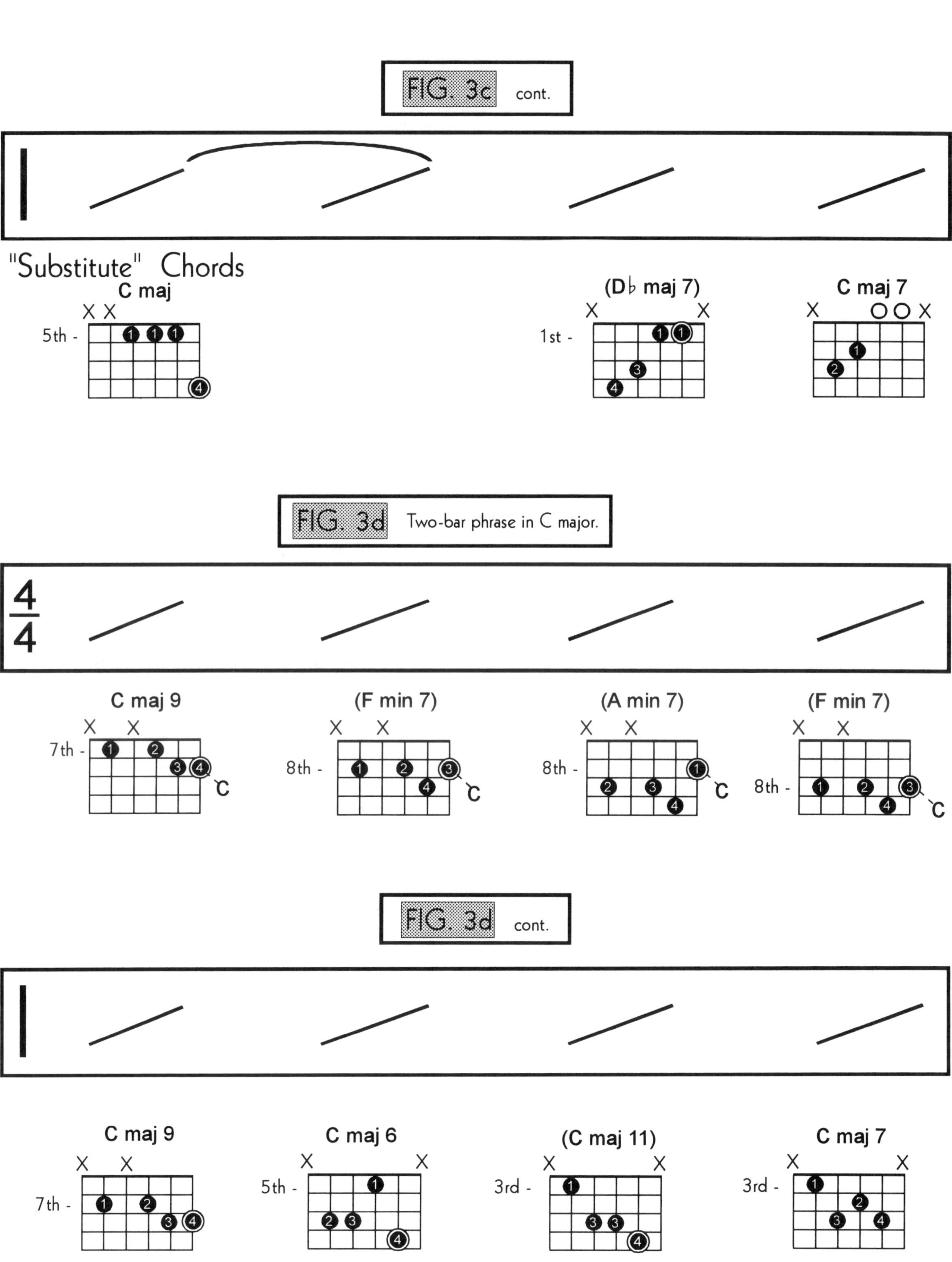
FIG. 3c cont.
"Substitute" Chords
C maj
5th -
(D♭ maj 7)
1st -
C maj 7
FIG. 3d Two-bar phrase in C major.
C maj 9
7th -
(F min 7)
8th -
(A min 7)
8th -
(F min 7)
8th -
FIG. 3d cont.
C maj 9
7th -
C maj 6
5th -
(C maj 11)
3rd -
C maj 7
3rd -

FIG. 3e As for 3c and 3d.

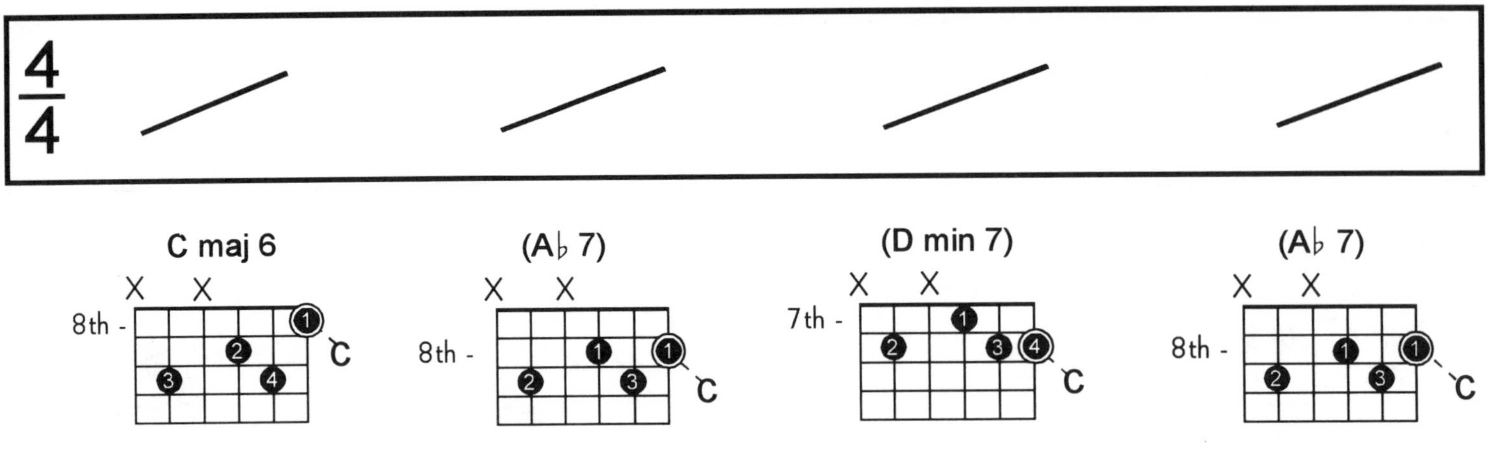

4/4

C maj 6 — 8th
(A♭ 7) — 8th
(D min 7) — 7th
(A♭ 7) — 8th

FIG. 3e cont.

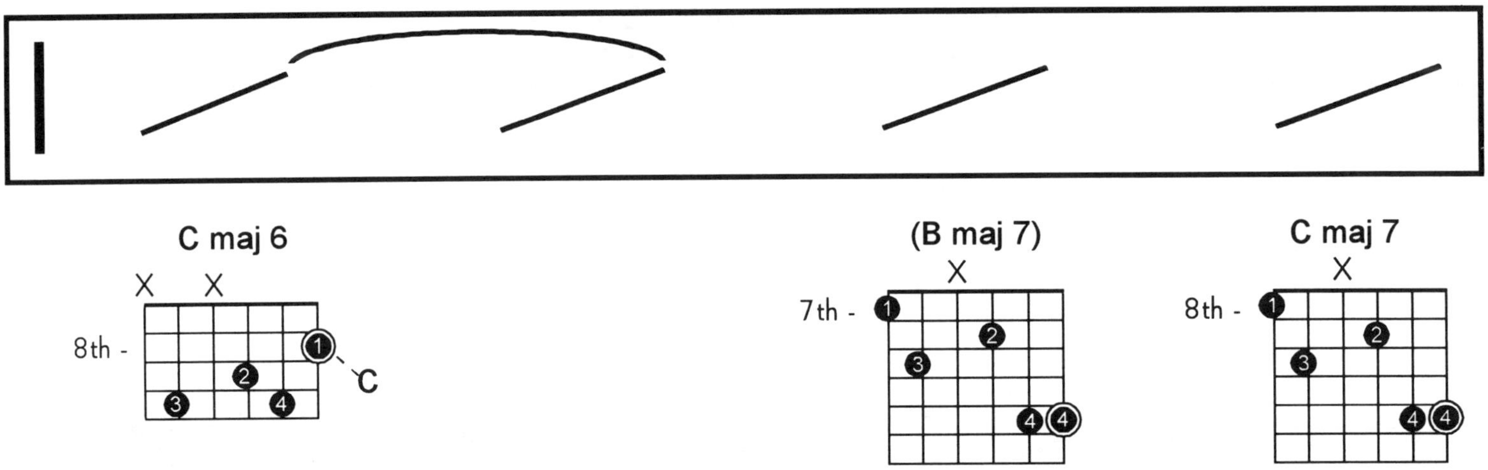

C maj 6 — 8th
(B maj 7) — 7th
C maj 7 — 8th

FIG. 3f As for 3e.

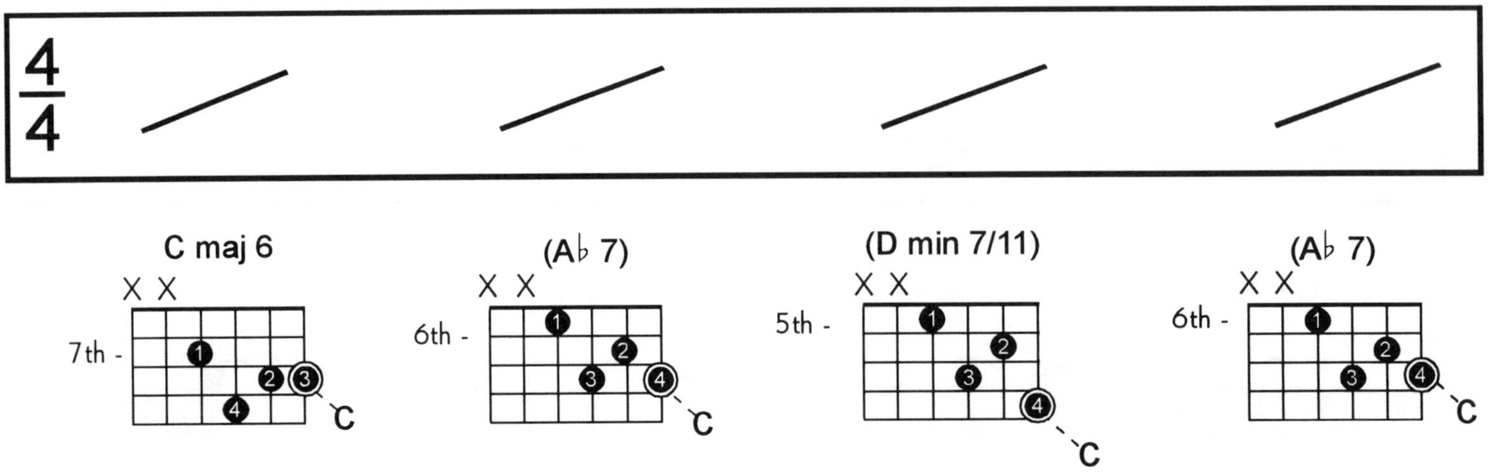

4/4

C maj 6 — 7th
(A♭ 7) — 6th
(D min 7/11) — 5th
(A♭ 7) — 6th

FIG. 3f cont.

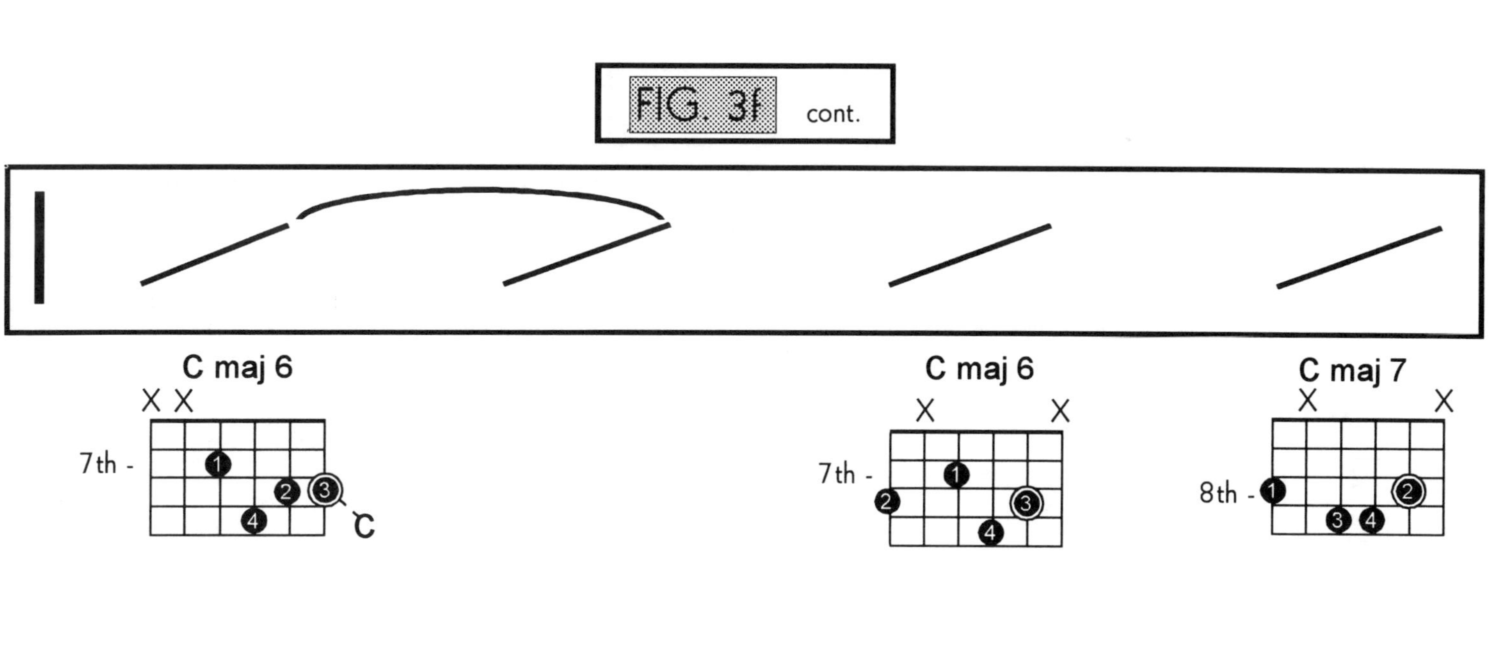

FIG. 3g As for 3c to 3f but the whole chord-form is moved.

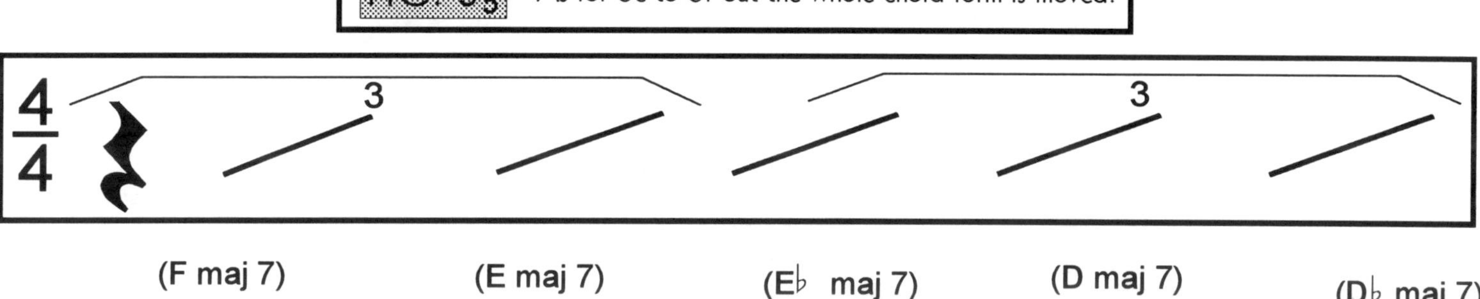

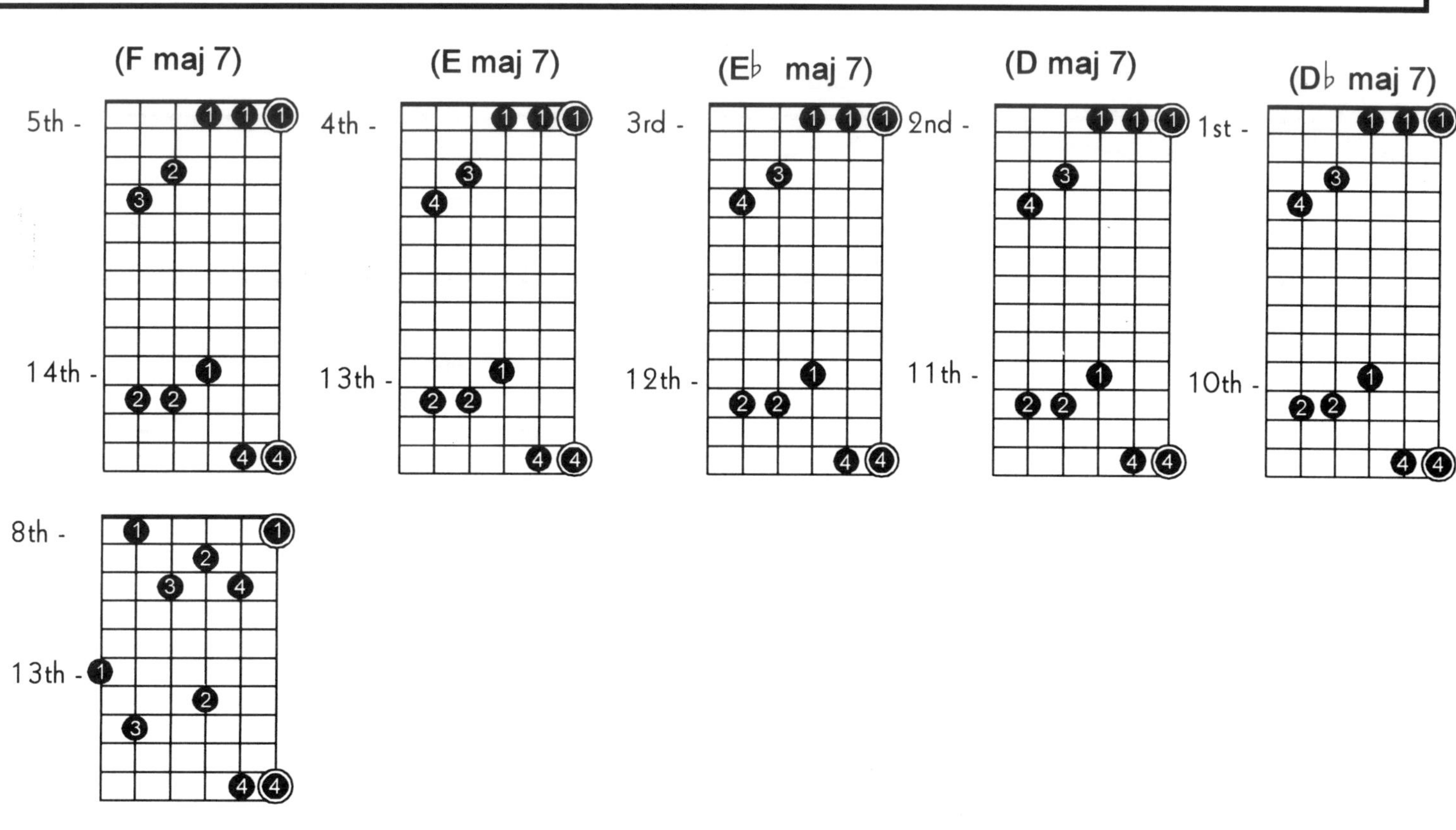

FIG. 3g cont.

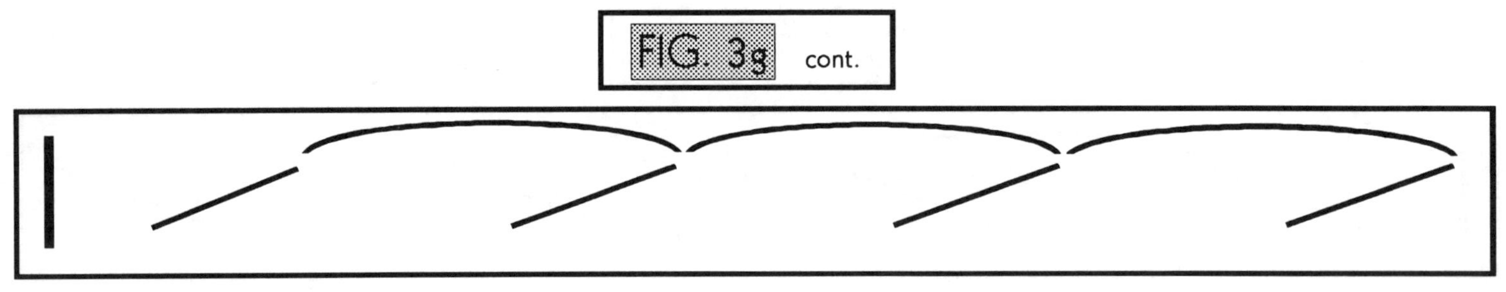

C maj 7

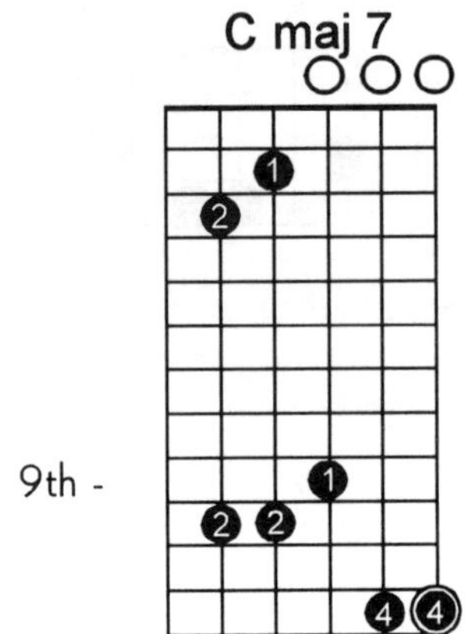

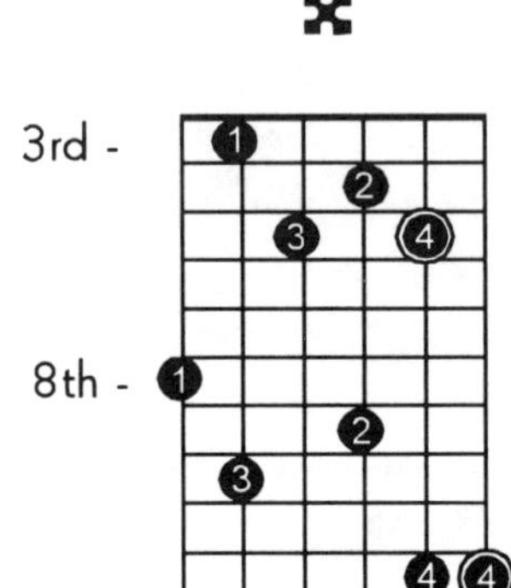

Chords with this mark are alternatives for starting and ending the phrase.

FIG. 3h As for 3g but with the chord moving in reverse direction.

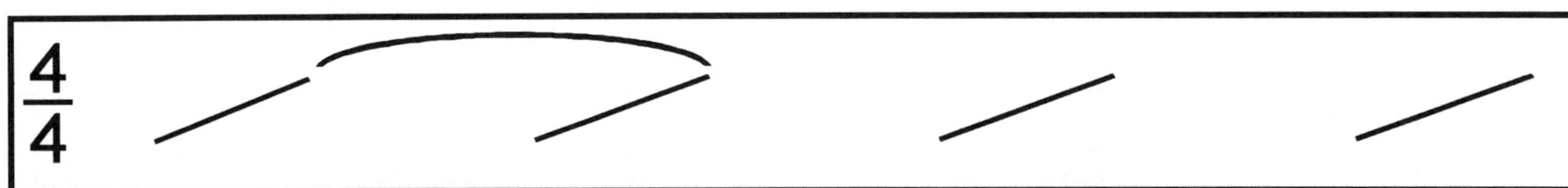

C maj 6

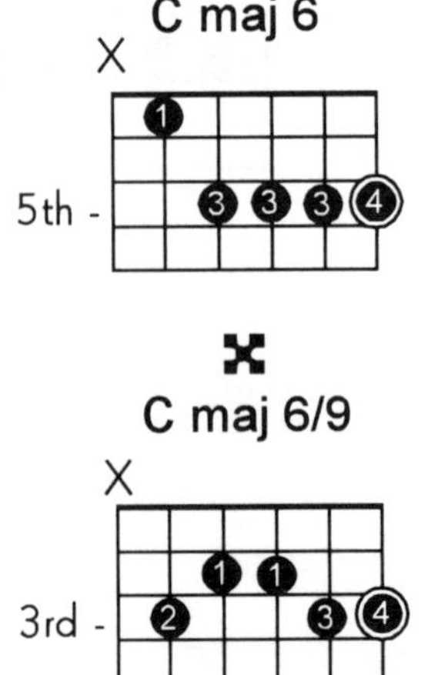

(B♭ maj 6)

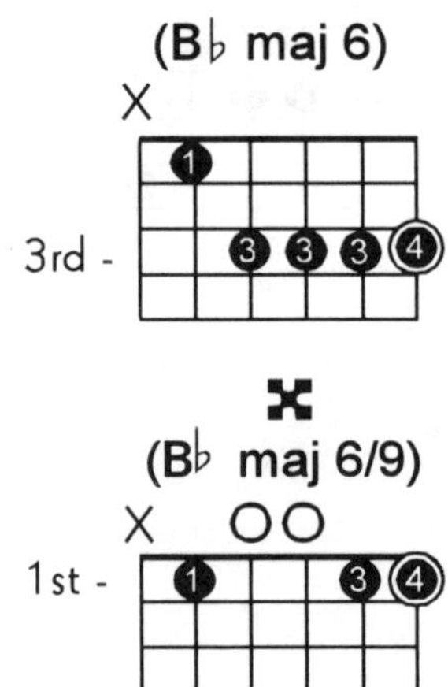

B maj 6

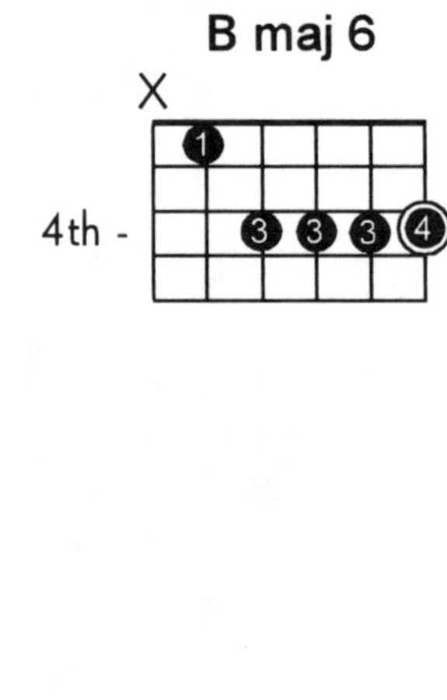

FIG. 3h cont.

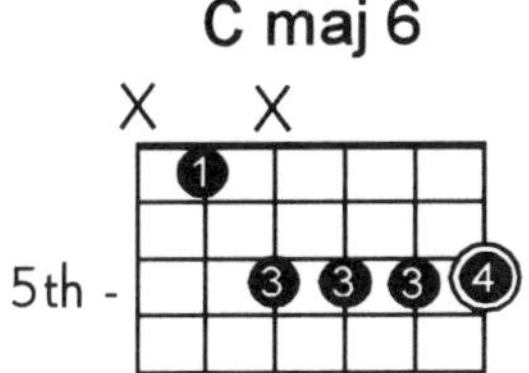

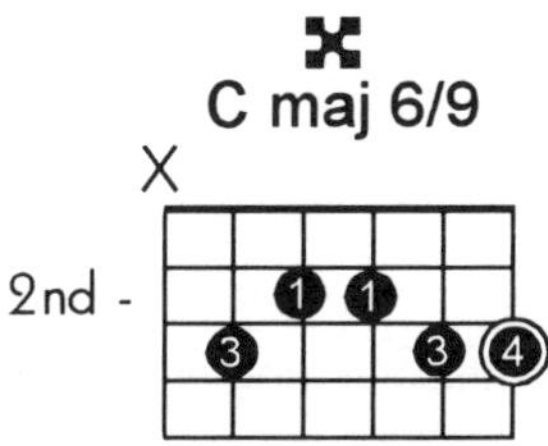

A useful method is to first decide upon a certain chord diagram on which to finish a passage or ending of a chord progression and then glance back for several beats and decide upon one of these beats on which the starting chord of a sequence of "approach" chords could be played. This "approach" chord, and the chords used in-between it and the "final" chord, could be derived from the final chord by "bending" the latter in the manner illustrated in the examples just given.

Notice that in the examples given in figs. (c) to (h) the notes move in what is known as "similar" or "parallel" motion, except in the progressions in which the "lead" note is retained in one position throughout a sequence, in which case only the notes in the harmony parts proceed in similar motion. In consecutive steps of a semitone each such progressions are termed "chromatic slithers" and are frowned upon by exponents of harmony text-book progressions. Nevertheless, these "chromatic slithers" are often effective when used with discretion and they are most useful for 'fill-in' purposes.

As a change from sequences in which the notes move in parallel motion we have sequences in which the "bent" chord forms produce "contrary motion" between the "lead" note and the bass note, as shown in Fig. (I). In this sequence the top note ascends in steps of a half-tone while the bass descends in like manner: -

FIG. 3i As for 3h but with the "lead" note ascending in steps of half-tone while the bass note descends in steps of a semitone.

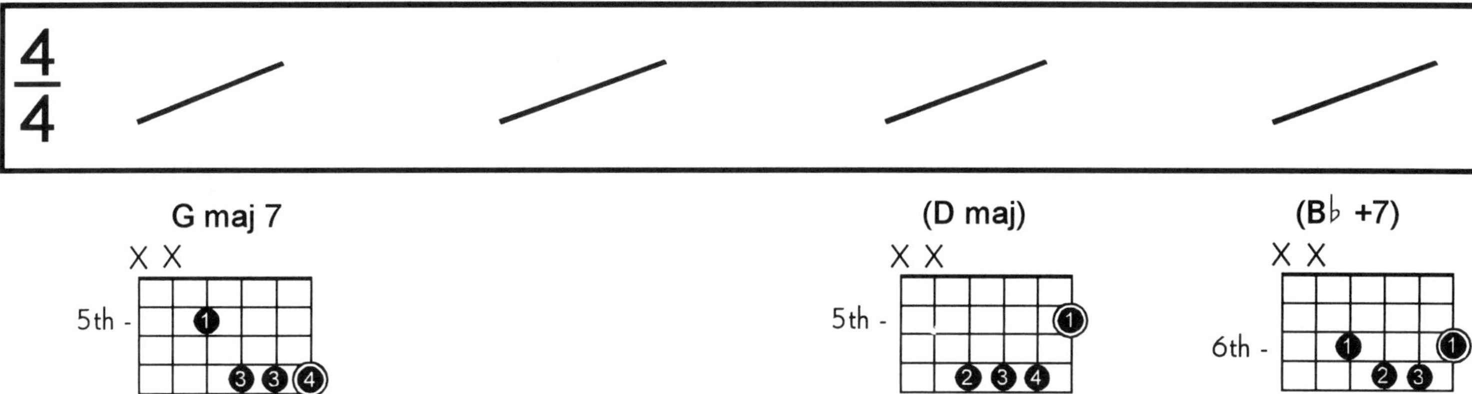

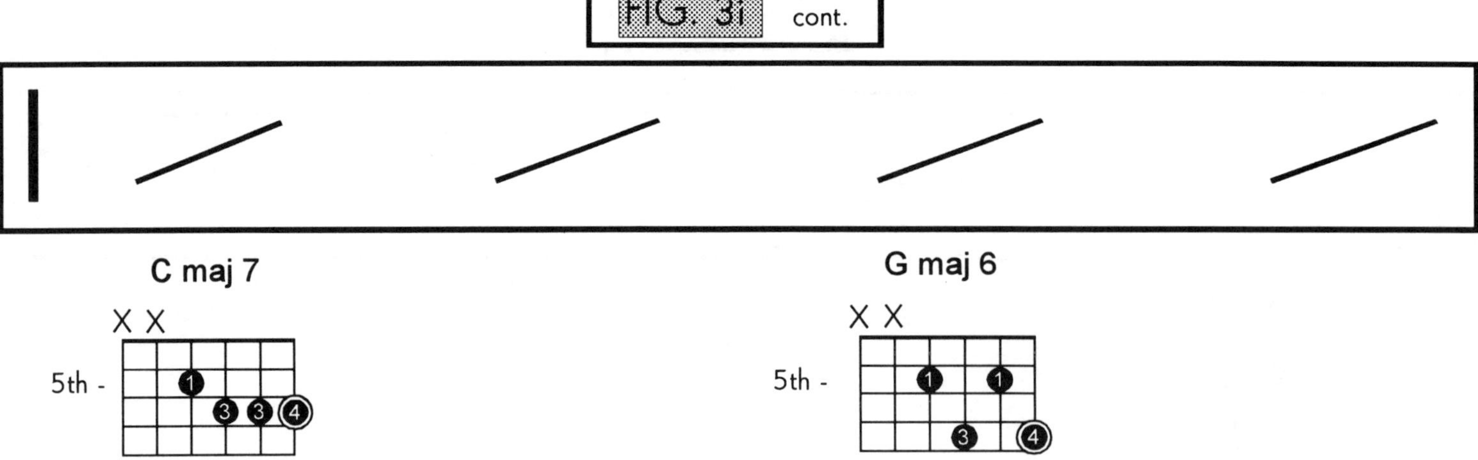

Many other examples could be added to those already given but these should be sufficient as a guide to the readers own experiments since there is considerable scope for individual experimental work in this field.

The choice of the most acceptable chord forms derived from the "bending" of the notes of selected chords, or chords indicated by chord symbols in a given chord-progression, will depend mainly on the reader's instinct for good harmony. Failing the possession of a natural "bent" for harmony , the latter may be considered as a training of the ear by listening with close attention to the sounds produced by all the chord you play and to the "melodic lines" created in the linking of chords in all harmonic progressions - not only to the "line" created by the movement of the "lead" note of each chord but also to (1) the lines produced by the bass notes and, (2) the lines produced by the notes of the harmony parts.

"Doubling" of the "lead", or melody, note in the bass part should generally be avoided except in the case of doubling the "lead" for the purpose of strengthening the melodic line. Otherwise, stepwise movements, ascending and/or descending are preferable, particularly when such steps are in "contrary motion" to that of the melody-line. Leaps and falls of an interval larger than a fifth are also to be avoided, generally speaking, in the bass part. Readers who wish to proceed further with the use of "substitute" chords and "approach" chords may find the method described and illustrated in the following examples to be of some interest.

As shown in some of the examples starting on page 85 the "lead" note of any given chord symbol chord-form can, at various times, be an "interval" or scale-note of any major, minor or dominant scale besides being a scale note of the given chord. For the purpose of example, suppose we take the note on fret position eight, on the first string, as a "lead" note and then proceed to apply the notes of any chord symbol (of your own choice) to the harmony parts. Depending on which chord symbol is chosen the alphabetical name for the note on P.8, first string, can be "B sharp" (as in E major (aug.5th); "C", as in C major, C minor, etc.) or "D double-flat", (as in G flat major, dim.5). Therefore, if we regard the flat", (as in G flat major, (dim.5th). Therefore, if we regard the note, for the time being, as just a "sound", we can take each one, (in turn) of the twelve sounds of the scale of semitones, (or "chromatic scale" as it is commonly known), and call this note the fundamental note of the chord-form which is to be applied to the harmony parts for the "lead" note selected for the example. The following illustration shows, (Fig. 1), the example "lead note" on P.8, first string, together with its alternative names and (Fig. 2), the table of chord-forms which can, at various times, be applied to the example "lead" note.

Note that, for the purpose of simplification, the fundamental notes in the table of chord forms are taken in the order in which they ascend the chromatic scale from the note having the same sound as the "lead" note. The reason for this is to allow for the table of symbol names to be in the same order whenever any particular "lead" note replaces the note used for the example, E.G., supposing the new "lead" note is on P.3, first string, and the same note is taken to be the commencing fundamental note of the chromatic scale ascending from it, the same order of chord symbols as in the table can be followed, (excepting, or course for the alphabetical names, I.E., instead of reading "C major" for the first chord-form in the table, you would read "G major" - (G being a commonly-used name for the note on P.3, (first string). (see page 71 for the alternative names for each note).

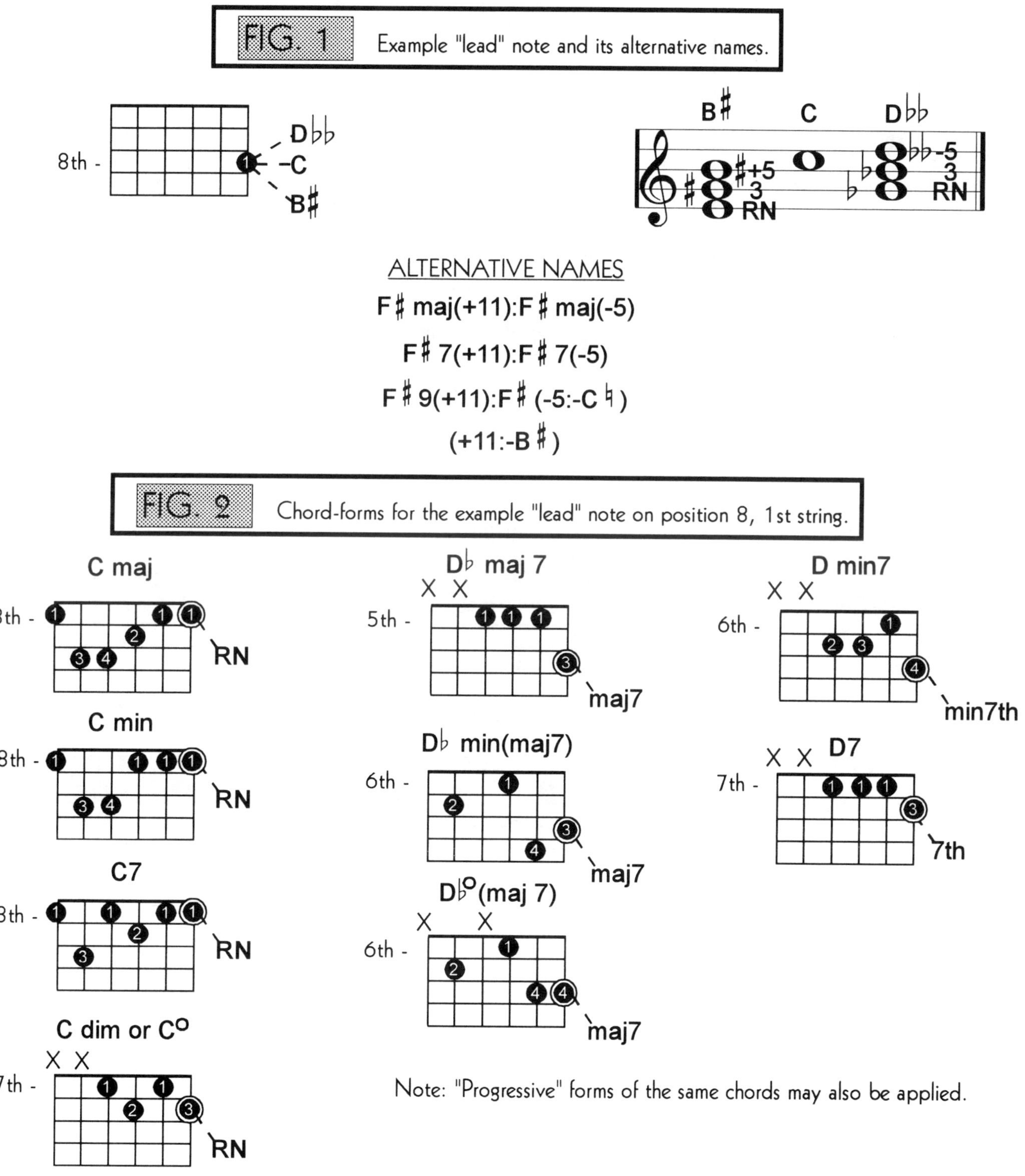

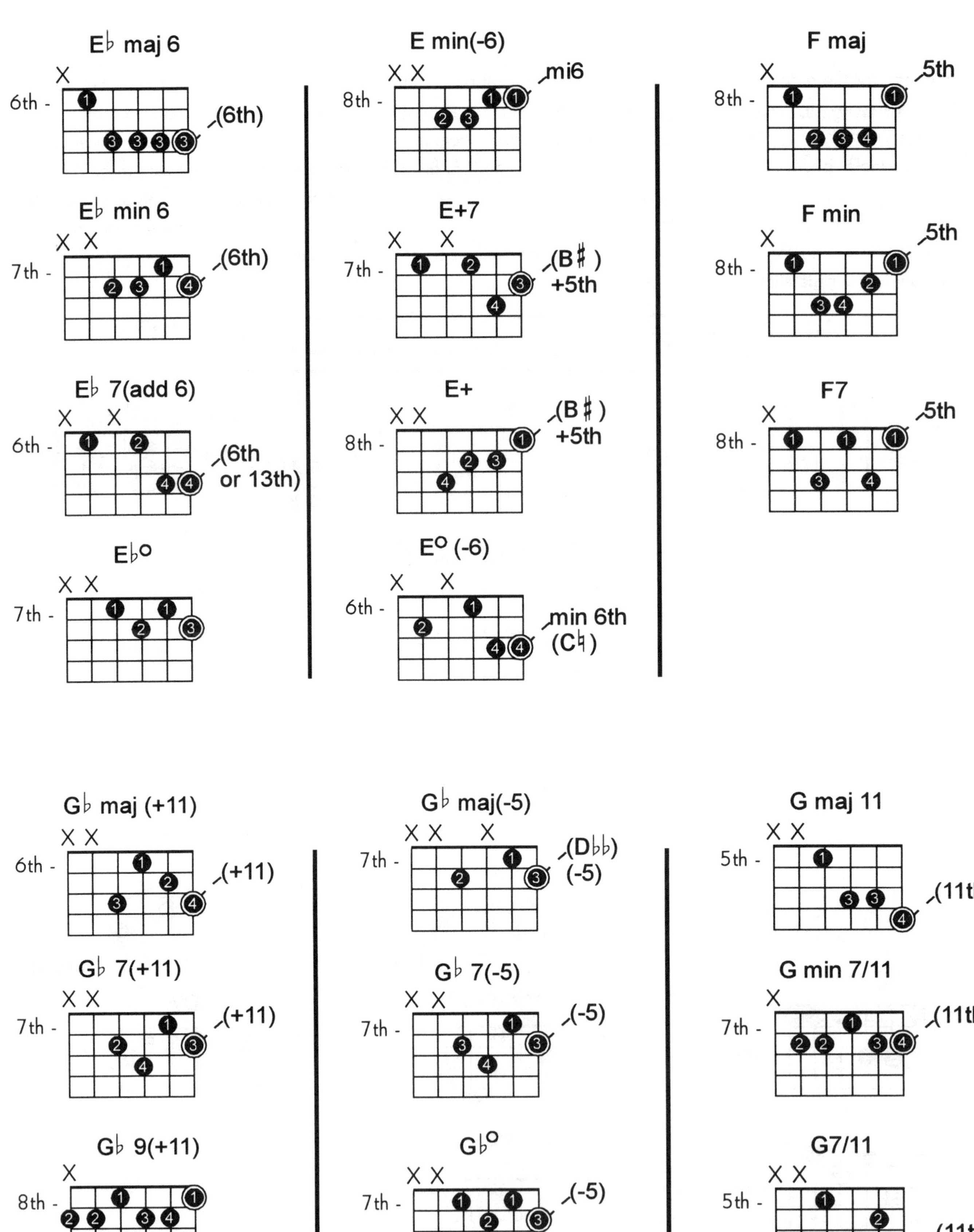

Go (add11)

6th -

(11th)

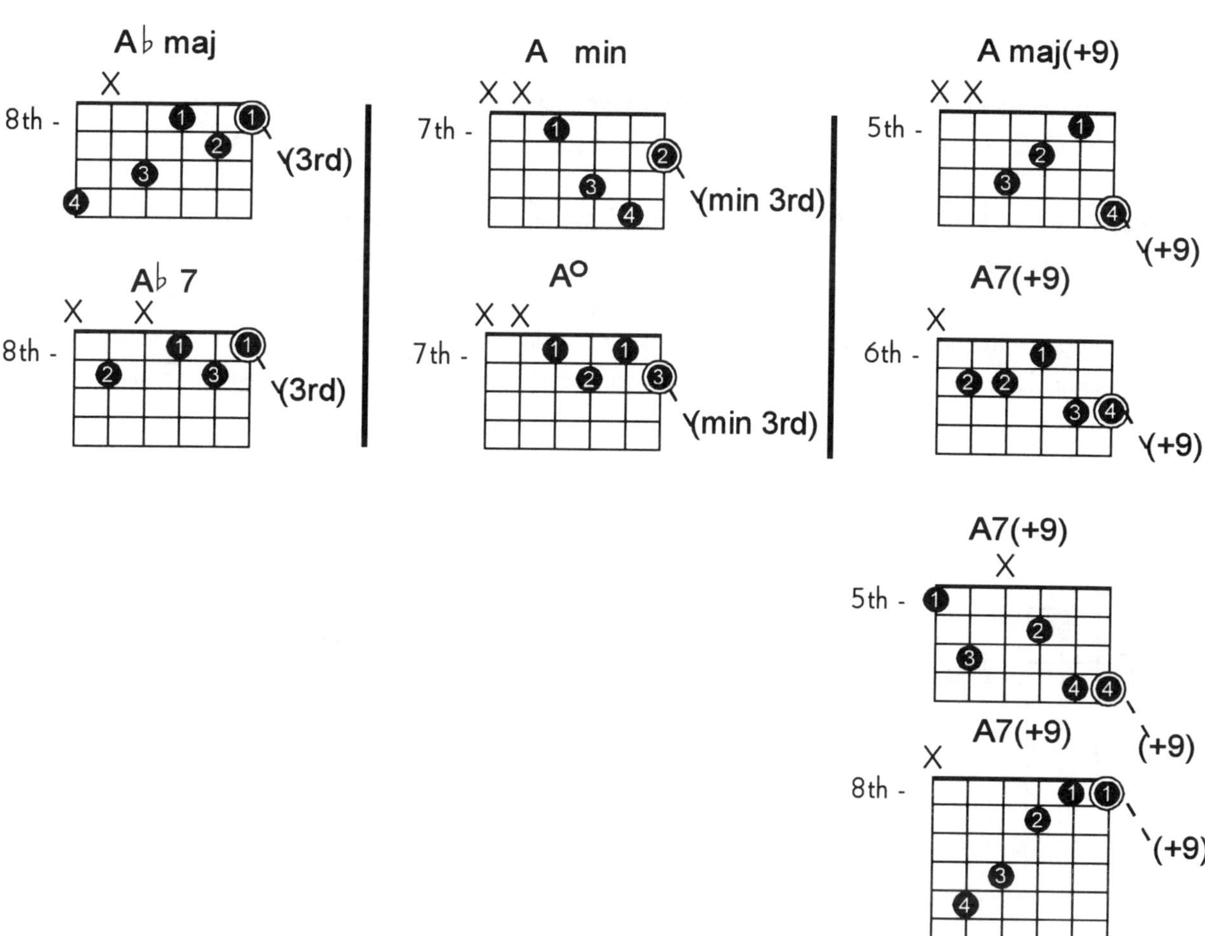
A♭ maj
8th -
(3rd)
A♭ 7
8th -
(3rd)
A min
7th -
(min 3rd)
A°
7th -
(min 3rd)
A maj(+9)
5th -
(+9)
A7(+9)
6th -
(+9)
A7(+9)
5th -
(+9)
A7(+9)
8th -
(+9)

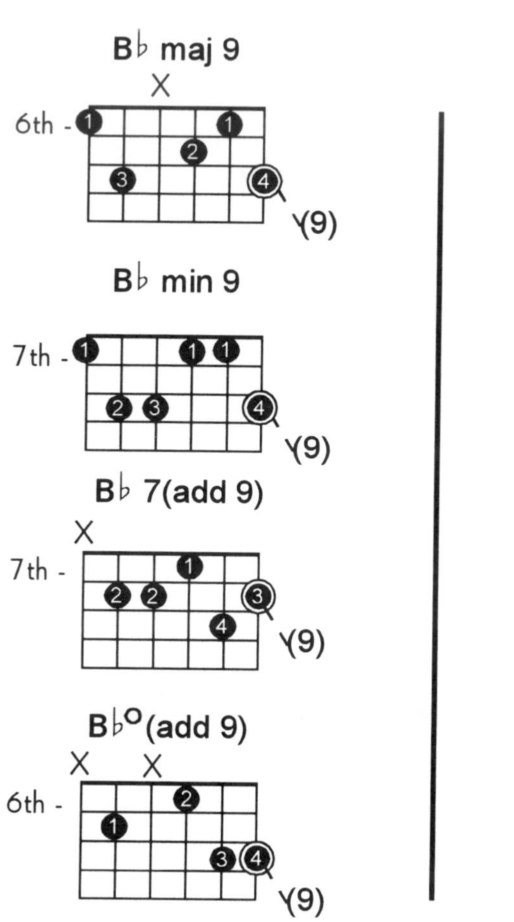
B♭ maj 9
6th -
(9)
B♭ min 9
7th -
(9)
B♭ 7(add 9)
7th -
(9)
B♭°(add 9)
6th -
(9)

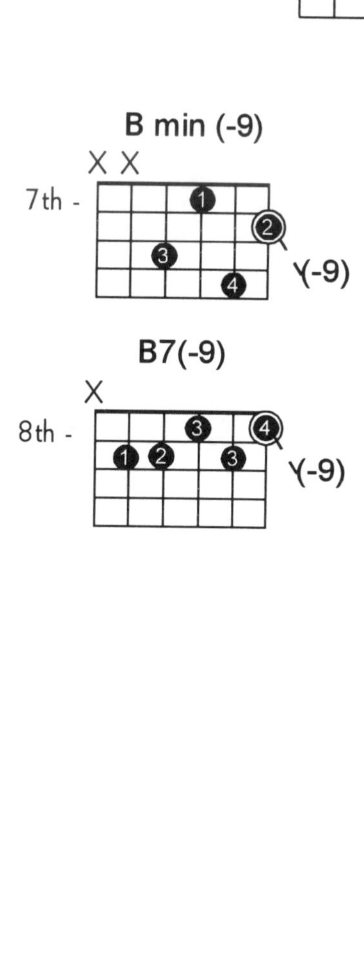
B min (-9)
7th -
(-9)
B7(-9)
8th -
(-9)

The same chord symbols may also be used for the alternative fingerboard positions of the example "lead" note, I.E., on P.1 (low position), and P. 13, on second string, (the same sound as on P.8 of the first string)

Refer to Fig. 2 in part 1, 2, 3 and 4 and choose a chord diagram given for the keynote, (in parts 1 and 2), and for the "V" note, (in parts 3 and 4), and note the finger given for the "lead" note; now place this finger directly on P.1 (low position), or on P.13, (high position), on the second string and then form the chord by placing the remaining fingers as given for the notes in the harmony parts of the chord, as shown in the following example of chord forms for chord symbols C major, C minor, C 7 and C dim.7, moved from the positions given in the book for G major, G minor, D 7 and D dim.7: -

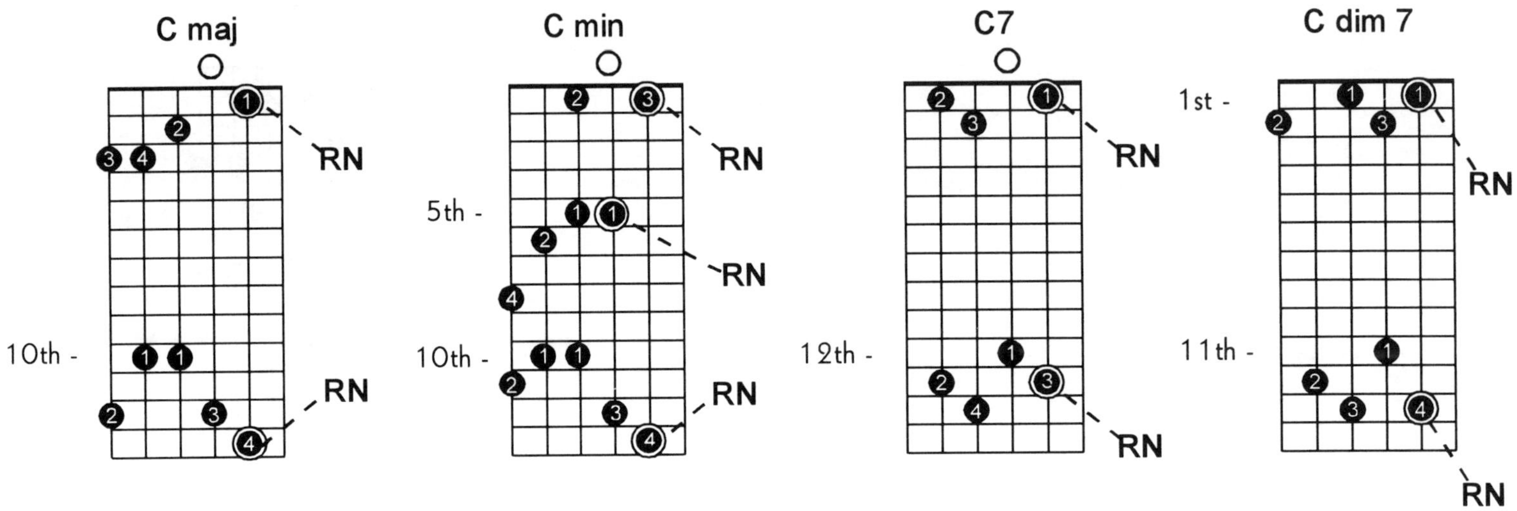

Other chord forms for the same chord symbols and the same "lead" can replace those given in these examples.

A Project For You

Fig. 4 is a two-bar phrase in common tempo, with C major harmony and with C,(P.8, first string), in the "lead" and sustained throughout the two bar measure. In this instance, instead of playing chord-links consisting of C major "progressive" chord-forms, choose a few of the chords from those given in the table, Fig.2 (just dealt with) and after playng the chords in various links of, say two chords at a time, make up a selection of forms which blend satisfactorily with each other and will lead back nicely to the finishing chord. Let your ear be the judge when deciding on the chord forms to be used as substitute chords or "approach" chords to the final chord.

Two-bar "melody-phrase" with C "lead" and C major chord harmony: substitute chords are introduced on the fourth beat of the first bar and on beats one, two and three of the second bar, followed by the C major chord on the last beat. "Lead" note C, (sustained for two bars): chord symbol C major.

4/4

C maj 6 — 8th

C maj 9 — 7th

G° (add 11) — 6th

FIG. 4 cont.

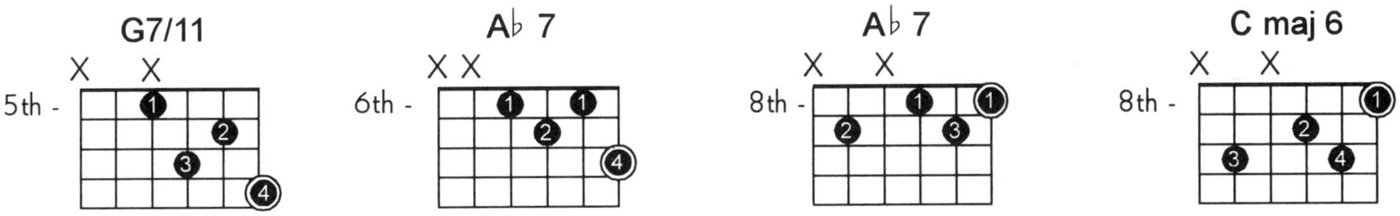

G7/11 — 5th

A♭ 7 — 6th

A♭ 7 — 8th

C maj 6 — 8th

In similar phrases in which the chords are used for accompaniment purposes and it is not essential to sustain particular "lead" note throughout the whole two-bar measure you can use various chords which, when linked together to form a chord sequence, produce a melody-line, or counter-melody phrase designed to provide an interesting "backing" to solo voice or instrument and also in ensemble playing. Fig. 5, below, is an example of such a chord sequence: -

FIG. 5 Two-bar "Harmony-Phrase" with C major harmony as the given chord symbol.

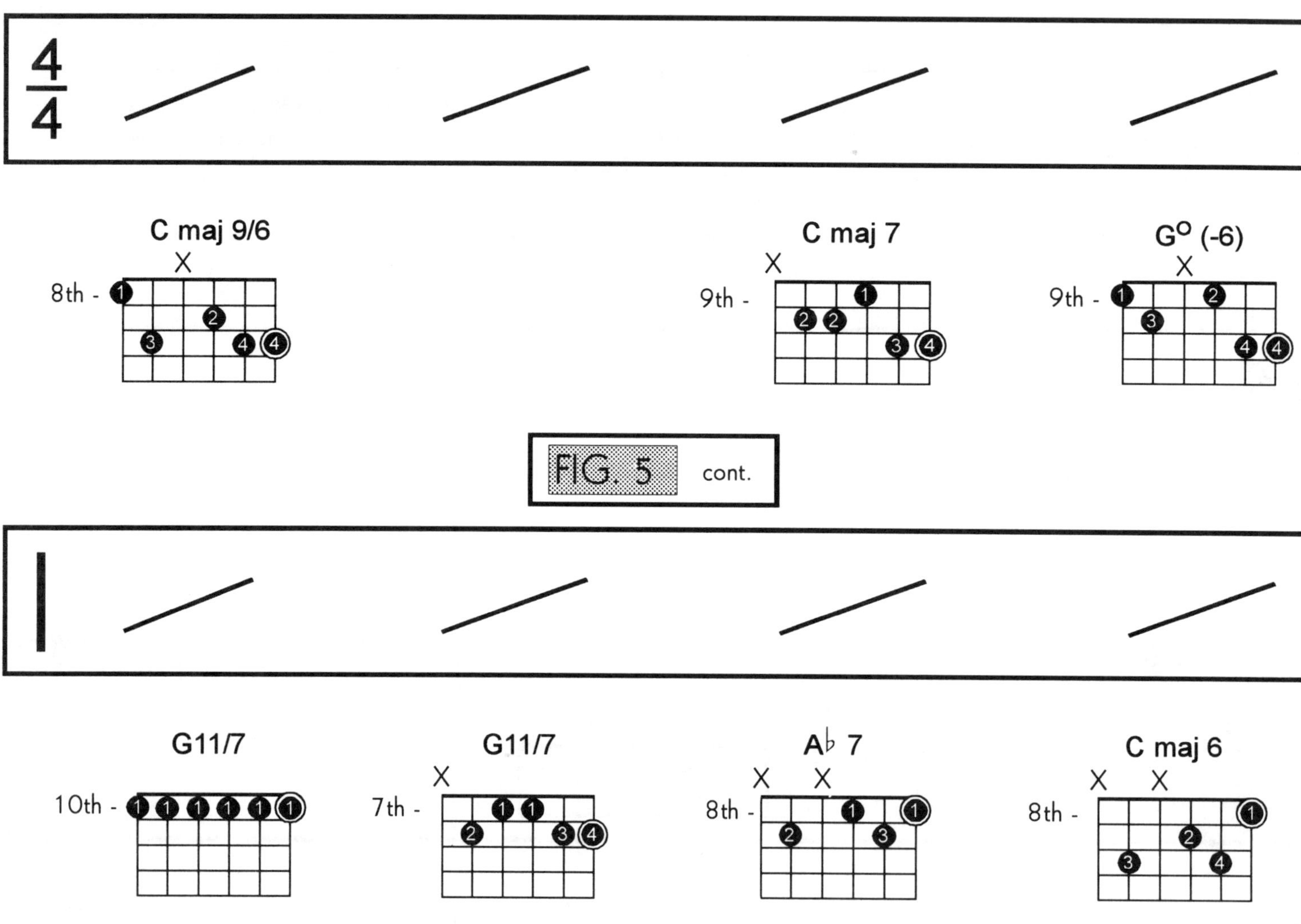

Many other two-bar, and also one-bar chord sequences can be devised by selecting various combinations of chords from the table given in Fig. 2 and then linking them together, and although it must be admitted that harmonic progressions derived from the use of the methods described in this book are "shots in the dark" in comparison with the skilled scoring of professional music arrangers it must be recognized that the majority of guitarists have neither the time nor the inclination to pursue a detailed study of text book harmony, therefore, in both accompaniment and in chord solo playing on the guitar they must rely almost exclusively upon their ears and a fair sense of harmony acquired by listening with close attention to the playing of experienced players.

Chord Forms For Scale Notes And "Altered" Notes In Popular Songs

As mentioned in "chord solo playing-self-arranged", page 19, the notes of any popular songs consist of scale-notes and "altered" notes belonging to the scales indicated by the chord symbols given, in most song sheets, for the harmonic accompaniment to the song, therefore, to avoid taking up unnecessary time and space by repeating the directions given on page 19, the reader is requested to refer to said page as an aid to readily understanding the explanations and illustrations in the following example in converting the notes of the song to their scale-note names, according to the chord symbols given in the harmony accompaniment.

Incidentally, the majority of song sheets include the tonic sol-fa names for the melody notes. In the voice part of the song, as an aid to vocalists who are unfamiliar with music-notation. Theses tonic sol-fa names are, however, in accordance with the scale of the key in which a song is written and they have no connection with the scale note names of the various keys indicated by the chord symbols.

In the following extract from the traditional song "Greensleeves", (1642), the notes are written an octave above their actual sounds, as is usual in writing for the guitar, but instead of including the sol-fa names of the notes I have given the alphabetical names for the convenience of players who are also unfamiliar with notation.

Directly over each note of the song a figure represents the scale-note name according to the chord symbol. This is intended to serve as an example in converting the notes of the song to their scale-note names, according to the chord symbols. Assuming that the reader applies the procedure to his/her favorite songs it is a simple matter to decide on the most convenient positions, on guitar, for the melody notes and then, (after referring to the reference tables of scale notes and altered scale-notes for any required key or scale), writing the scale note name over each melody note.

The next step, after writing the scale-note names of the notes of the song, is to turn to the "scale notes in chord form" in parts 1 to 4 and make up a selection of chord diagrams for the purpose of playing the song in "chord-solo style". As in the example of chord-forms selected for playing "Greensleeves" in chord form.

A Selection From The Song "Greensleeves"

Now, taking each chord symbol and its scale-notes, as they occur in the melody-line and dealing with the minor chord symbols first, refer to the chord forms in part 2 and sketch out a few of the chord diagrams given for scale notes in minor keys. Against the "lead" note of each selected diagram, jot down the fret positions on which the "lead"-note finger is to be placed when forming the chord on guitar. (later, when you have decided on the chords you wish to use for the notes of the song, you can indicate the fret position for the first finger, in the usual manner, if preferred; otherwise, the diagrams may be positioned according to the "lead" note fingering).

Secondly, treat the major chord symbols and their scale-notes (in the melody) in the same manner and turn to part 1 to select the chord diagrams. Follow the same procedure with dominant chord and "diminished" chord symbols and the "V-scale-notes" in the song; the chord diagrams for these are given in parts 3 and 4.

Here is an example of selections of chord diagrams as applied to the extract from "Greensleeves": -

Greensleeves for solo guitar

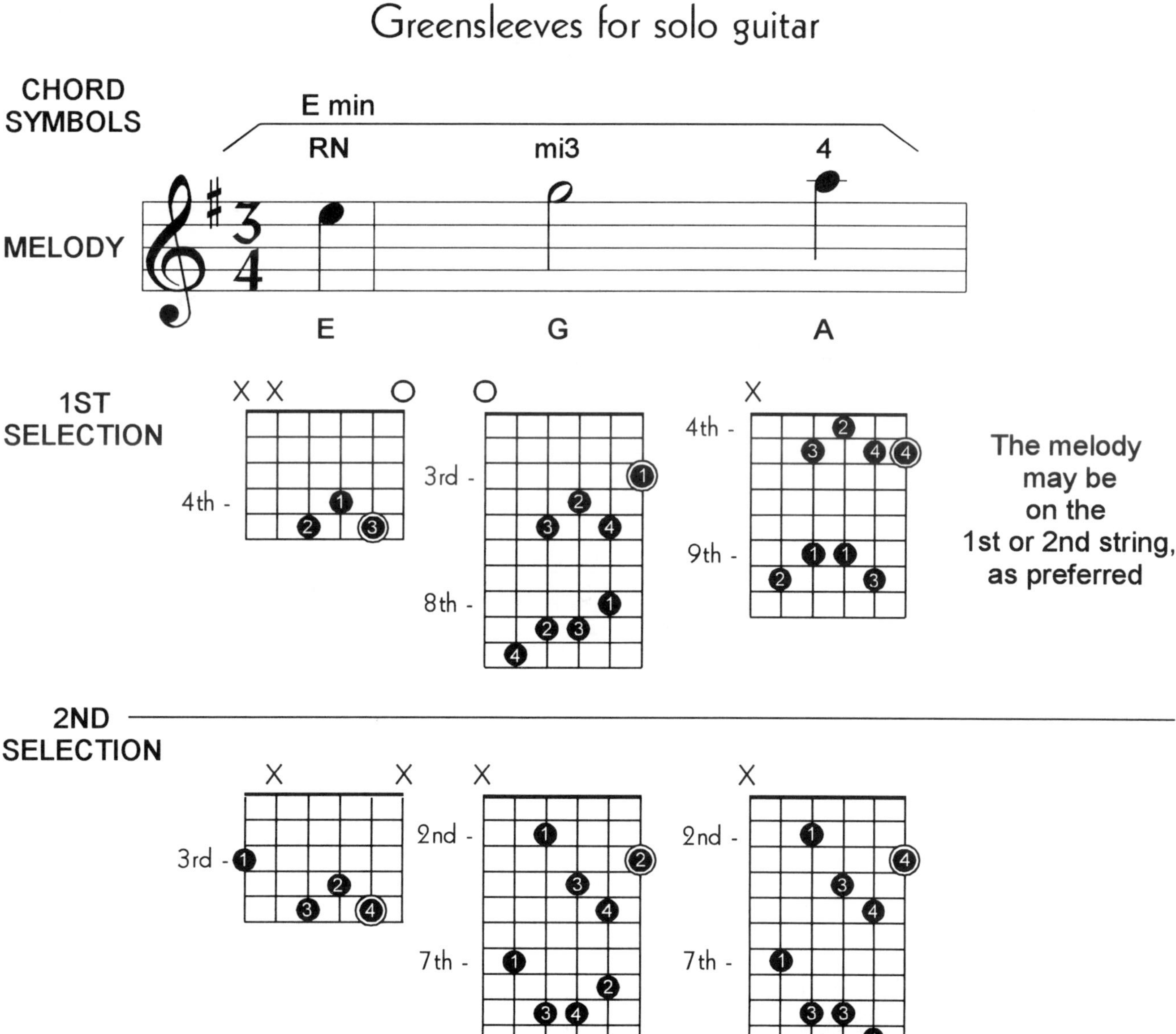

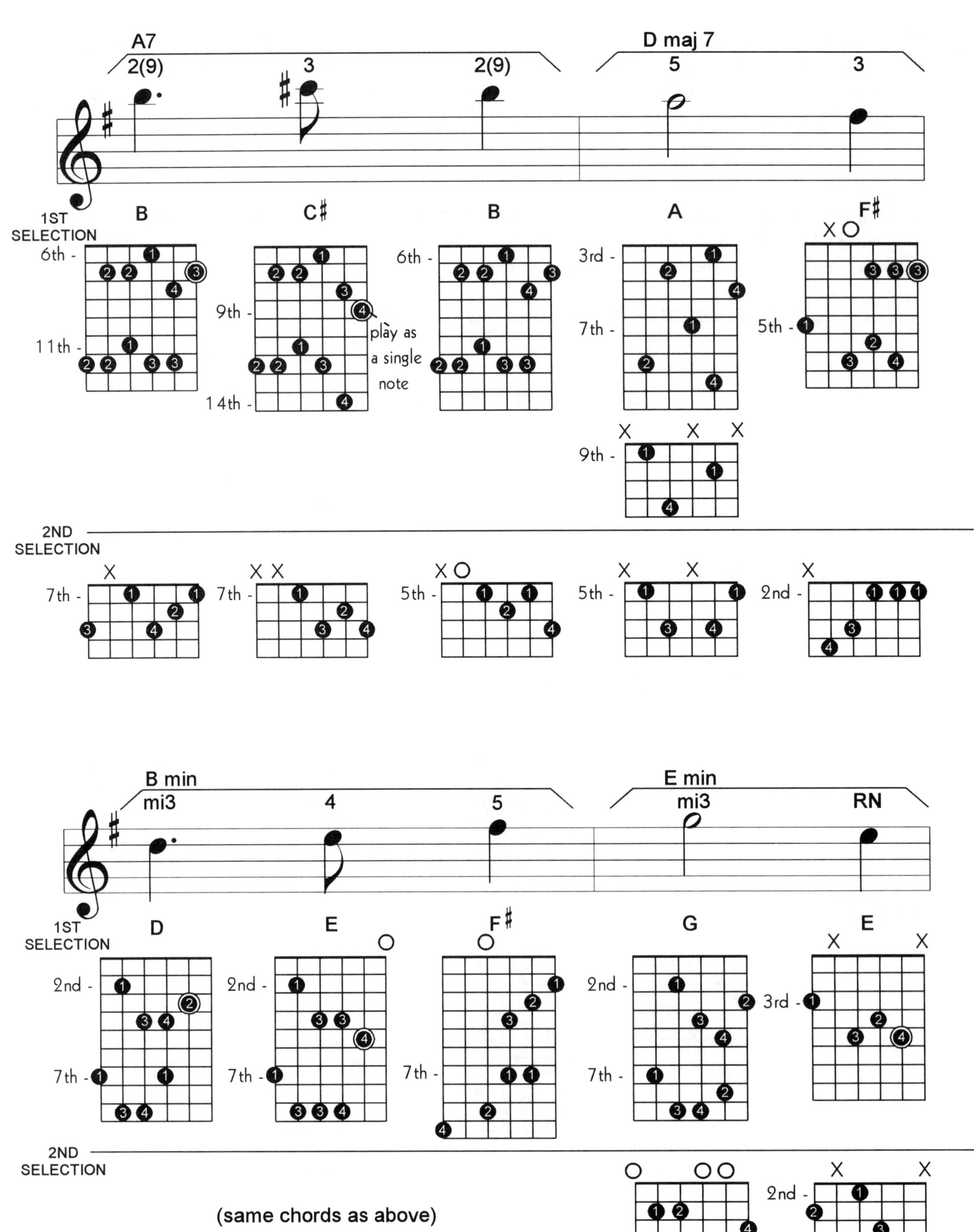

A7
2(9)
3
2(9)
D maj 7
5
3
1ST SELECTION
B
C♯
B
A
F♯
6th -
11th -
9th -
14th -
play as a single note
6th -
3rd -
7th -
5th -
9th -
2ND SELECTION
7th -
7th -
5th -
5th -
2nd -
B min
mi3
4
5
E min
mi3
RN
1ST SELECTION
D
E
F♯
G
E
2nd -
7th -
2nd -
7th -
7th -
2nd -
7th -
3rd -
2ND SELECTION
(same chords as above)
2nd -

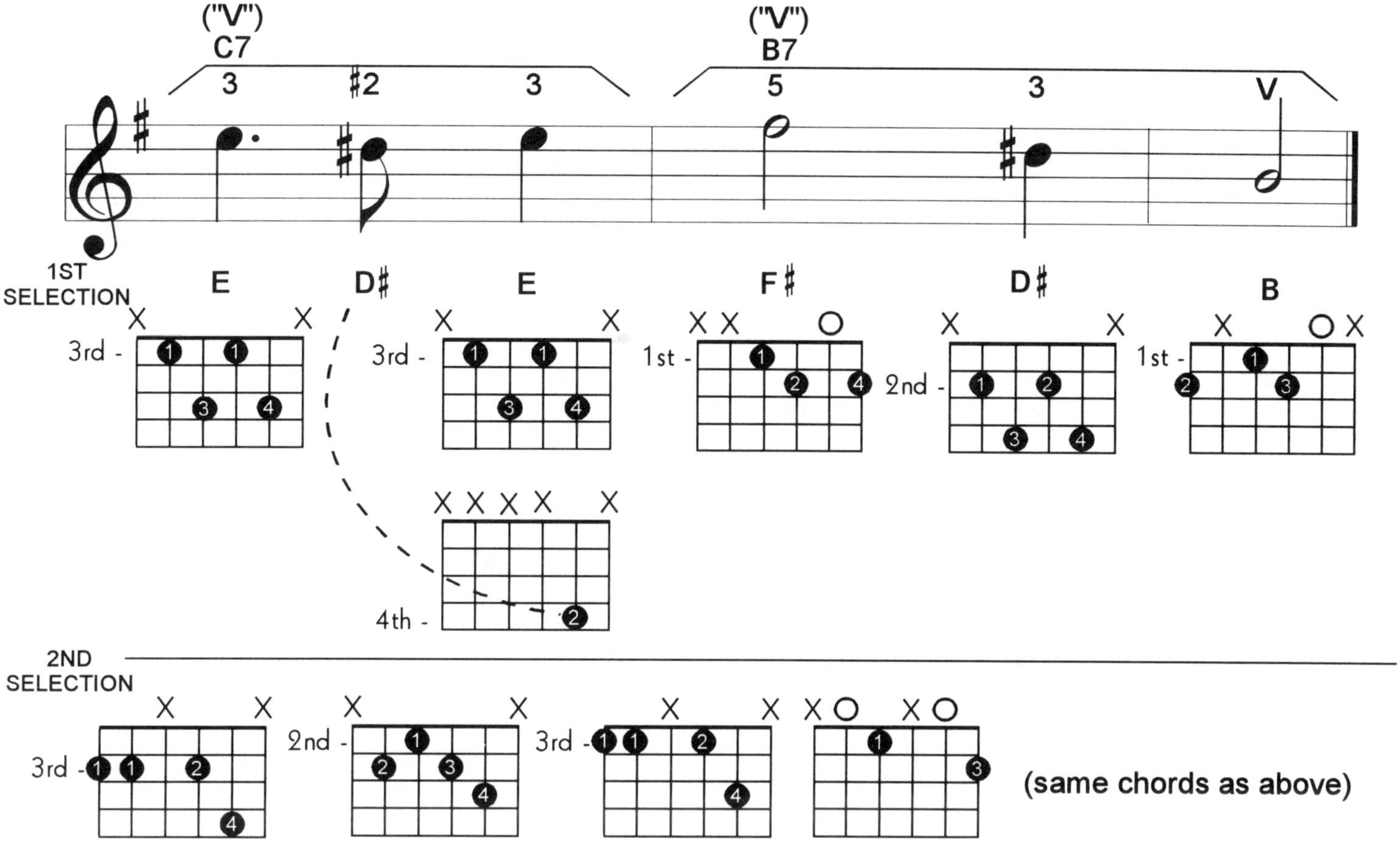

The first selection of "melody-chords" consists of more or less straight-forward chord forms as used in simplified scores of chord solo playing, while the second selection is rather more ambitious. Both selections are for the first eight bars of the extract from "Greensleeves" and this should be sufficient for the purpose of illustrating the procedure described on page 91: the remaining eight bars of the extract have been purposely left so as to provide for individual choice, by the reader, of chord diagrams to be used as "melody-chords" for those bars the latter project is, or course, optional and the reader may prefer to work out their own chord-solo scores of favorite songs, the notes of which are easily located, by ear, on the fingerboard, since the procedure is exactly the same as for the chord solo score of "Greensleves". In the case of songs in which the melody is rather "busy" it is common practice to employ a combination of melody-chords and single notes, the reason for this being obvious.

Remember that you can substitute "progressive" chord-forms in place of "common" major and minor chords given in song sheets, or you can introduce "added" or "altered" scale-notes in the harmony parts as in the following example, again in the first eight bars of "Greensleeves" : -

"Progressive" chords substituted for "common" chords.

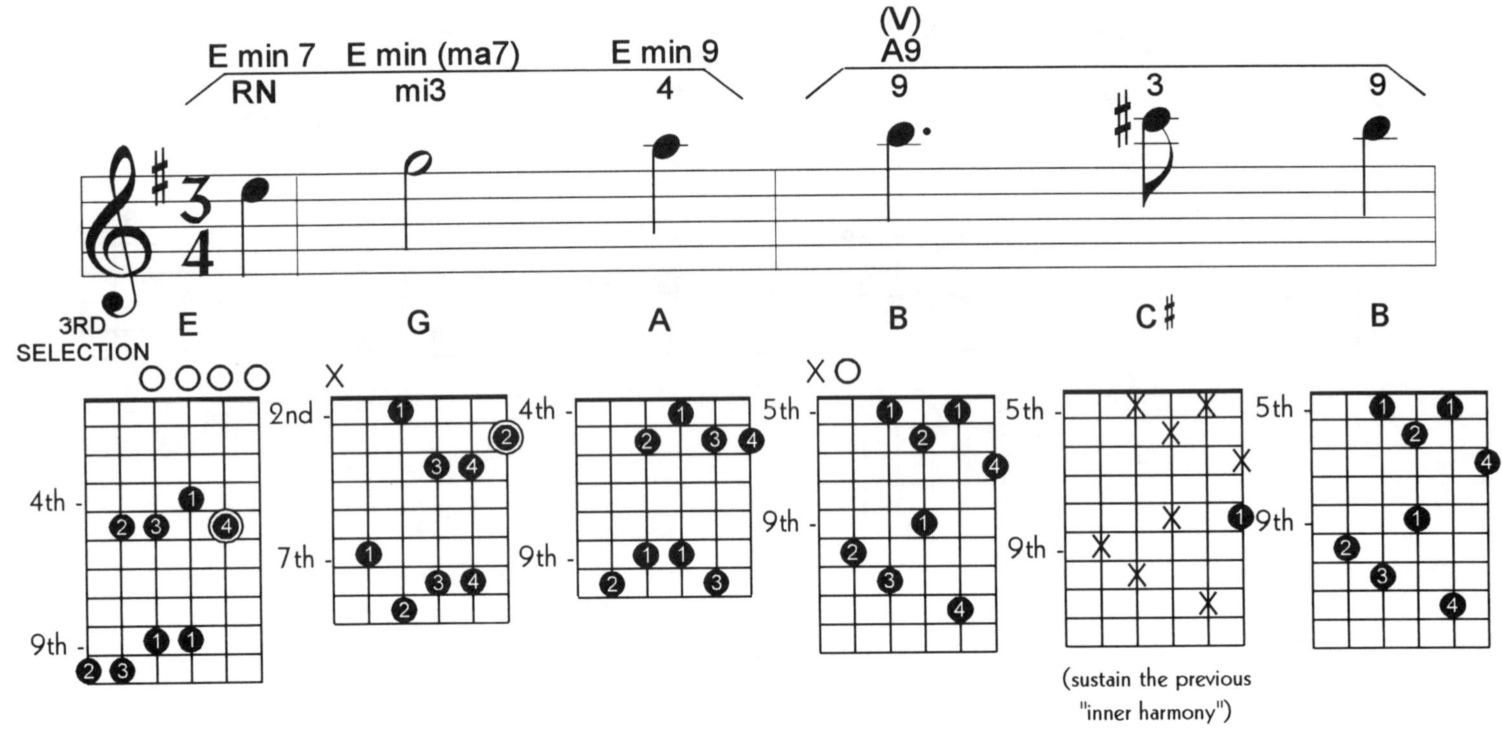

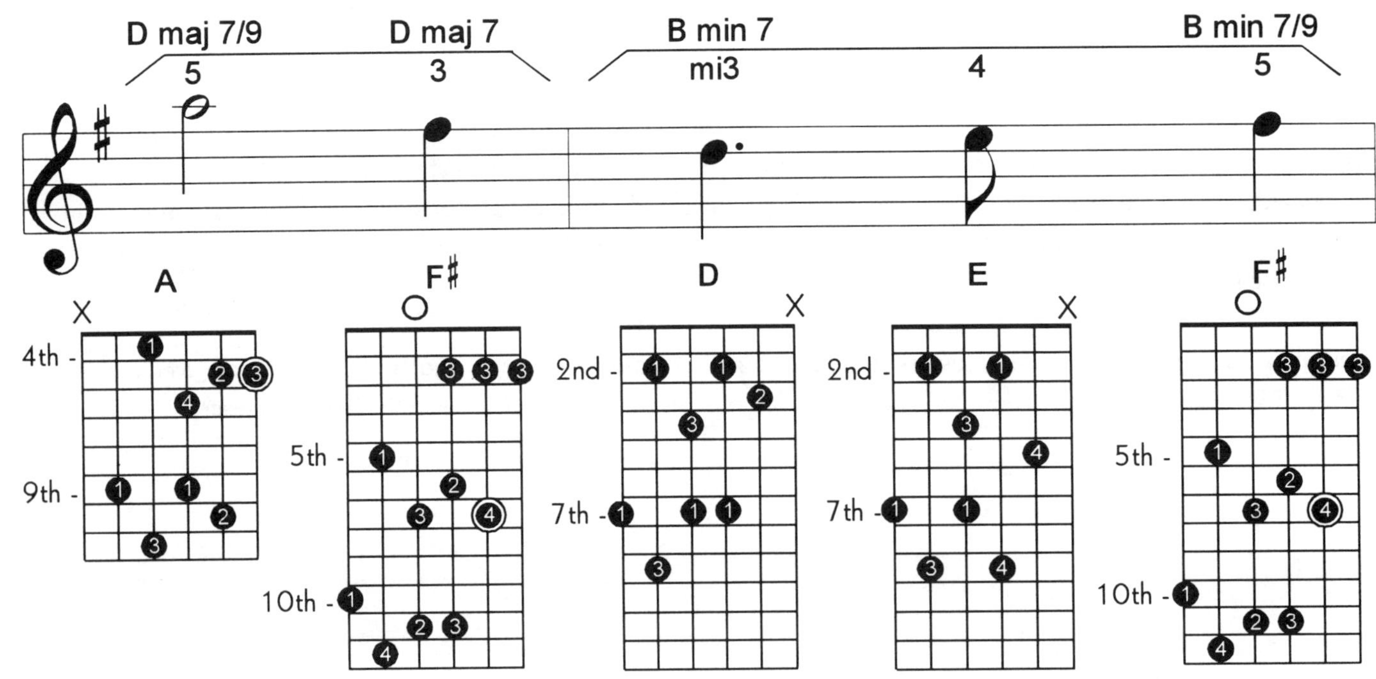

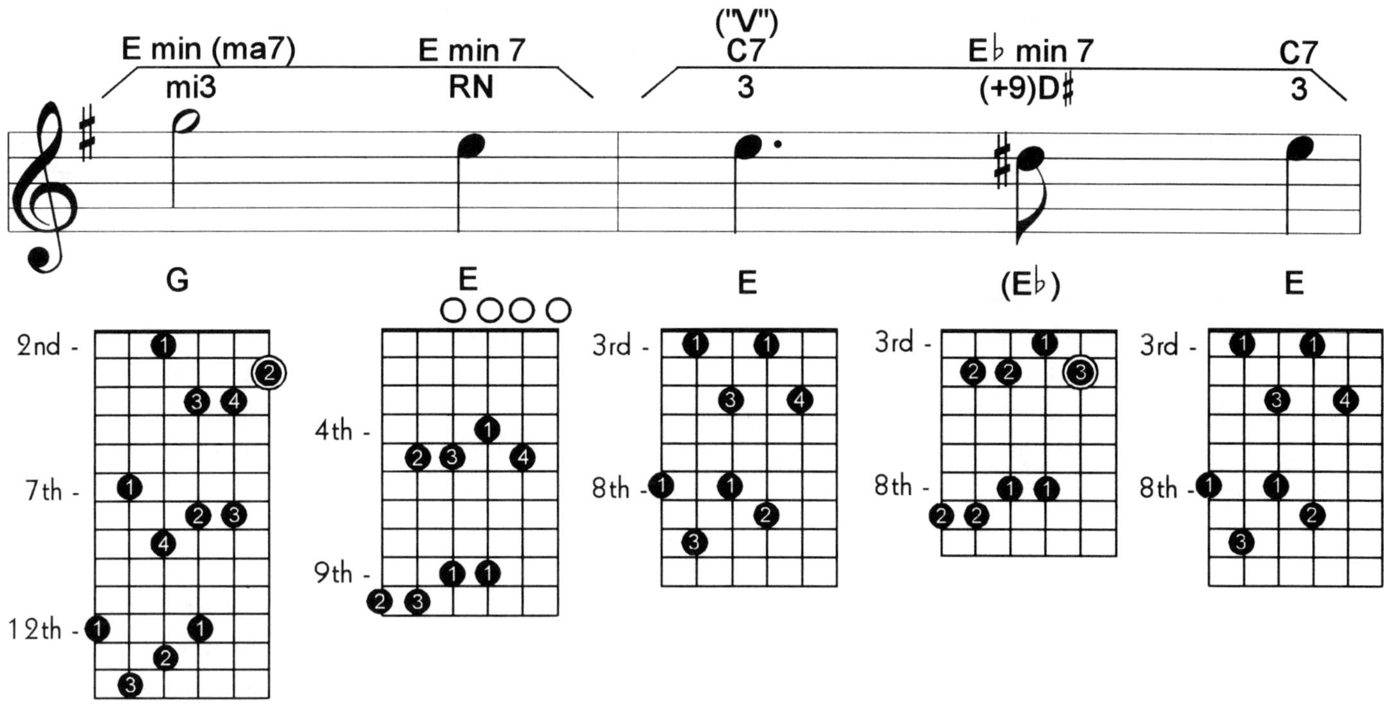

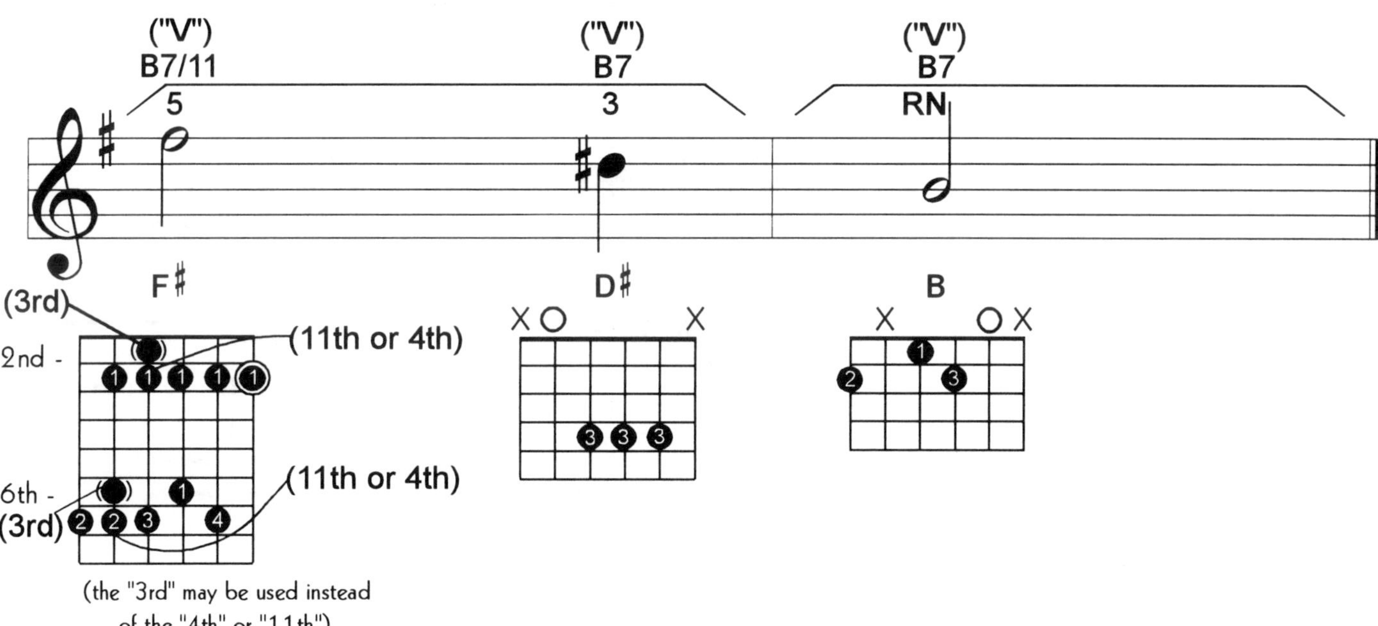

(the "3rd" may be used instead of the "4th" or "11th")

A common fault in the use of substitute chords, particularly with "progressive" chords with two or more "added" notes, is the inclusion of too many of such chords in a single arrangement of a piece of music, resulting in the harmonic progression being overloaded with them. Also, the melodic-lines created by the inner parts of the harmony are often erratic and ill-constructed, therefore discretion is called for in the selection of such chords for either accompaniment work or for solos.

In conclusion I trust that I have made a useful contribution in helping the reader to aquire a useful working-knowledge of the use of chord-forms, on guitar, for accompaniment work and in chord solo scores and also to the building of a useful repertoire of chord forms.

Musically yours,
Allan Holdsworth

Supplement

Reference tables "lead", or melody-notes on the 1st and 3rd strings and their "scale-note", or "interval", names according to any chord symbol, for major, minor, dominant and diminished dominant harmony - at-a-glance.

These tables may be used as an alternative to the reference tables of fingerboard positions of scale-notes and altered scale-notes in all major, minor, dominant and diminished dominant scales, particularly when converting the notes of a favorite song into scale-note names per the chord symbols given, in song sheets, for the harmonic accompaniment.

Chord forms for each "lead" note are given in diagram form, in parts 1 to 4. All the chord forms are easily applied to any given, or chosen, "lead note" on the 1st., 2nd., and 3rd. strings; the method is as follows: - assuming the fingerboard position of your "lead" note is known - (as determined by ear) - the reference tables give you the scale-note name of the note according to the chord symbol given for its accompaniment for the purpose of example, supposing the "lead" note is on P.3, (1st. string) and the given chord symbol is B+7, reference table (1) tells you the scale-note name for your "lead" note is "augmented 5th, (+5). Therefore, turn to Fig. 1 part 3, and choose a chord diagram given for that scale-note.

Now, to play that chord diagram for your "lead" note on P.3, (1st. string), simply place the finger (given on the diagram, for the "lead" note), on its new position and then position the other fingers in the "shape" of the chord, E.G.: -

FIG. 1 Chord forms with "aug.5th" lead, selected from part 3, (dominant scales in chord form).

"Lead" note, "aug.5th";D+7 chord

3rd -

(11th)

5th -

3rd -

10th -

11th -

Arrow indicates the finger for the "lead"

FIG. 2 Chords with "aug.5th" lead. As in fig. 1, with the "lead" note on position 3, (1st string) or on position 8, (2nd string). This method avoids having to count from the fret positions given for the first finger when transposing chords to other scales.

"Lead" note, "aug.5th";B+7 chord

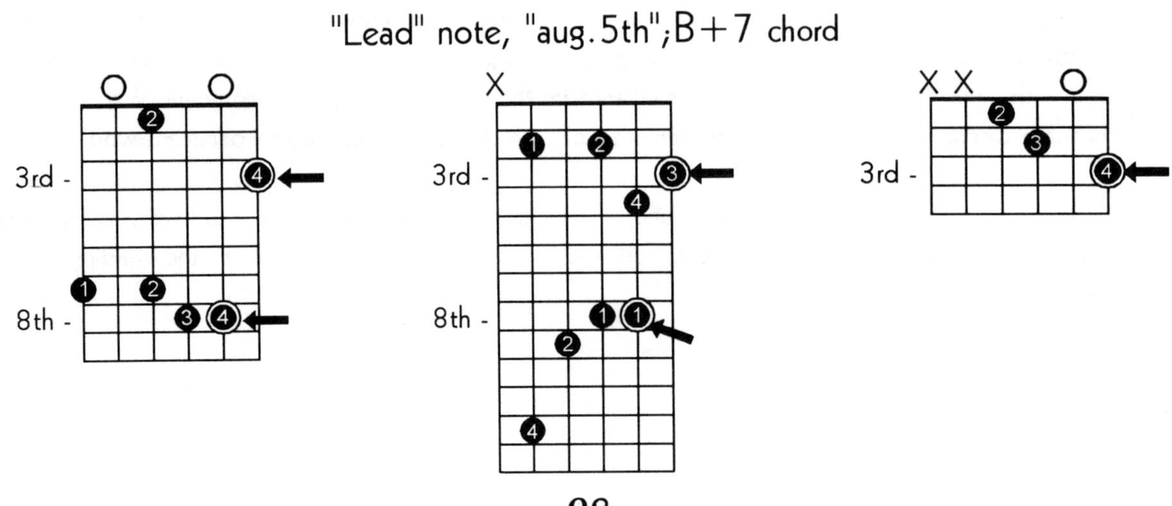

Reference Tables

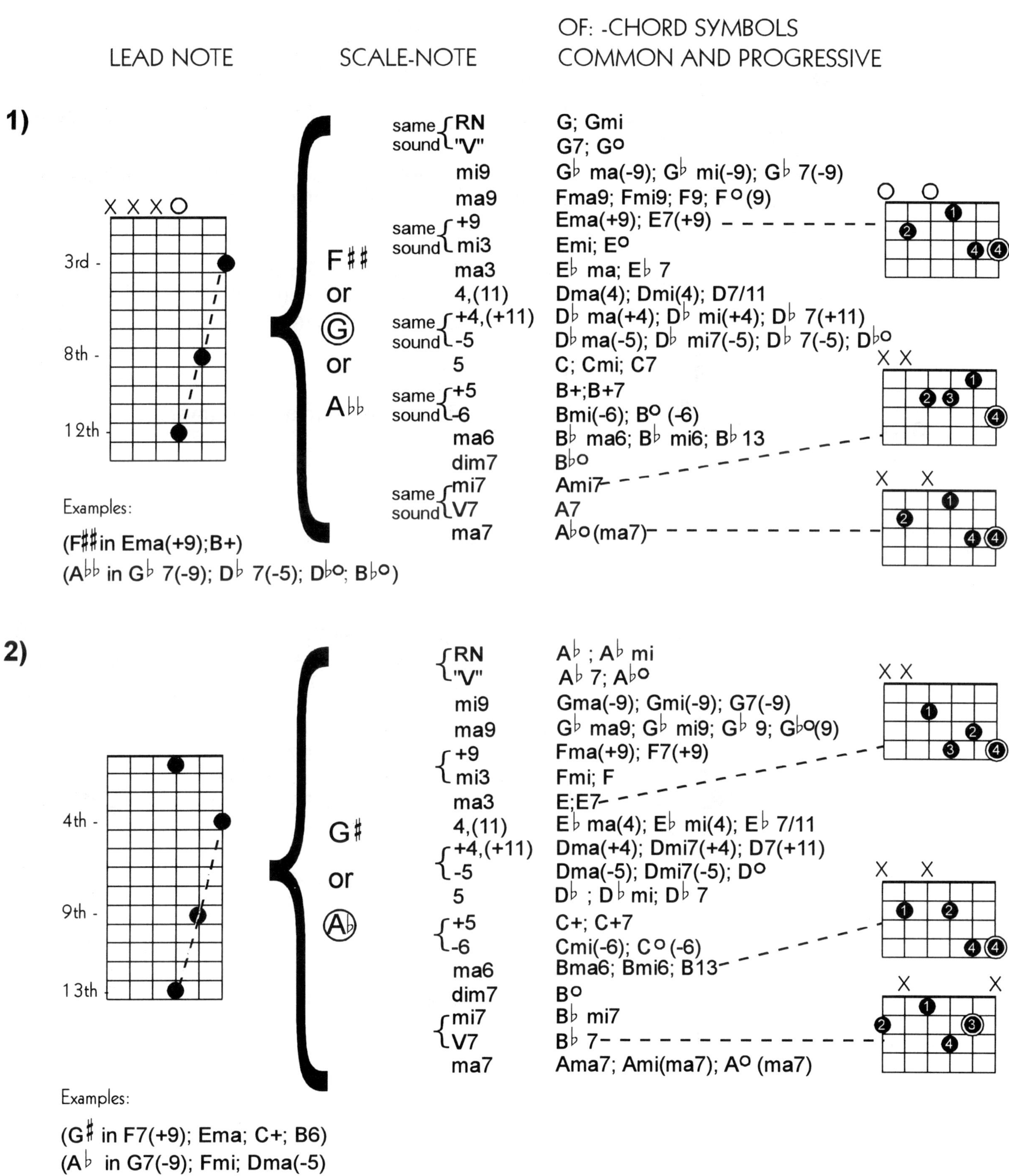

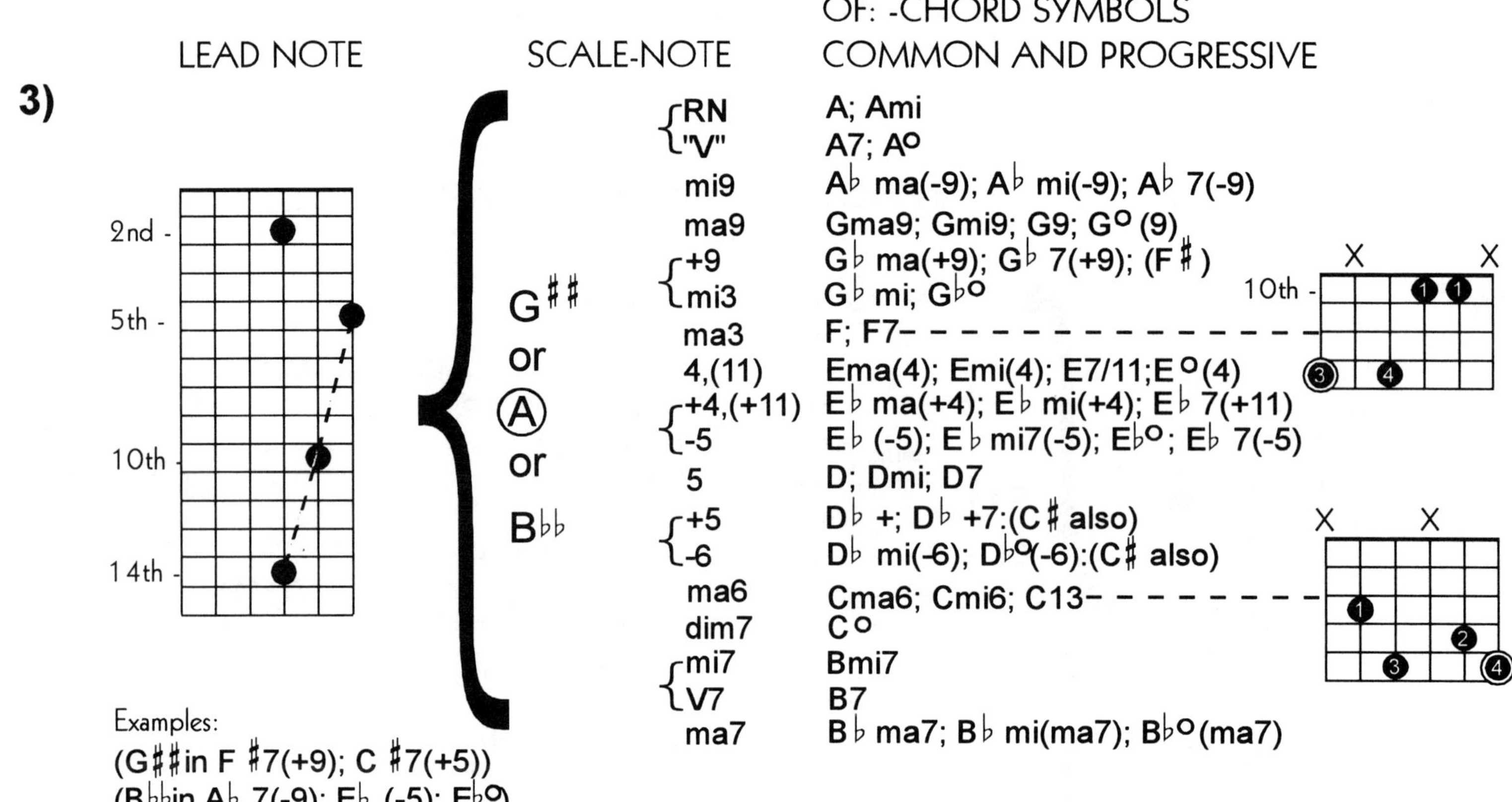
LEAD NOTE
SCALE-NOTE
OF: -CHORD SYMBOLS
COMMON AND PROGRESSIVE
3)
2nd -
5th -
10th -
14th -
G♯♯
or
Ⓐ
or
B♭♭
RN A; Ami
"V" A7; A°
mi9 A♭ ma(-9); A♭ mi(-9); A♭ 7(-9)
ma9 Gma9; Gmi9; G9; G° (9)
+9 G♭ ma(+9); G♭ 7(+9); (F♯)
mi3 G♭ mi; G♭°
ma3 F; F7
4,(11) Ema(4); Emi(4); E7/11; E°(4)
+4,(11) E♭ ma(+4); E♭ mi(+4); E♭ 7(+11)
-5 E♭ (-5); E♭ mi7(-5); E♭°; E♭ 7(-5)
5 D; Dmi; D7
+5 D♭ +; D♭ +7:(C♯ also)
-6 D♭ mi(-6); D♭°(-6):(C♯ also)
ma6 Cma6; Cmi6; C13
dim7 C°
mi7 Bmi7
V7 B7
ma7 B♭ ma7; B♭ mi(ma7); B♭°(ma7)
X X
10th -
X X
Examples:
(G♯♯in F♯7(+9); C♯7(+5))
(B♭♭in A♭ 7(-9); E♭ (-5); E♭°)

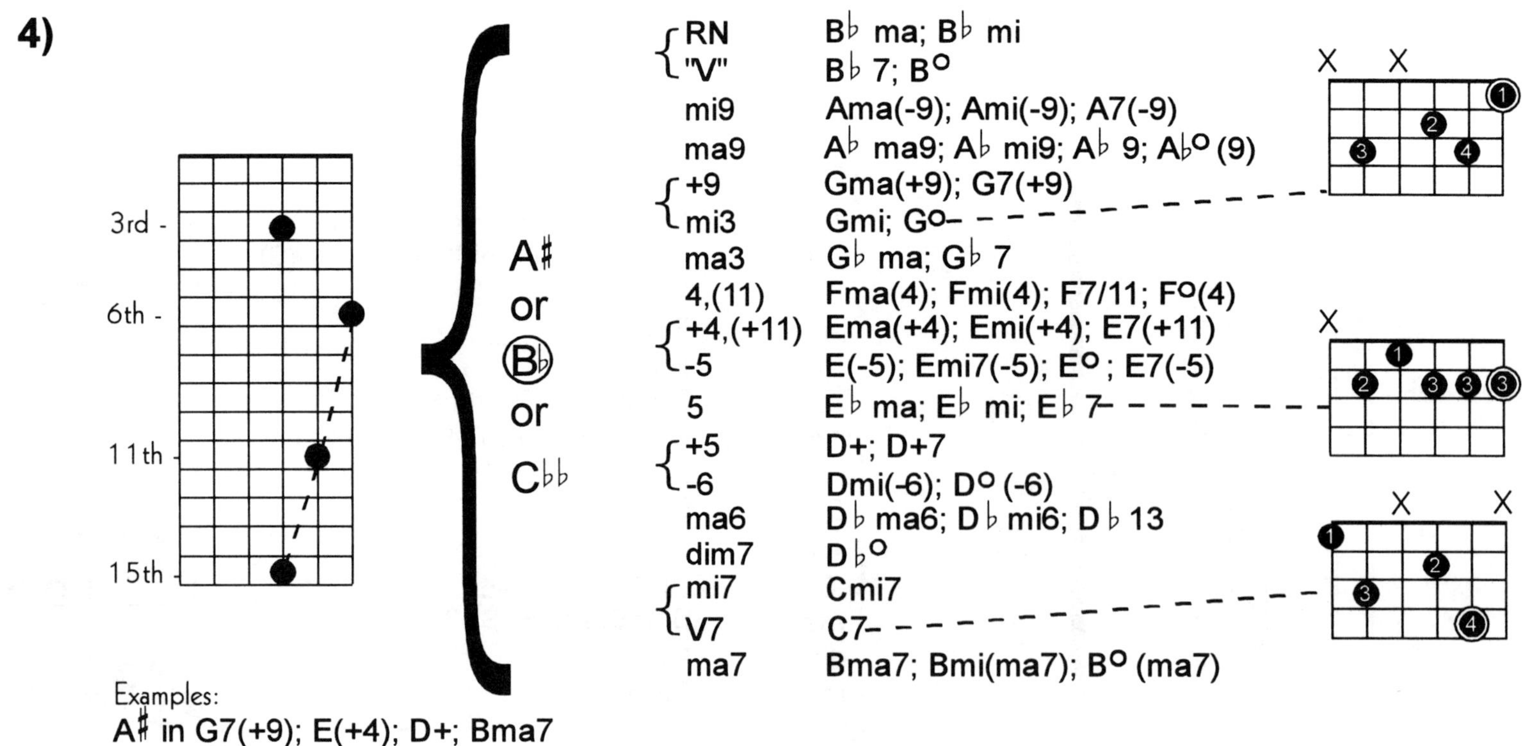
4)
3rd -
6th -
11th -
15th -
A♯
or
B♭
or
C♭♭
RN B♭ ma; B♭ mi
"V" B♭ 7; B°
mi9 Ama(-9); Ami(-9); A7(-9)
ma9 A♭ ma9; A♭ mi9; A♭ 9; A♭°(9)
+9 Gma(+9); G7(+9)
mi3 Gmi; G°
ma3 G♭ ma; G♭ 7
4,(11) Fma(4); Fmi(4); F7/11; F°(4)
+4,(11) Ema(+4); Emi(+4); E7(+11)
-5 E(-5); Emi7(-5); E°; E7(-5)
5 E♭ ma; E♭ mi; E♭ 7
+5 D+; D+7
-6 Dmi(-6); D° (-6)
ma6 D♭ ma6; D♭ mi6; D♭ 13
dim7 D♭°
mi7 Cmi7
V7 C7
ma7 Bma7; Bmi(ma7); B° (ma7)
X X
X
X X
Examples:
A♯ in G7(+9); E(+4); D+; Bma7
C♭♭ in D♭°

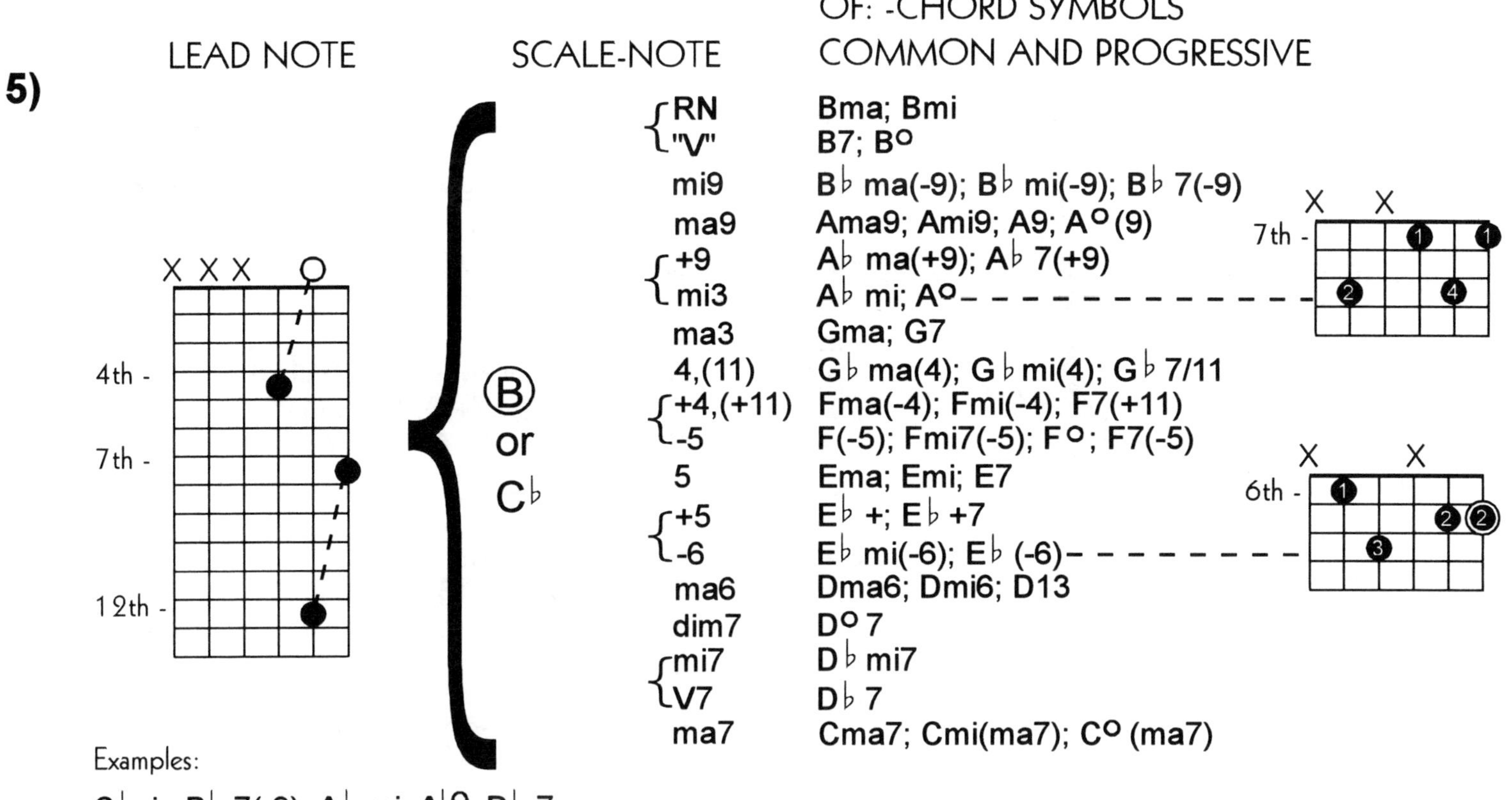
5)
LEAD NOTE
SCALE-NOTE
OF: -CHORD SYMBOLS
COMMON AND PROGRESSIVE
RN Bma; Bmi
"V" B7; B°
mi9 B♭ ma(-9); B♭ mi(-9); B♭ 7(-9)
ma9 Ama9; Ami9; A9; A° (9)
+9 A♭ ma(+9); A♭ 7(+9)
mi3 A♭ mi; A°
ma3 Gma; G7
4,(11) G♭ ma(4); G♭ mi(4); G♭ 7/11
+4,(+11) Fma(-4); Fmi(-4); F7(+11)
-5 F(-5); Fmi7(-5); F°; F7(-5)
5 Ema; Emi; E7
+5 E♭ +; E♭ +7
-6 E♭ mi(-6); E♭ (-6)
ma6 Dma6; Dmi6; D13
dim7 D° 7
mi7 D♭ mi7
V7 D♭ 7
ma7 Cma7; Cmi(ma7); C° (ma7)
B or C♭
X X X
4th -
7th -
12th -
7th -
6th -
Examples:
C♭ in B♭ 7(-9); A♭ mi; A♭°; D♭ 7

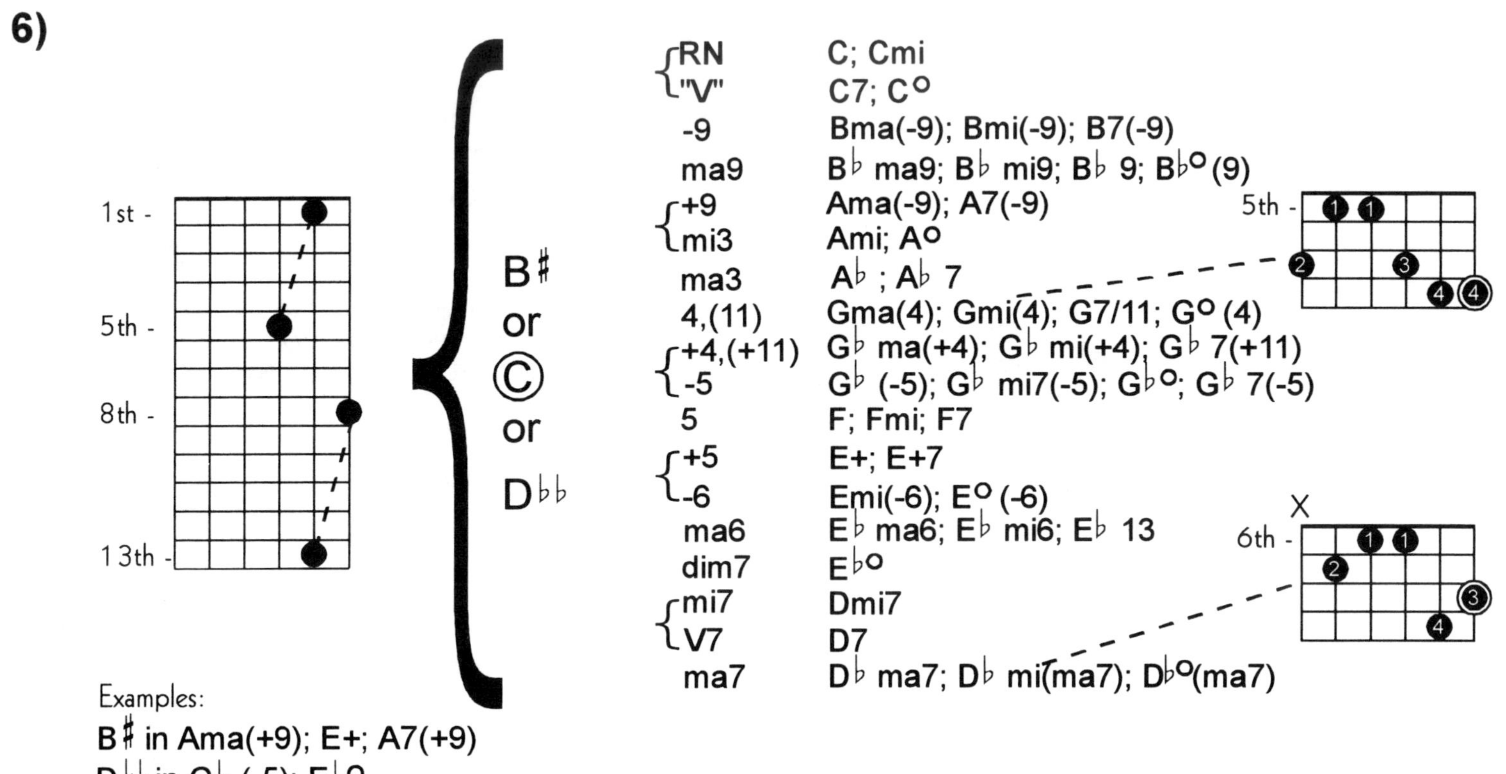
6)
RN C; Cmi
"V" C7; C°
-9 Bma(-9); Bmi(-9); B7(-9)
ma9 B♭ ma9; B♭ mi9; B♭ 9; B♭° (9)
+9 Ama(-9); A7(-9)
mi3 Ami; A°
ma3 A♭ ; A♭ 7
4,(11) Gma(4); Gmi(4); G7/11; G° (4)
+4,(+11) G♭ ma(+4); G♭ mi(+4); G♭ 7(+11)
-5 G♭ (-5); G♭ mi7(-5); G♭°; G♭ 7(-5)
5 F; Fmi; F7
+5 E+; E+7
-6 Emi(-6); E° (-6)
ma6 E♭ ma6; E♭ mi6; E♭ 13
dim7 E♭°
mi7 Dmi7
V7 D7
ma7 D♭ ma7; D♭ mi(ma7); D♭°(ma7)
B♯ or C or D♭♭
1st -
5th -
8th -
13th -
5th -
6th -
Examples:
B♯ in Ama(+9); E+; A7(+9)
D♭♭ in G♭ (-5); E♭°

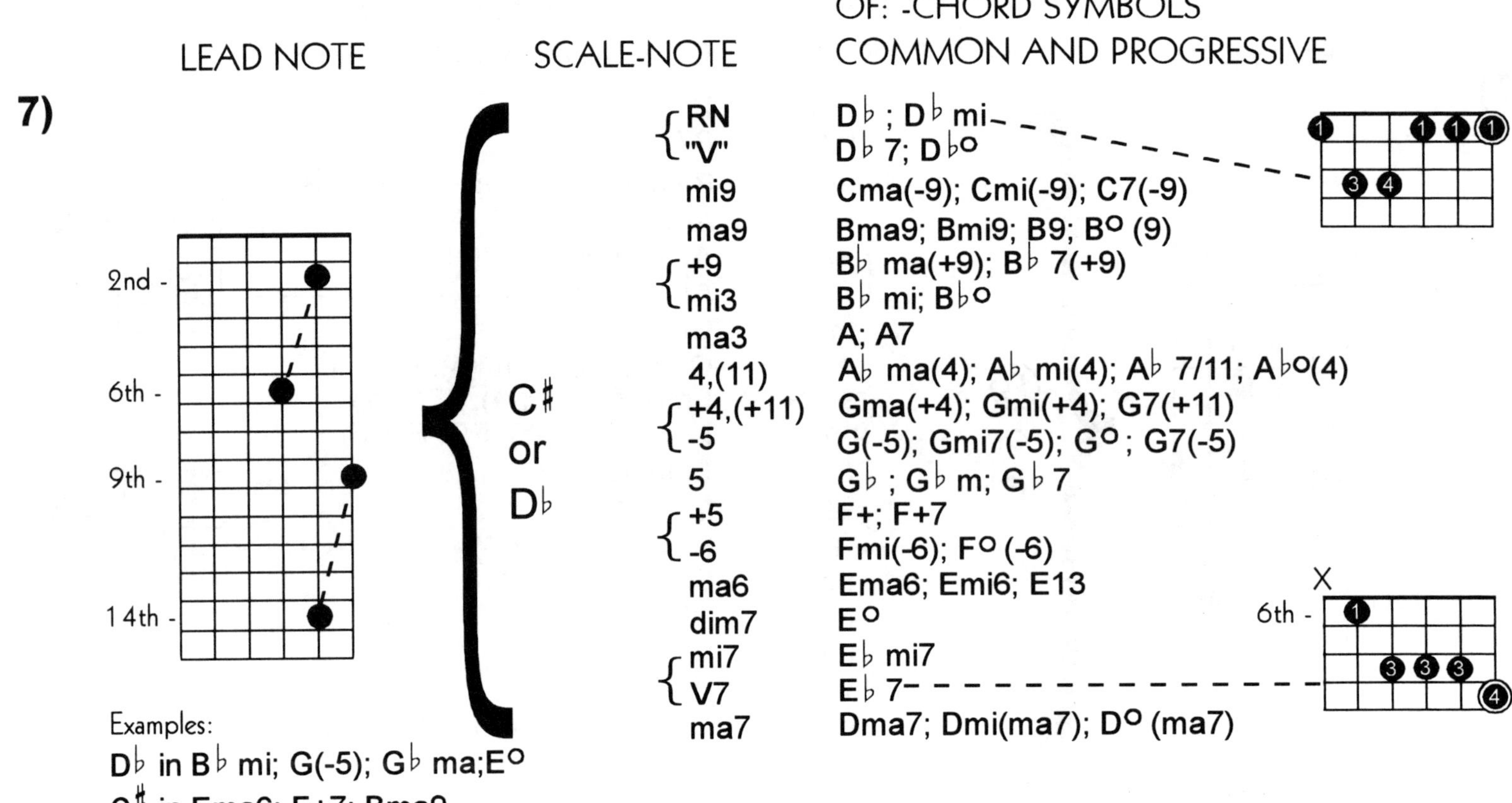
LEAD NOTE
SCALE-NOTE
OF: -CHORD SYMBOLS
COMMON AND PROGRESSIVE
7)
RN D♭; D♭ mi
"V" D♭ 7; D♭o
mi9 Cma(-9); Cmi(-9); C7(-9)
ma9 Bma9; Bmi9; B9; Bo (9)
+9 B♭ ma(+9); B♭ 7(+9)
mi3 B♭ mi; B♭o
ma3 A; A7
4,(11) A♭ ma(4); A♭ mi(4); A♭ 7/11; A♭o(4)
+4,(+11) Gma(+4); Gmi(+4); G7(+11)
-5 G(-5); Gmi7(-5); Go; G7(-5)
5 G♭; G♭ m; G♭ 7
+5 F+; F+7
-6 Fmi(-6); Fo (-6)
ma6 Ema6; Emi6; E13
dim7 Eo
mi7 E♭ mi7
V7 E♭ 7
ma7 Dma7; Dmi(ma7); Do (ma7)
C♯
or
D♭
2nd
6th
9th
14th
6th
X
Examples:
D♭ in B♭ mi; G(-5); G♭ ma; Eo
C♯ in Ema6; F+7; Bma9

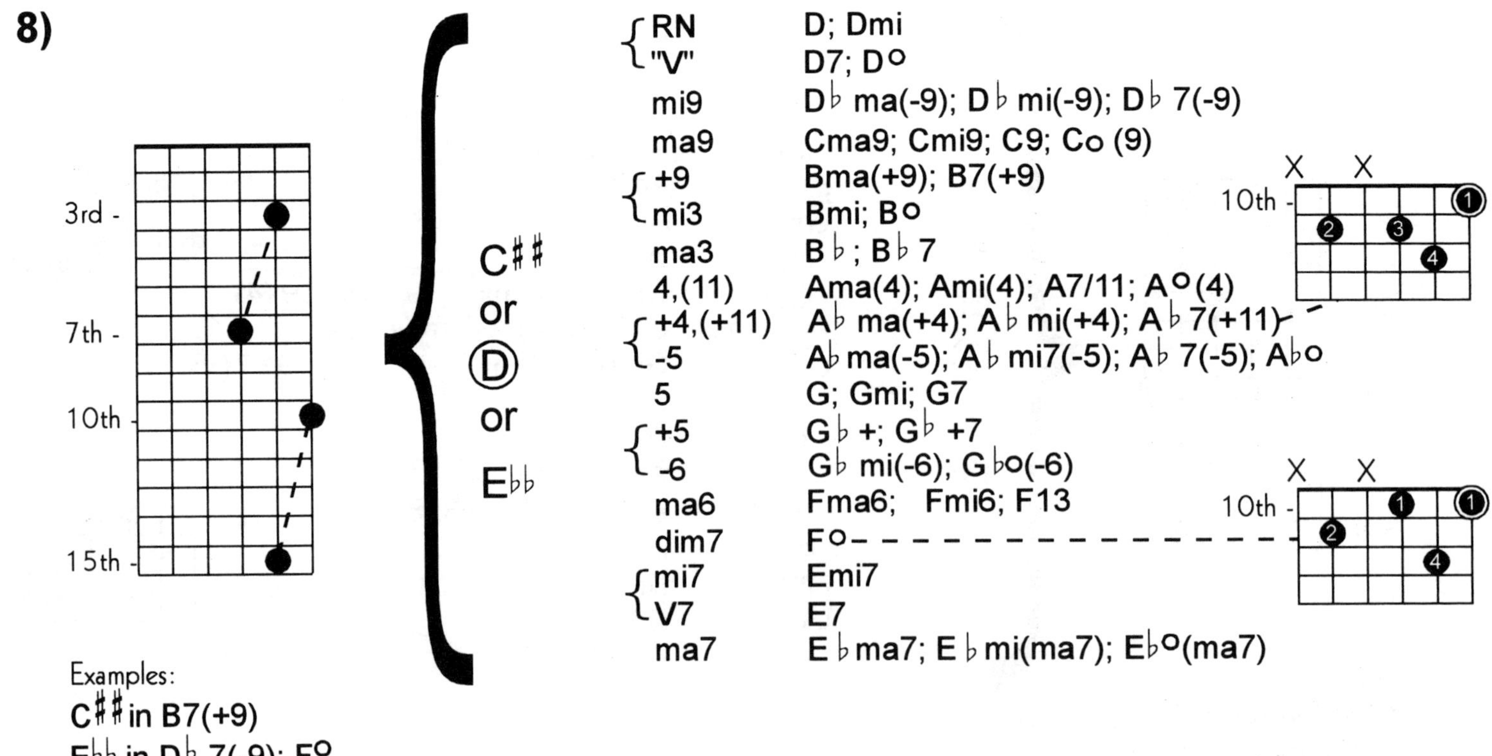
8)
RN D; Dmi
"V" D7; Do
mi9 D♭ ma(-9); D♭ mi(-9); D♭ 7(-9)
ma9 Cma9; Cmi9; C9; Co (9)
+9 Bma(+9); B7(+9)
mi3 Bmi; Bo
ma3 B♭; B♭ 7
4,(11) Ama(4); Ami(4); A7/11; Ao(4)
+4,(+11) A♭ ma(+4); A♭ mi(+4); A♭ 7(+11)
-5 A♭ ma(-5); A♭ mi7(-5); A♭ 7(-5); A♭o
5 G; Gmi; G7
+5 G♭ +; G♭ +7
-6 G♭ mi(-6); G♭o(-6)
ma6 Fma6; Fmi6; F13
dim7 Fo
mi7 Emi7
V7 E7
ma7 E♭ ma7; E♭ mi(ma7); E♭o(ma7)
C𝄪
or
D
or
E𝄫
3rd
7th
10th
15th
10th
10th
X X
X X
Examples:
C𝄪 in B7(+9)
E𝄫 in D♭ 7(-9); Fo

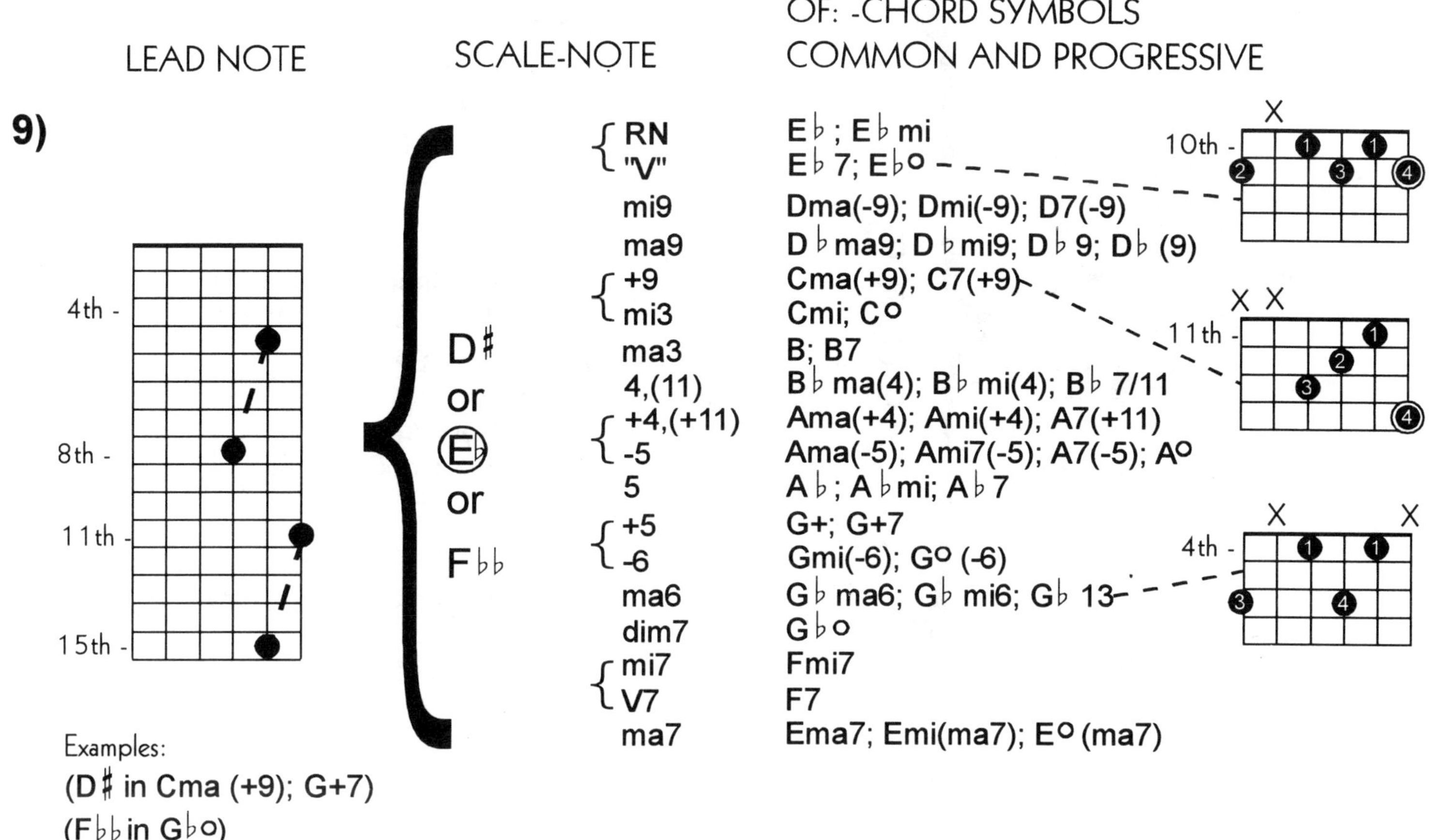
OF: -CHORD SYMBOLS
LEAD NOTE
SCALE-NOTE
COMMON AND PROGRESSIVE
9)
4th -
8th -
11th -
15th -
D♯
or
E♭
or
F♭♭
RN
"V"
mi9
ma9
+9
mi3
ma3
4,(11)
+4,(+11)
-5
5
+5
-6
ma6
dim7
mi7
V7
ma7
E♭; E♭mi
E♭7; E♭o
Dma(-9); Dmi(-9); D7(-9)
D♭ma9; D♭mi9; D♭9; D♭(9)
Cma(+9); C7(+9)
Cmi; Co
B; B7
B♭ma(4); B♭mi(4); B♭7/11
Ama(+4); Ami(+4); A7(+11)
Ama(-5); Ami7(-5); A7(-5); Ao
A♭; A♭mi; A♭7
G+; G+7
Gmi(-6); Go (-6)
G♭ma6; G♭mi6; G♭13
G♭o
Fmi7
F7
Ema7; Emi(ma7); Eo (ma7)
10th -
11th -
4th -
X
Examples:
(D♯ in Cma (+9); G+7)
(F♭♭ in G♭o)

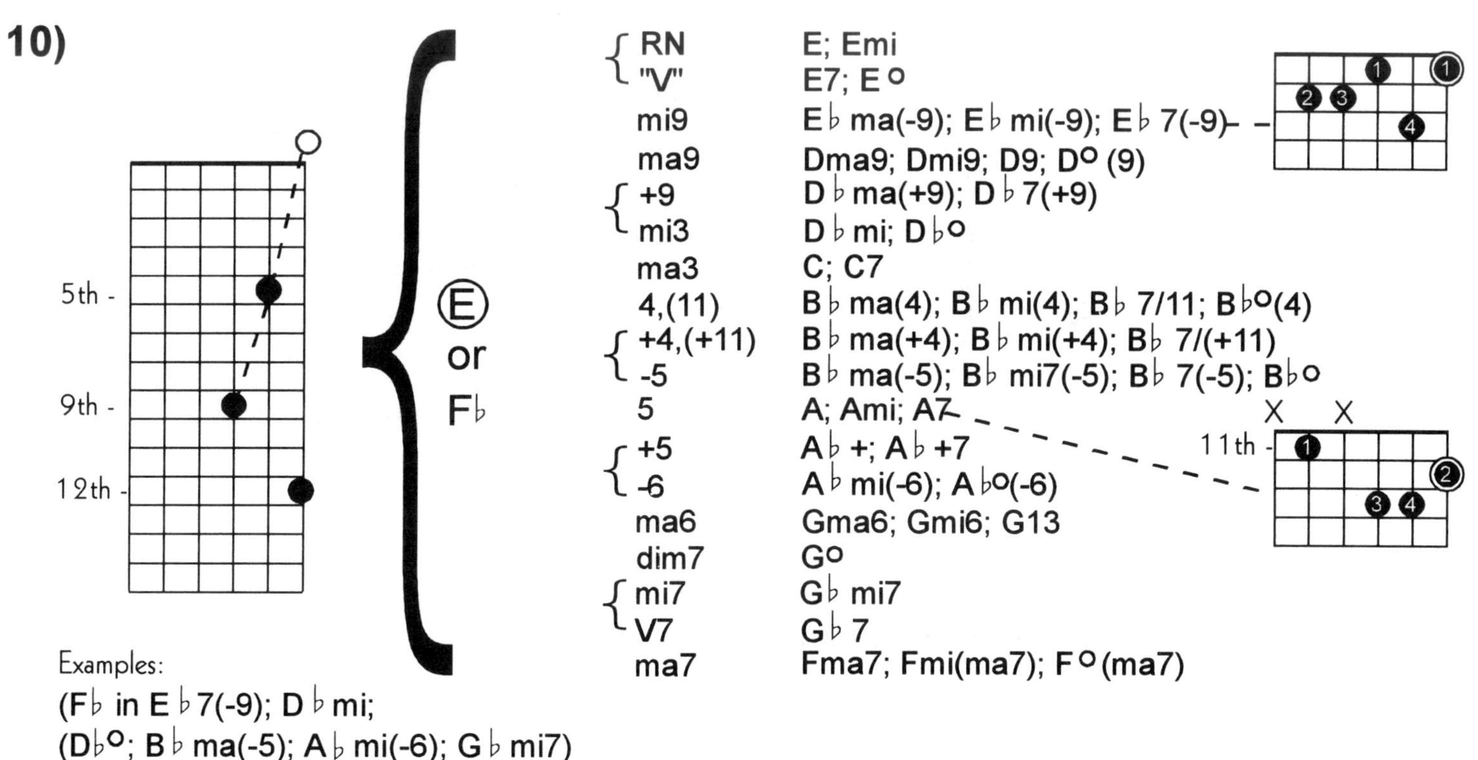
10)
5th -
9th -
12th -
E
or
F♭
RN
"V"
mi9
ma9
+9
mi3
ma3
4,(11)
+4,(+11)
-5
5
+5
-6
ma6
dim7
mi7
V7
ma7
E; Emi
E7; Eo
E♭ma(-9); E♭mi(-9); E♭7(-9)
Dma9; Dmi9; D9; Do (9)
D♭ma(+9); D♭7(+9)
D♭mi; D♭o
C; C7
B♭ma(4); B♭mi(4); B♭7/11; B♭o(4)
B♭ma(+4); B♭mi(+4); B♭7/(+11)
B♭ma(-5); B♭mi7(-5); B♭7(-5); B♭o
A; Ami; A7
A♭+; A♭+7
A♭mi(-6); A♭o(-6)
Gma6; Gmi6; G13
Go
G♭mi7
G♭7
Fma7; Fmi(ma7); Fo (ma7)
11th -
X
Examples:
(F♭ in E♭7(-9); D♭mi;
(D♭o; B♭ma(-5); A♭mi(-6); G♭mi7)

LEAD NOTE	SCALE-NOTE	OF: -CHORD SYMBOLS COMMON AND PROGRESSIVE

11)

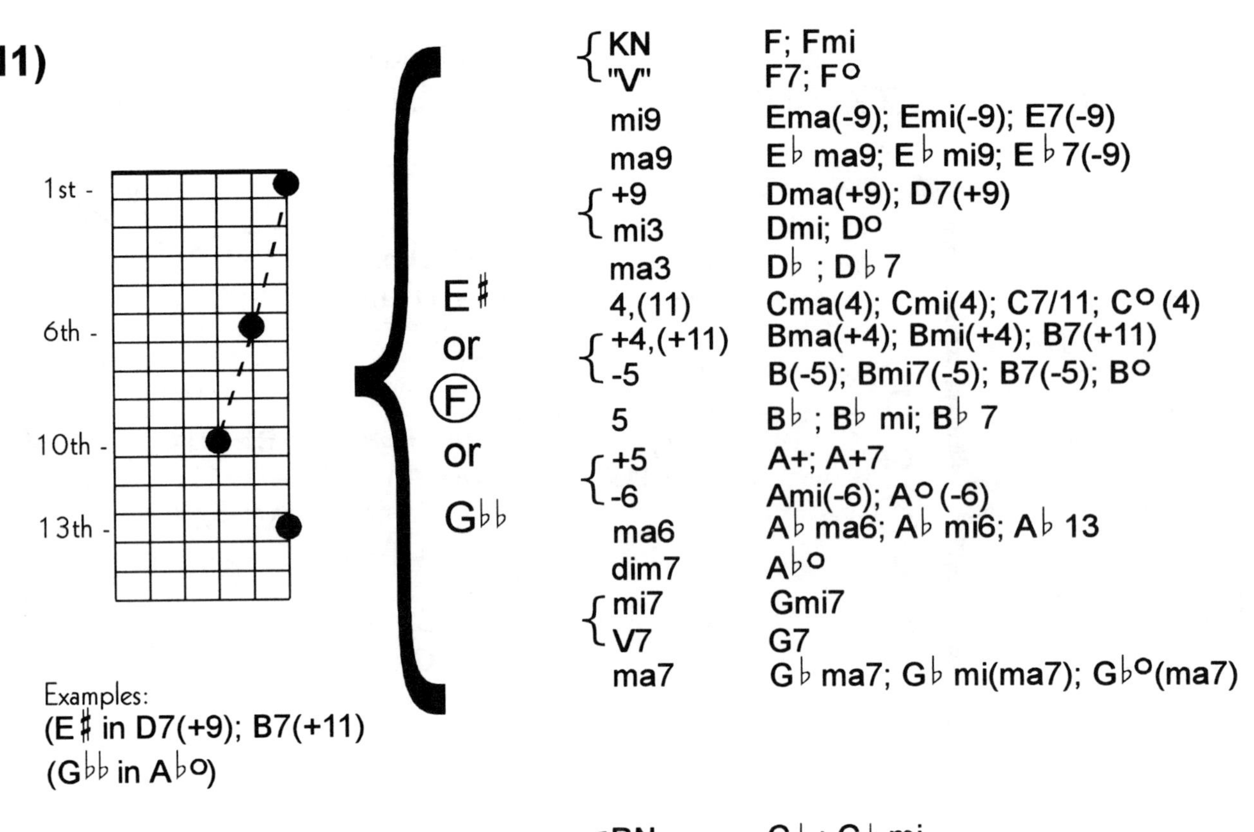

Scale-note	Chord symbols
KN	F; Fmi
"V"	F7; F°
mi9	Ema(-9); Emi(-9); E7(-9)
ma9	E♭ ma9; E♭ mi9; E♭7(-9)
+9	Dma(+9); D7(+9)
mi3	Dmi; D°
ma3	D♭ ; D♭7
4,(11)	Cma(4); Cmi(4); C7/11; C° (4)
+4,(+11)	Bma(+4); Bmi(+4); B7(+11)
-5	B(-5); Bmi7(-5); B7(-5); B°
5	B♭ ; B♭ mi; B♭ 7
+5	A+; A+7
-6	Ami(-6); A° (-6)
ma6	A♭ ma6; A♭ mi6; A♭ 13
dim7	A♭°
mi7	Gmi7
V7	G7
ma7	G♭ ma7; G♭ mi(ma7); G♭°(ma7)

Examples:
(E♯ in D7(+9); B7(+11)
(G♭♭ in A♭°)

12)

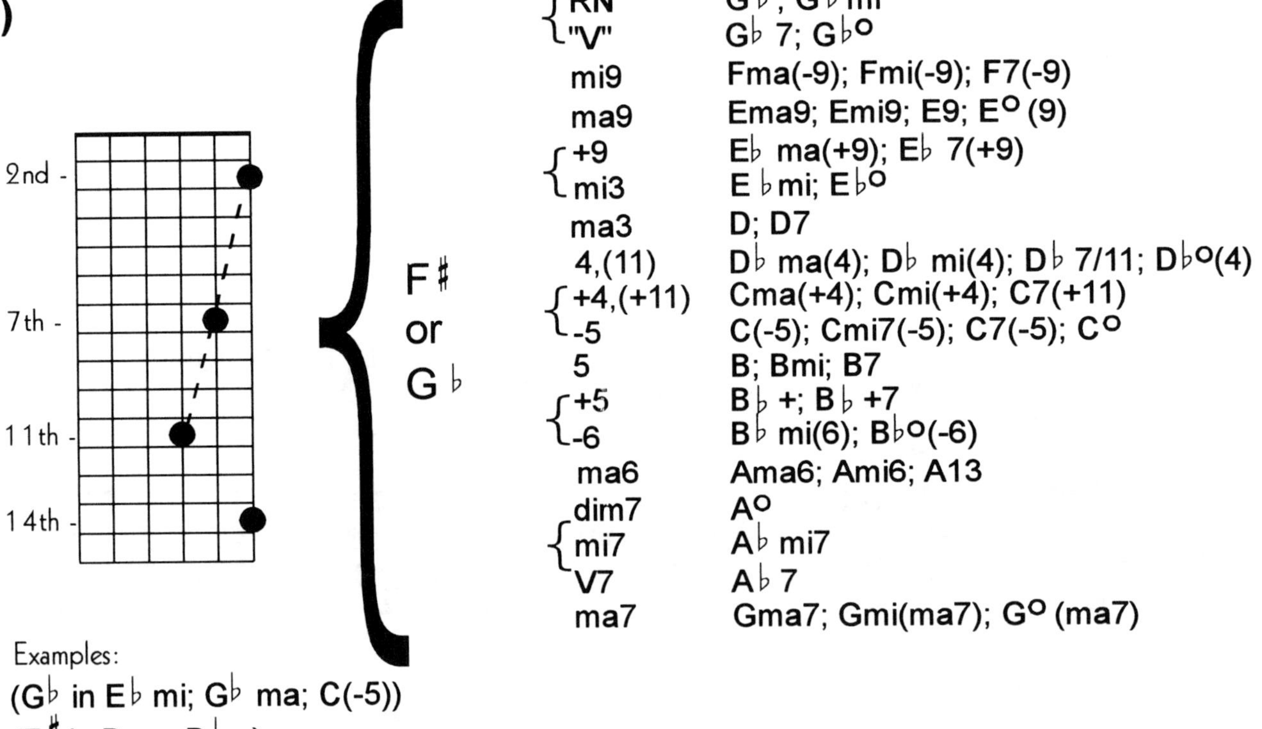

Scale-note	Chord symbols
RN	G♭ ; G♭ mi
"V"	G♭ 7; G♭°
mi9	Fma(-9); Fmi(-9); F7(-9)
ma9	Ema9; Emi9; E9; E° (9)
+9	E♭ ma(+9); E♭ 7(+9)
mi3	E♭mi; E♭°
ma3	D; D7
4,(11)	D♭ ma(4); D♭ mi(4); D♭ 7/11; D♭°(4)
+4,(+11)	Cma(+4); Cmi(+4); C7(+11)
-5	C(-5); Cmi7(-5); C7(-5); C°
5	B; Bmi; B7
+5	B♭ +; B♭ +7
-6	B♭ mi(6); B♭°(-6)
ma6	Ama6; Ami6; A13
dim7	A°
mi7	A♭ mi7
V7	A♭ 7
ma7	Gma7; Gmi(ma7); G° (ma7)

Examples:
(G♭ in E♭ mi; G♭ ma; C(-5))
(F♯ in Bma; B♭ +)

The "lead" notes in the tables are given in the following order:

1) G; (F♯♯); (A♭♭)	**4)** B♭ ; (A♯); (C♭♭)	**7)** D♭ ; C♯	**10)** E; (F♭)
2) A♭ ; (G♯)	**5)** B; (C♭)	**8)** D; (C♯♯); (E♭♭)	**11)** F; (E♯); (G♭♭)
3) A; (G♯♯); (B♭♭)	**6)** C; (B♯); (D♭♭)	**9)** E♭ ; D♯; (F♭♭)	**12)** F♯ ; G♭

A Selection From The Song "Londonderry Air"

The following "chord solo" of an extract from "Londonderry Air" is included as another example in converting the notes of the melody to scale-note names - (or "intervals") - of the chord symbols given for the harmony accompaniment to the melody.

Taking each note in turn and locating the fingerboard position of the note, - (by ear, if you like) - refer to the tables and first glance at the chord symbols given for the note; opposite this symbol, the column of scale notes tells you the "interval name" for the note. Jot this name down, directly above the melody note and then, when all the notes of the melody have been treated in this manner, turn to "scale-notes in chord form" and make up a selection of chord forms having the "lead" notes required for the chord-solo.

Following the directions given on page 19, your selection of chords for the solo of "Londonderry Air" could be similar to the selection given here: -

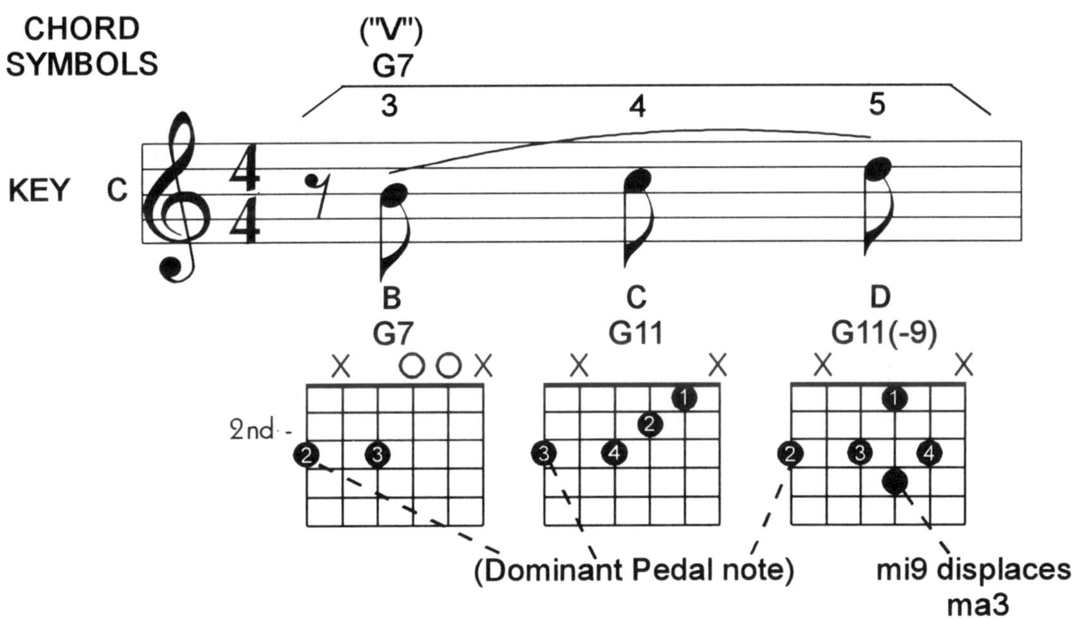

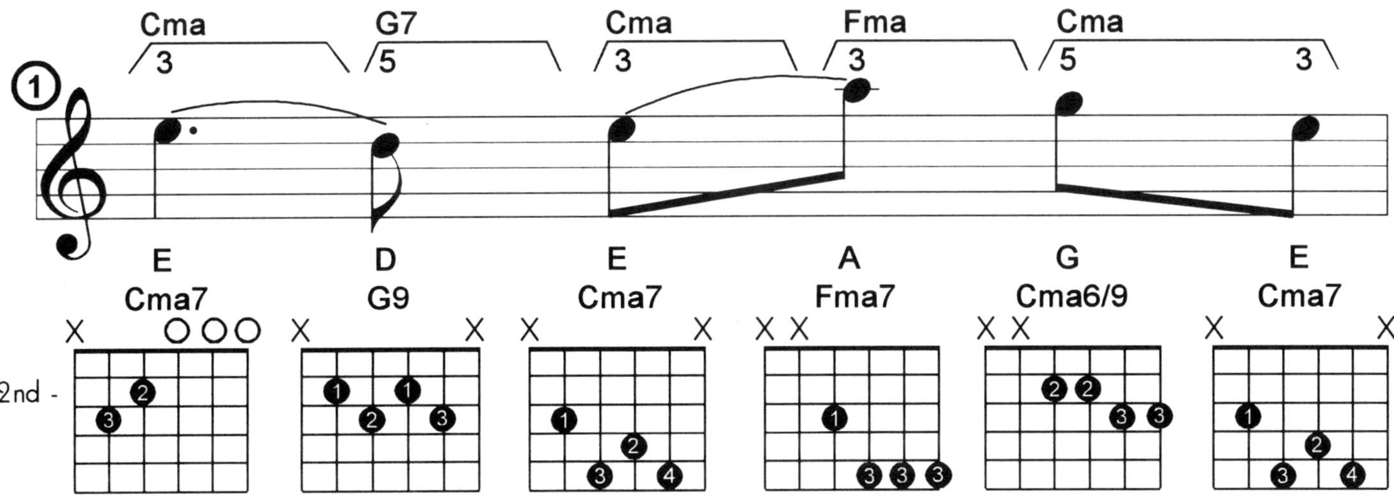

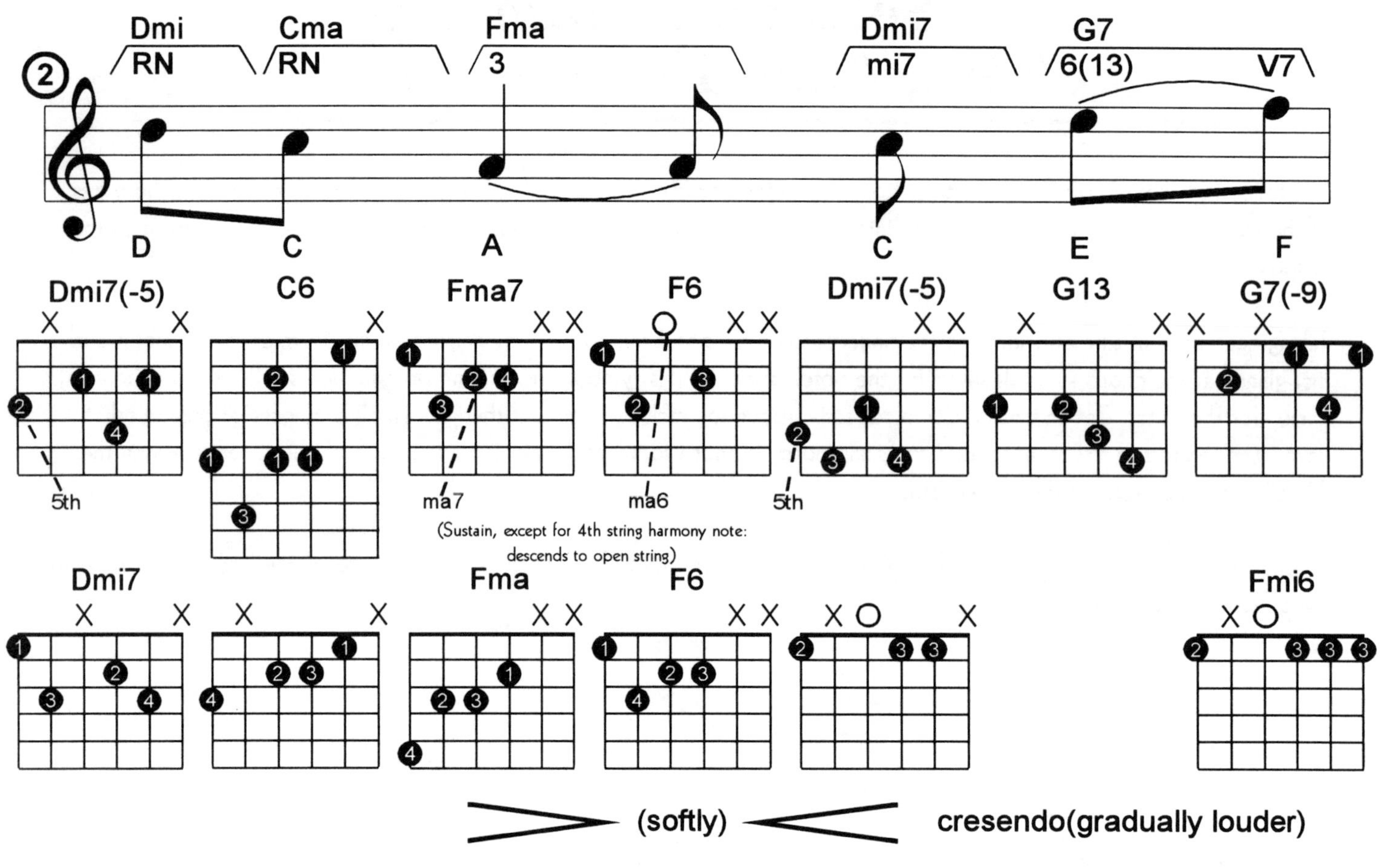

2
Dmi
RN
Cma
RN
Fma
3
Dmi7
mi7
G7
6(13)
V7
D
C
A
C
E
F
Dmi7(-5)
C6
Fma7
F6
Dmi7(-5)
G13
G7(-9)
5th
ma7
ma6
5th
(Sustain, except for 4th string harmony note: descends to open string)
Dmi7
Fma
F6
Fmi6
(softly)
cresendo(gradually louder)

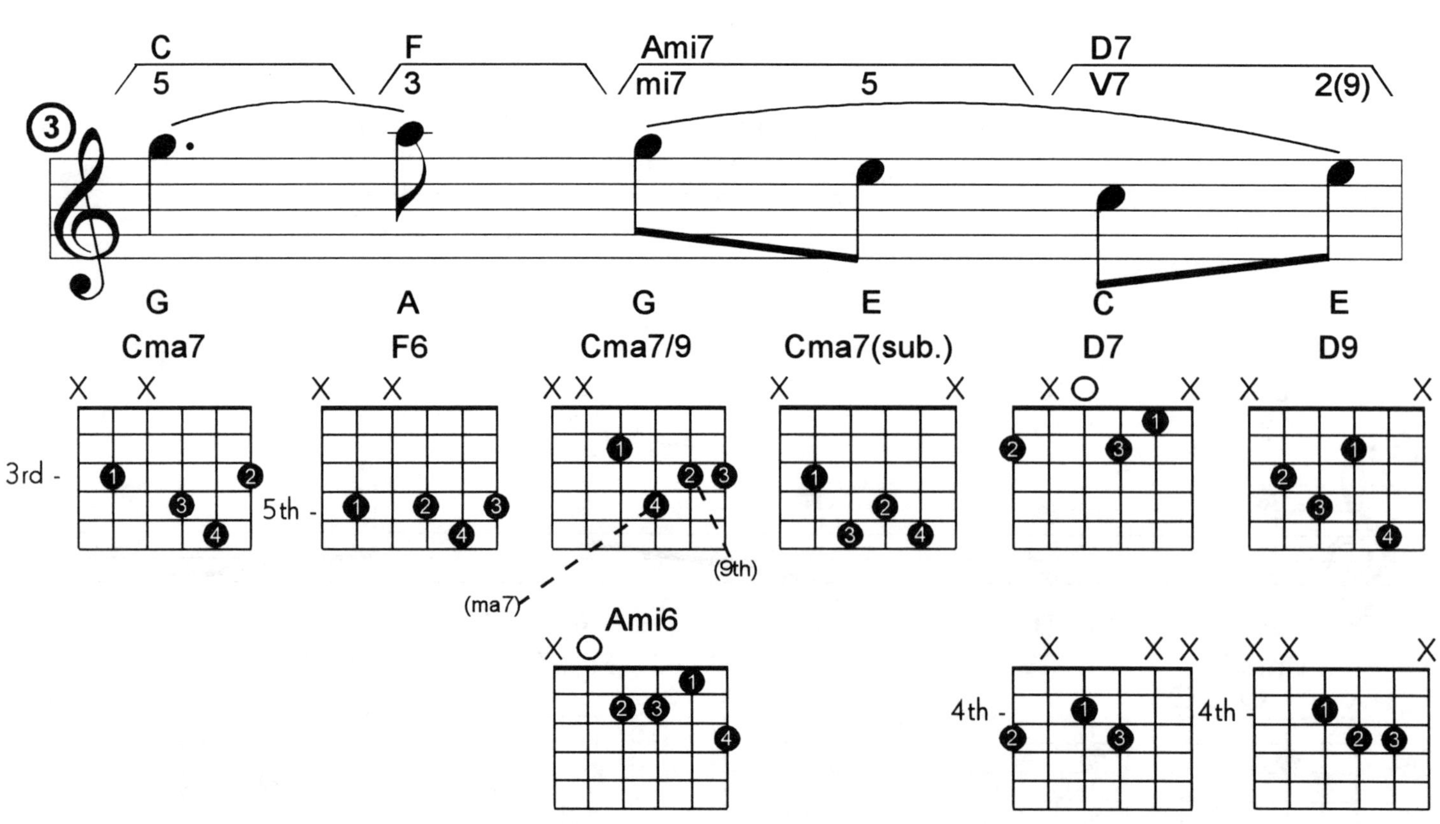

3
C
5
F
3
Ami7
mi7
5
D7
V7
2(9)
G
A
G
E
C
E
Cma7
F6
Cma7/9
Cma7(sub.)
D7
D9
3rd -
5th -
(9th)
(ma7)
Ami6
4th -
4th -

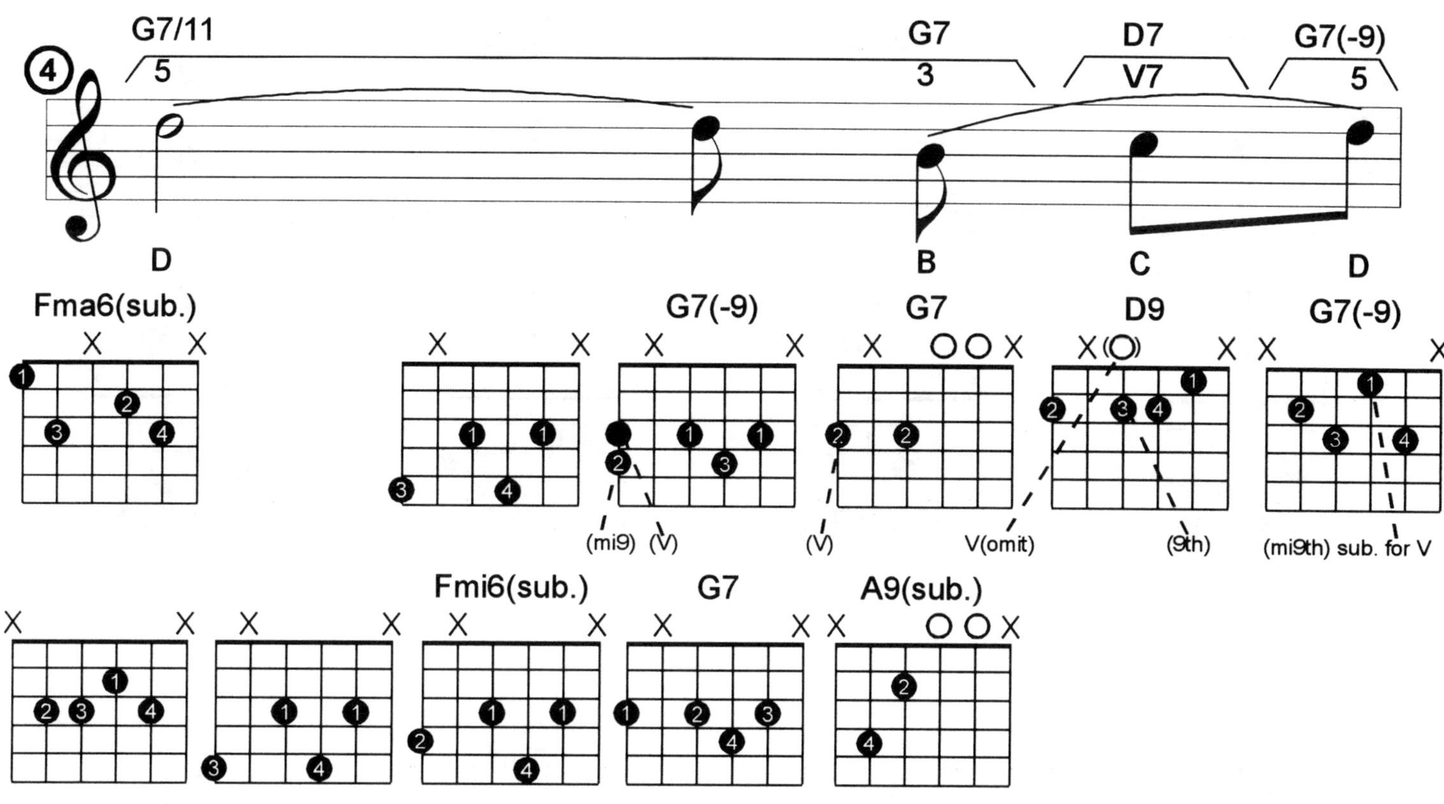

4
G7/11
5
G7
3
D7
V7
G7(-9)
5
D
B
C
D
Fma6(sub.)
G7(-9)
G7
D9
G7(-9)
(mi9) (V)
(V)
V(omit)
(9th)
(mi9th) sub. for V
Fmi6(sub.)
G7
A9(sub.)

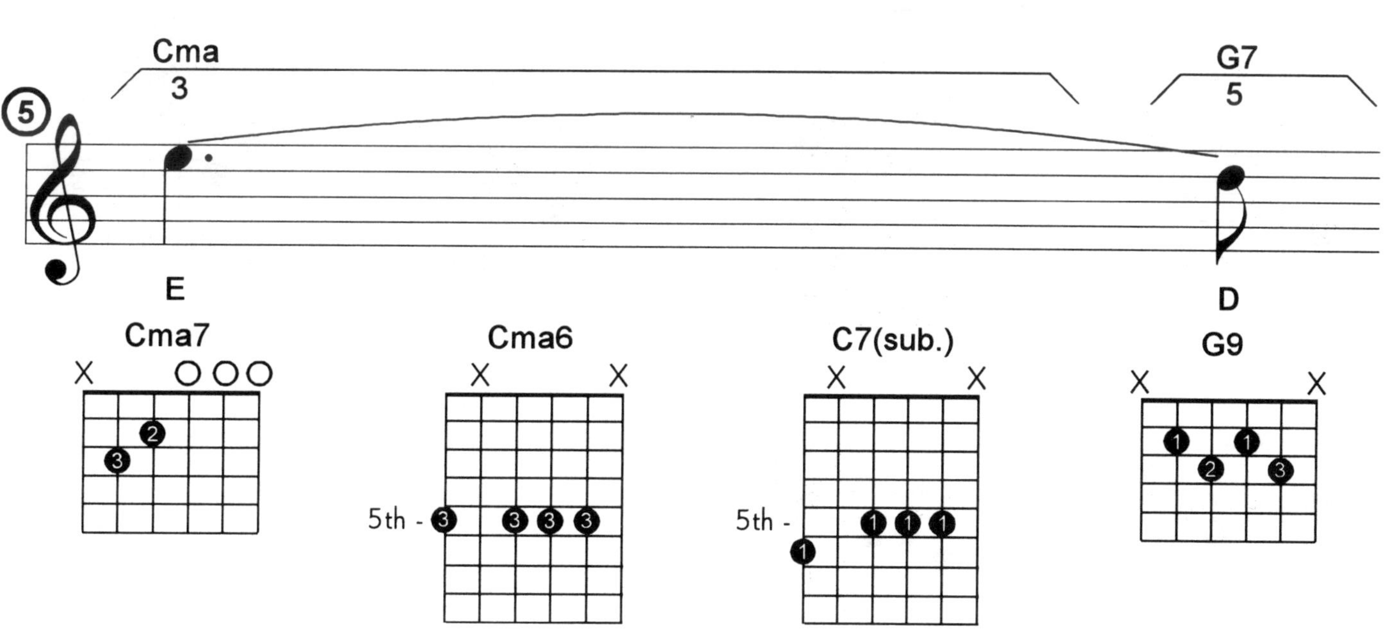

5
Cma
3
G7
5
E
D
Cma7
Cma6
C7(sub.)
G9
5th -
5th -

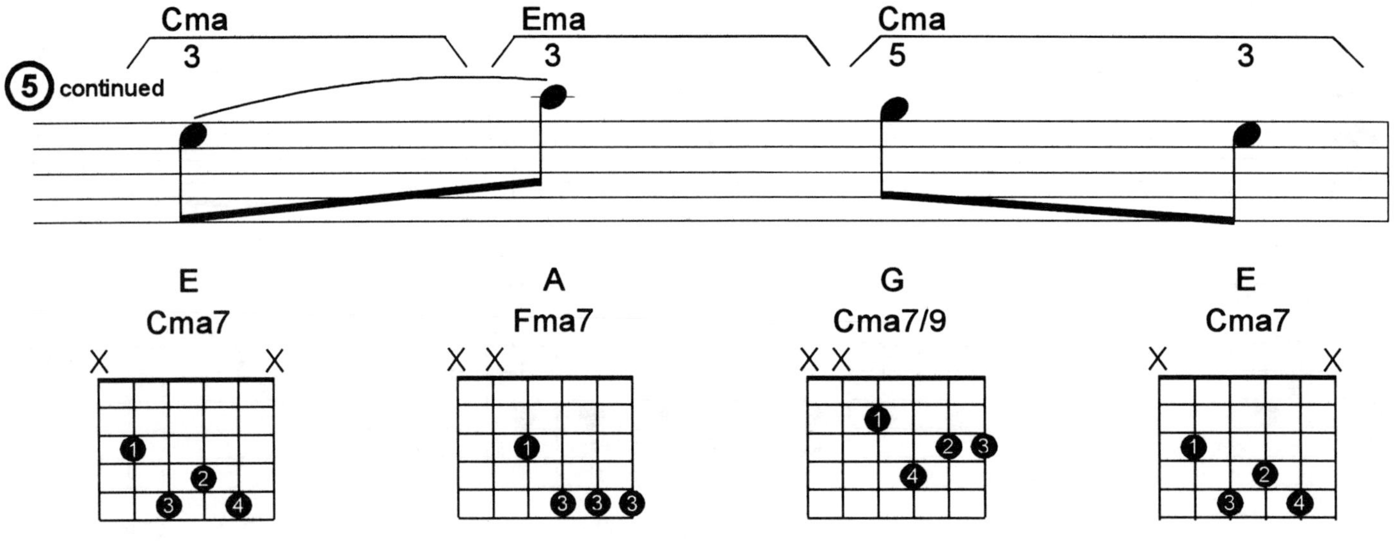
Cma
3
Ema
3
Cma
5
3
5 continued
E
Cma7
A
Fma7
G
Cma7/9
E
Cma7

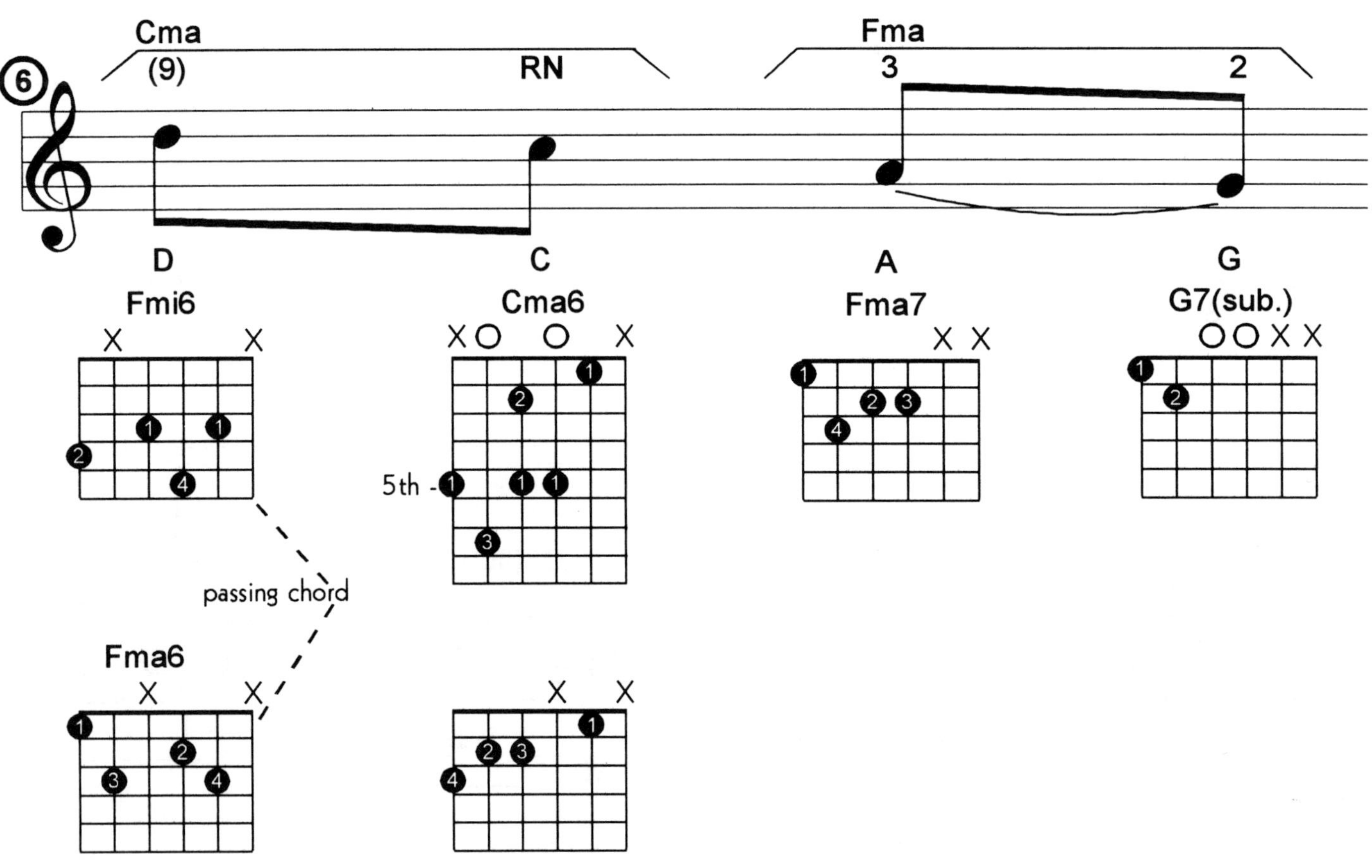
Cma
(9)
RN
Fma
3
2
6
D
Fmi6
C
Cma6
A
Fma7
G
G7(sub.)
5th
passing chord
Fma6

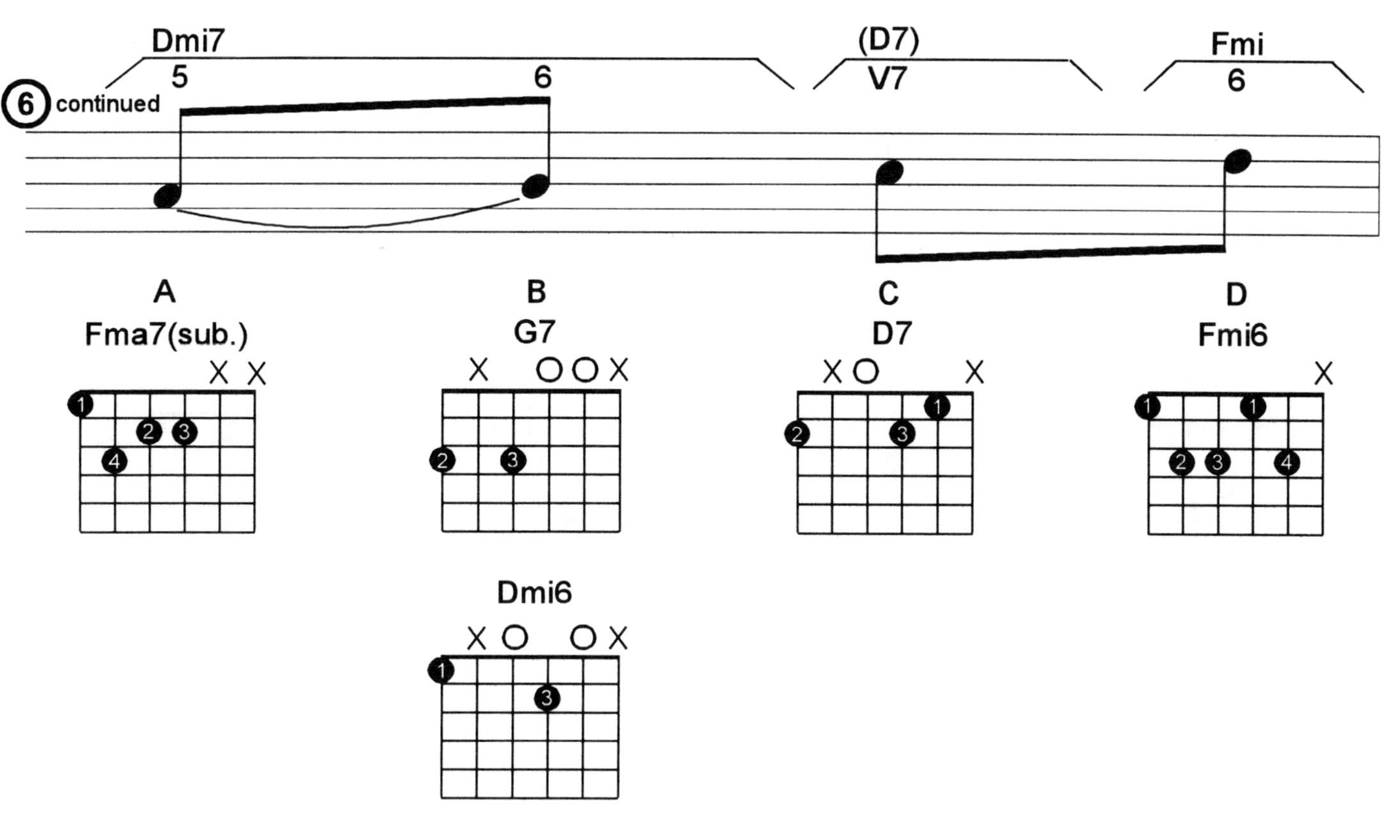

Dmi7
5
6
6 continued
(D7)
V7
Fmi
6
A
Fma7(sub.)
B
G7
C
D7
D
Fmi6
Dmi6

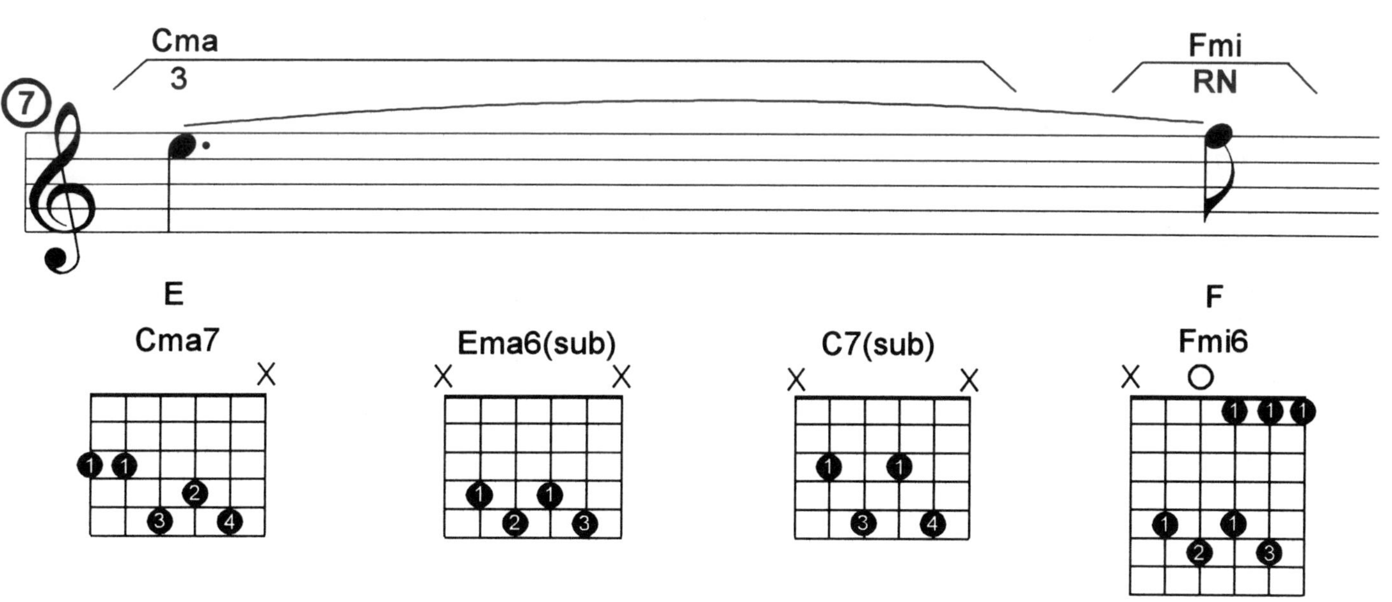

7
Cma
3
Fmi
RN
E
Cma7
Ema6(sub)
C7(sub)
F
Fmi6

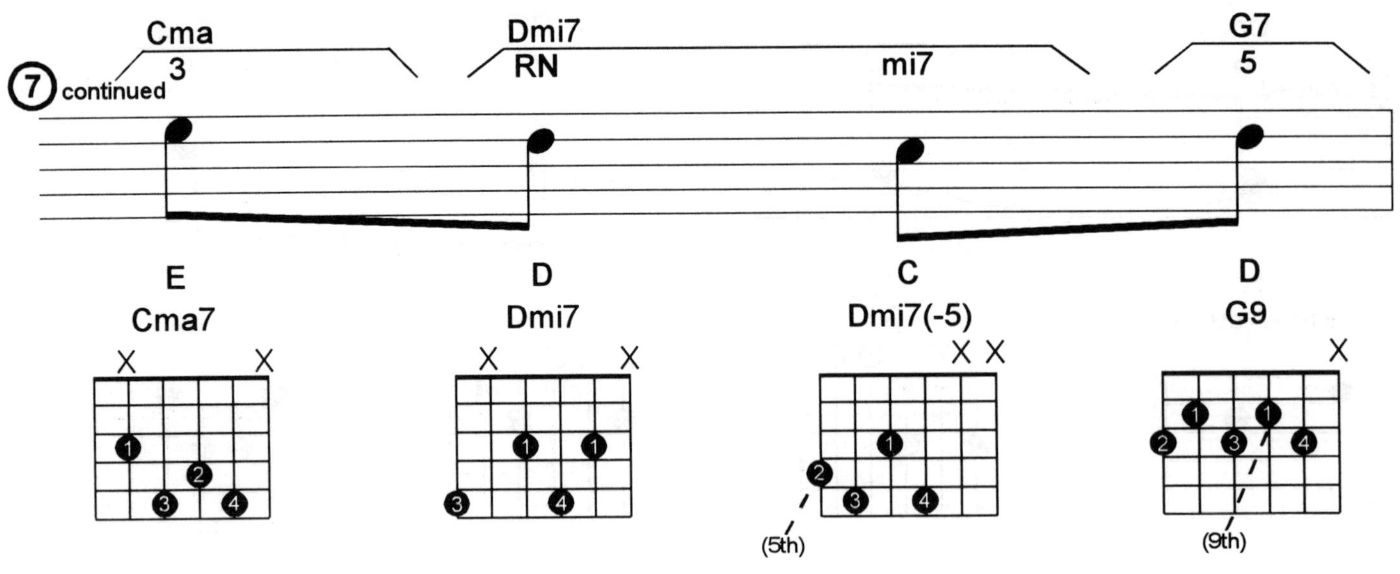

7 continued
Cma
3
Dmi7
RN
mi7
G7
5
E
D
C
D
Cma7
Dmi7
Dmi7(-5)
G9
(5th)
(9th)

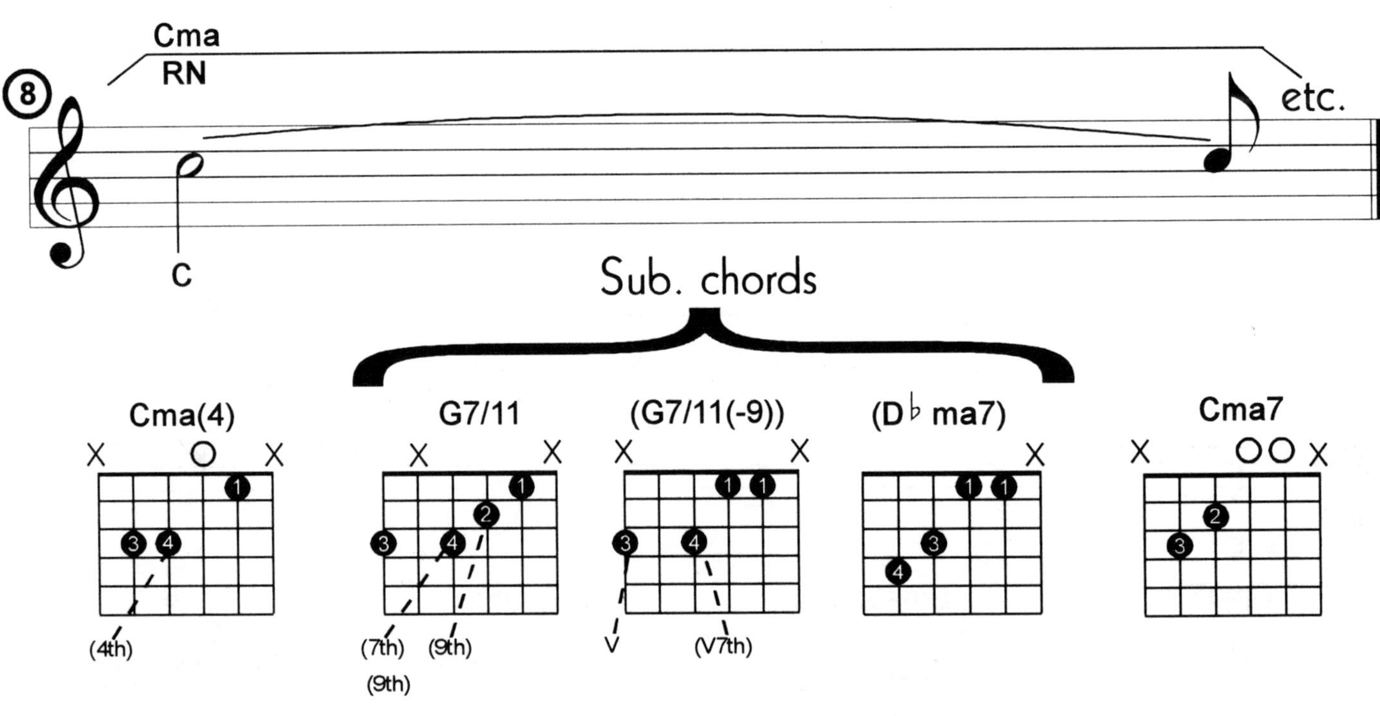

8
Cma
RN
etc.
C
Sub. chords
Cma(4)
G7/11
(G7/11(-9))
(D♭ ma7)
Cma7
(4th)
(7th)
(9th)
(9th)
V
(V7th)

Alternative Selections:

(Note the use of "substitute" chords and adjusted chord forms.)

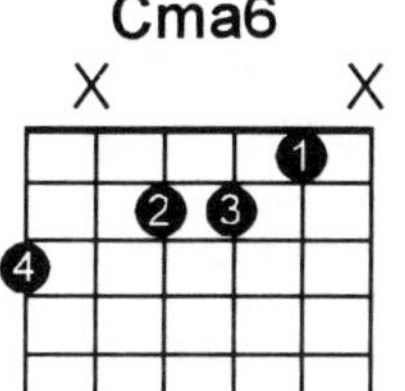

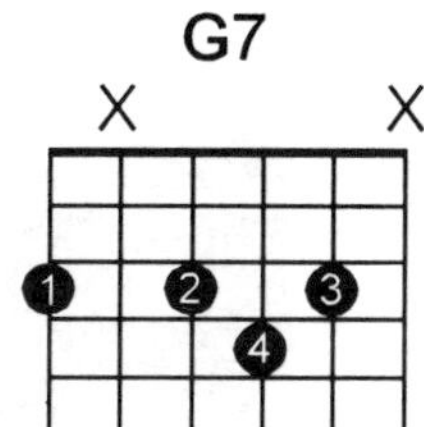

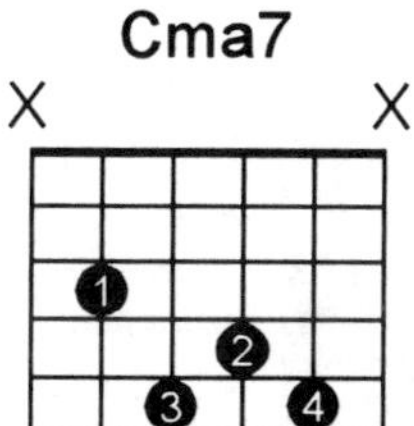

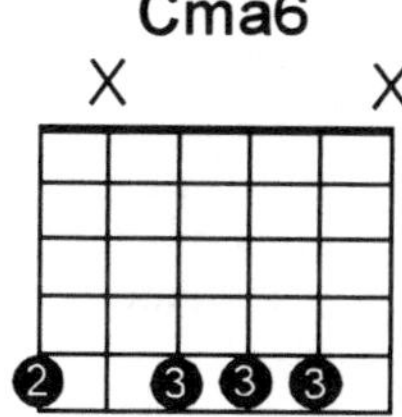

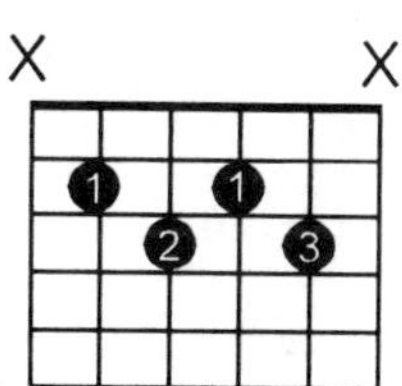
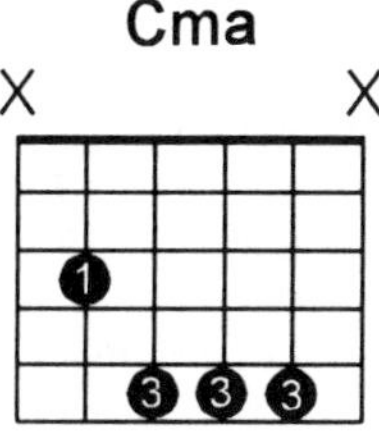

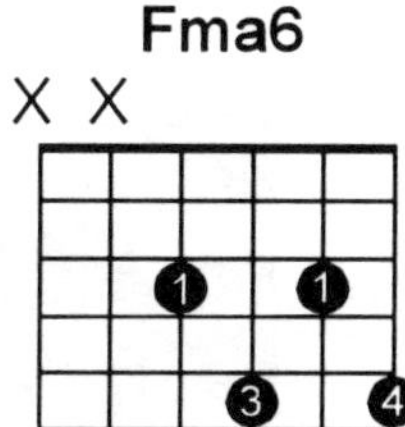

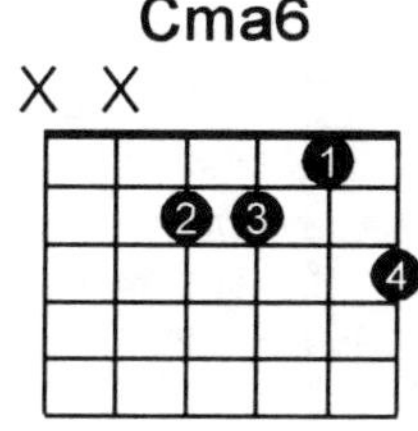

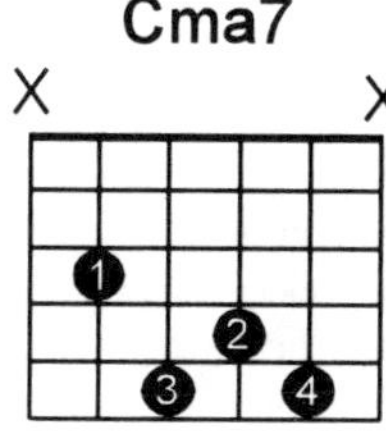

Alternative Score:

Chordal forms in combonation with single notes.

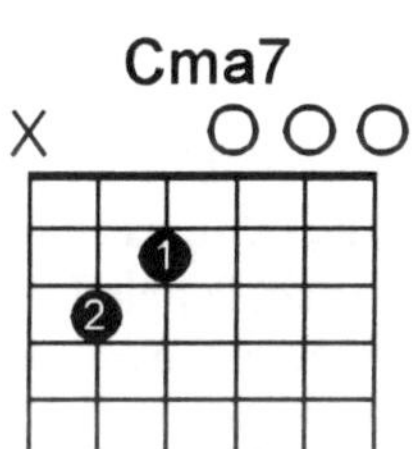

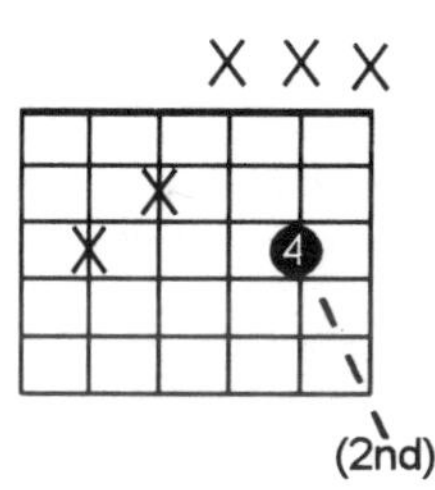

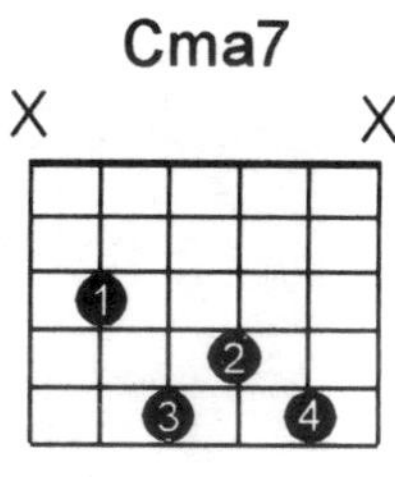

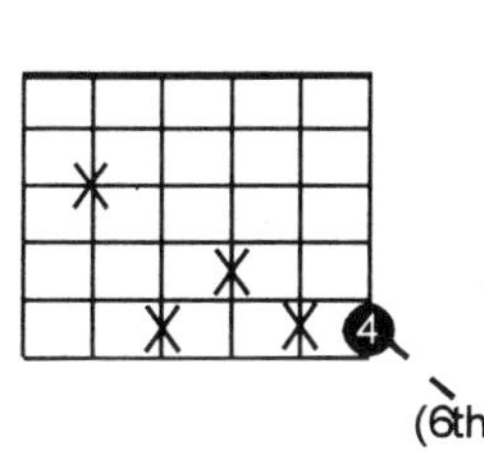

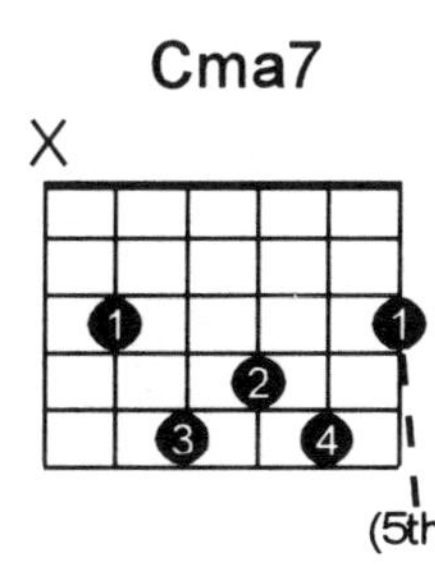

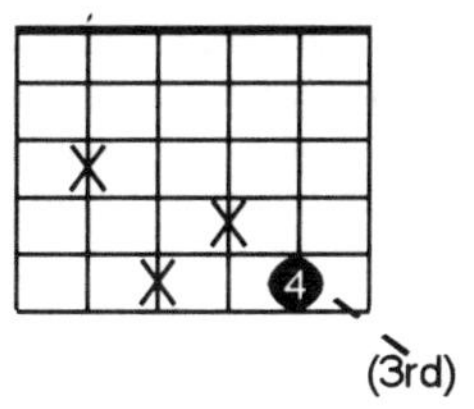

As already stated in the explanation given in the introductionary comments preceding the chord solo of the first eight bars of "Londonderry Air", the solo is intended to serve chiefly as an example in converting the notes of a melody into scale-note names, according to chord symbols given for the harmonic accompaniment and secondly to illustrate how chord-forms given in parts 1 to 4 (and also the "adjusted" versions of those chord-forms) may be applied to the notes of the chosen melody .

The melody just mentioned is of the kind in which the chord changes are much more frequent than in the majority of popular tunes although it is not imperative for every single note of the melody to be treated chordally. The solo could consist, therefore, of a combination of chord forms intermixed with single-note phrases in which the single notes are treated as "passing notes" in between appropriately placed chordal forms. As in the example given in bar no. 5.

You'll Like What You Hear!

Guitar books from Centerstream Publishing

P.O. Box 17878 - Anaheim Hills, CA 92807 (714) -779-9390

Guitar Chords Plus

by Ron Middlebrook
Centerstream Publishing

A comprehensive study of normal and extended chords, tuning, keys, transposing, capo, and more. Includes lots of helpful photos and diagrams, a key to guitar symbols, and a glossary of guitar terms.

00000011 ....$11.95

Blues Guitar Legends

by Kenny Sultan
Centerstream Publishing

This book/CD package allows you to explore the styles of Lightnin' Hopkins, Blind Blake, Mississippi John Hurt, Blind Boy Fuller, and Big Bill Broonzy. Through Sultan's arrangements, you will learn how studying the masters can help you develop your own style.

_______00000181 Book/CD Pack $19.95

Flying Fingers*

by Dave Celentano
Centerstream Publications

Your fingers will be flying over the guitar neck as this book/cassette demonstrates proven techniques that increase speed, precision and dexterity. 32 examples cover alternate picking, sweep picking and circular picking. Cassette demonstrates techniques at three speeds: slow, medium and fast.

_______00000103 Book/Cassette Pack $15.95

Survival Licks & Bar Room Tricks*

by Mark & J.R.
Centerstream Publications

A survival guide for today's music scene – from learning how to solo in a variety of styles to how to protect yourself from flying bottles. After reading this book, you will be equipped with the knowledge and confidence it takes to pull any gig off. Includes country, blues, rock, metal and jazz fusion licks in notes and tab.

_______00000133 ....$8.95

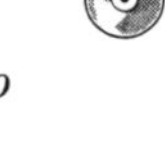

Over The Top

by Dave Celentano
Centerstream Publications

A new book/CD pack by Dave Celentano for guitarists who want to concentrate on their 2-hand tapping tech-nique.

_______00000166 Book/CD Pack.....................$17.95

Pedal Steel Licks For Guitar*

by Forest Rodgers
Centerstream Publishing

Learn to play 30 popular pedal steel licks on the guitar. All 30 examples are played three times on the accompanying CD. Also features tips for the best steel guitar sound reproduction, and steel guitar voiced chords.

_______00000183 Book/CD Pack $15.95

SCALES AND MODES IN THE BEGINNING

by Ron Middlebrook
Centerstream Publications

The most comprehensive and complete scale book written especially for the guitar. Divided into four main sections: 1) Fretboard Visualization, the breaking down of the whole into parts; 2) Scale Terminology – a thorough understanding of whole and half steps, scale degrees, intervals, etc.; 3) Scales And Modes – the rear of the book covers every scale you will ever need with exercises and applications; 4) Scale To Chord Guide – ties it all together, showing what scale to use over various chords.

_______00000010...$11.95

Modal Jams And Theory

Using The Modes For Solo Guitar
by Dave Celentano
Centerstream Publications

Not only will this book show you how to play the modes, it will also show you the theory behind mode construction, how to play any mode in any key, how to play the proper mode over a given chord progression, and how to write chord progressions for each of the seven modes. The accompanying CD includes two rhythm tracks (drums, bass, keyboard and rhythm guitar), and a short solo for each mode so guitarists can practice their solos with a "real" band.

_______00000163 Book/CD Pack.....................$17.95

The Complete Book Of Chords, Scales, Arpeggios For The Guitar*

by Al Politano
Centerstream Publications

Every chord, scale and arpeggio is plotted out in every practical position and with some dedicated study, one could play all of them in every position and in all keys. Written with just a minimum amount of verbalization. Use this book for improvisation, studying or playing exercises. This is the best, most complete reference book you can buy.

_______00000021 ....$8.95

Electric Blues Guitar

by Derek Cornett
Centerstream Publications

An introduction to the most commonly used scales and techniques for the modern blues player, complete with CD. Includes musical examples to show how scales are used in improvisation, and play-along tunes that provide a "hands-on" start to improvisation.

_____00000165 Book/CD Pack.........................$17.95

POWER RHYTHM GUITAR

by Ron Middlebrook with Dave Celentano
Centerstream Publications

This book/CD pack features 31 lessons for rhythm guitar that you can play by yourself, in a band, or as a back-up musician. Includes full band examples in many musical styles, including basic rock, country, hard rock, heavy metal, reggae, blues, funk, and more.

_______00000113 Book/CD Pack $17.95

Guitar Tuning For The Complete Idiot (For Smart People Too)*

Centerstream Publications
By Ron Middlebrook

A complete book on how to tune up. Tuning record included. Contents include: Everything You Need To Know About Tuning – with several methods explained; Intonation – what it is and how to set your guitar up; Strings – How To Find The Right Ones For You; 12 String Tuning; Picks; and much more.

_______00000002 ....$5.95

Open Guitar Tunings*

Centerstream Publications

The only book that illustrates over 75 different tunings in easy-to-read diagrams. Includes tunings used by artists such as Chet Atkins, Michael Hedges, Jimmy Page, Joe Satriani and more for rock, blues, bluegrass, folk and country styles including open D (for slide guitar), Em, open C, modal tunings and many more.

_______ 00000130 ....$4.95

P.O. Box 17878 - Anaheim Hills, CA 92807 (714) - 779-9390